E____ P.tl

W9-BJV-502

THE AMERICAN PRESIDENT

By the same author

THE PRESS, POLITICS AND THE PUBLIC
THE POLITICAL IMPACT OF MASS MEDIA

THE AMERICAN PRESIDENT

Power and Communication

Colin Seymour-Ure

St. Martin's Press   New York

Wingate College Library

© Colin Seymour-Ure 1982

All rights reserved. For information, write:
St. Martin's Press, Inc., 175 Fifth Avenue, New York, NY 10010
Printed in Hong Kong
First published in the United States of America in 1982

ISBN 0-312-02786-9

Library of Congress Cataloging in Publication Data

Seymour-Ure, Colin, 1938–
  The American president.

  Bibliography: p.
  Includes index.
  1. Presidents – United States. 2. Executive
power – United States. 3. Communication in
politics – United States. 4. United States – Politics
and government – 1945 – . I. Title.
JK518.S45 1982 353.03′2 82-5772
ISBN 0-312-02786-9 AACR2

093704

For Judy, Kirsty and Bruce

Contents

Acknowledgements

This sort of book – really a long essay – should be written at one sitting. Actually it has been written in uneven spasms over nearly four years, during the last three of which I was virtually a full-time academic administrator. The bulk of the reading and research was carried out on study leave in the USA in 1976–7. My thanks are due to the American Council of Learned Societies and the University of Kent for making this financially possible; also to the Department of Politics at the University of Massachusetts for its hospitality, and to friends on other campuses too for their warm welcome and for invitations enabling me to develop ideas in seminars, conference papers and informal discussions. For invitations of this kind or for comment on various bits of manuscript, I owe thanks in particular to Michael Baer, Elmer E. Cornwell Jr, Ed Fogelmann, John Hart, Milda Hedblom, Jerry Kline, Kurt and Gladys Lang, Richard E. Neustadt, David Paletz, Nelson Polsby, George E. Reedy and George Sulzner. For similar invitations to seminars in the United Kingdom I am grateful to Jay Blumler and David Morgan. I am also grateful to members of the Ford and Carter news staffs for interviews and facilities, and to many people in Washington and elsewhere who provided help or hospitality; among them were Stuart Adam, Les Aspin, Tony Auth, Fred Barnes, David Bell, Bob and Asta Cooper, Maurice and Fran Cutler, Isik and Erica Erim, Lionel and Barbara Feldman, Bill Garrison, Jack Germond, Michael and Marilyn Hodges, Wilson and Bailey Morris, and Pat Oliphant. Eric and Kirsten Einhorn were especially generous throughout our time in the States. Lastly, I am most grateful to Mrs Barbara Fisher for turning my handwriting, about which I am vain but which people find illegible, into unblemished typescript.

It remains to say that responsibility for the opinions expressed and for any errors or omissions is my own.

Every effort has been made to trace all the copyright-holders, but if any have been inadvertently overlooked, the publishers will be pleased to make the necessary arrangements at the first opportunity.

April 1981   COLIN SEYMOUR-URE

Introduction

This is an essay on the relationship between the President's public communication and his power.

What determines the President's approach to public communication? Does his communication give him the kinds of power needed to achieve his goals?

With few exceptions, analysts of presidential power do not stress communication factors and communication specialists do not analyse presidential power. There is a gap in the literature: a seemingly important dimension of presidential power is little explored.

Communication is central to the idea of power, and public communication is an inescapable part of presidential behaviour. By examining the communication processes involved in different kinds of power and the forms of public communication open to the President, surely the nature of the President's power should become clearer.

That, at any rate, is the argument. This essay makes no exaggerated claim to enlightenment itself. It seeks only to develop and illustrate the argument and to offer ideas about what presidential power looks like if the factor of public communication *is* kept to the fore. (The conclusion, in a word, is – weak.) Chapter 1 analyses the relationship between communication processes and various types of power; Chapter 2, the factors influencing the President's public communication. Chapter 3 starts with a short critique of the literature on presidential power, evaluates the use of public communication as an instrument of power by presidents since 1945 and concludes with a comment on comparable questions in a cabinet system of government.

Two thoughts prompted the essay. One was about presidential elections and the other about Richard Nixon's famous dawn encounter with anti-war protesters at the Lincoln Memorial in 1970.[1]

The first was a straggly reflection upon the heroic assumptions that an election makes about what voters can expect to learn of the presidential candidates and about the sense in which they have a realistic choice. What can tens of millions of Americans really know of the contestants? Must it not be true, just as a matter of statistics, that some voters have an image of one candidate coinciding exactly with the image some voters have of the other? Did 'Kennedy' and 'Nixon' in 1960, 'Johnson' and 'Goldwater' in 1964, 'Humphrey' and 'Nixon' (a 'new' Nixon) in 1968 mean the same thing in Maine, Florida, New Mexico, Alaska? The campaign invites people to think they are voting for the same candidates across the nation, choosing between known alternatives. Yet what sense can attach to 'sameness' in such a ritual? And so on. Of course, presidential elections do not have to be explained solely in terms of democratic control and rational choice. They are permeated, none the less, with democratic values and rhetoric.

As to the Nixon episode, it seemed, when it happened, at once imaginative, helpless, sentimental – even romantic. Here was a leader in travail, reaching out towards ordinary people. In a drama heightened by spontaneity, by the hour of the day, by the anti-war vigil itself, by the historical associations and sheer bulk of the Memorial, Nixon engaged his critics literally at Lincoln's feet. The episode posed in a second way the question of presidential communication. What factors determine how and why the President communicates with Americans? What difference does that communication make to his exercise of power?

So much for the two thoughts. There remained the obvious objection that books on large themes such as presidential power ought to be left to long-term president-watchers, academic in-and-outers, journalists, presidents themselves.

The first consideration persuading me to go ahead was that those books are part of the source material for this one. This book is essentially an argument about how presidential power ought to be studied, not a contribution to the store of information about presidents on the public record. A second consideration was that through the generosity of the American Council of Learned Societies I had the opportunity to research for a year in the United States. One way of using the time would have been to till some modest corner of the foreign field as though I were not a visitor at all. Another, which I chose, was to indulge my status as a visitor, confront a large theme and trust in the adage (while acknowledging hubris) that fresh minds may bring new perspectives to a subject. Whether that is true in this book is for the reader to decide.

1 Power and Communication

Power is variously defined and the subject of endless classifications. For such a key concept this is not surprising; nor does it matter to the present study. Power and allied notions – authority, influence, manipulation, coercion – share the basic quality of being relational. That is to say, A cannot have power (authority, influence, etc.) unless there is B over whom he may exercise it. The essence of the relation consists in the capacity of A to make B do what A wants. Distinctions between power and those other concepts turn on the circumstances and limits of that capacity. In discussion here those distinctions can be disregarded. What is at issue is not the appropriate way of naming different forms of A's capacity to control B, but rather the relation between those forms and the communication processes involved. For the relational quality of power makes communication a pivotal factor. Questions about why B obeys (the sources of power) and about what sort of things B does (the scope of power), as well as about how many Bs there are (the domain of power), can all be expected to receive answers in which the communication factor plays a significant and perhaps determining part. The purpose of this chapter is to explore and illustrate that significance, not to discuss the concept of power at large.[1]

I THE SOURCES OF POWER

(a) Why does B obey A?

To put the question in terms of this book, why do people obey the President? Explanations often boil down to four. (Divergences, as one analyst observes, 'are a matter of finer or larger slices more often than of different categories'.)[2]

Rewards and punishments. People might obey the President because of what he could do to or for them. As commander-in-chief he has coercive powers: both within the armed services and between them and those they may confront, power rests on force. In the administration the President can hire and fire people. He has an armoury of patronage appointments from which to reward partisans, legislators, representatives of sectional and regional interests. For journalists the reward consists in communication itself: access to information about the President. Gradations of access, and changes up and down, are conventional forms of reward and punishment. Benjamin Bradlee's *Conversations with Kennedy* (1975) illustrates the practice well. Bradlee suffered occasional periods of exclusion from the Kennedy circle after stories unfavourable to the Kennedy presidency appeared in his magazine *Newsweek*.

Besides these material resources the President has a bottomless purse of psychological gratifications, from the vulgarly flamboyant to the hardly perceptible. Being psychological, the manner of their communication is all-important: to be photographed with the President loses all point if he is scowling.

Presidential photographs are a cliché of this kind of reward and are themselves open to gradations of presidential involvement. When papers published a picture of John Kennedy inscribed by him to Billie Sol Estes, the subject of a political scandal (at the time of publication, not of the inscription), Kennedy was resentful. 'Sixty thousand copies of that document were distributed by the Democratic National Committee,' he complained to Ben Bradlee, 'none of them actually signed by me, none of them sent to anyone with my particular knowledge.' Kennedy then told Bradlee he had recently been asked by a New Jersey politician 'to sign a picture of himself to one Axel Gottleib. "You can't help but wonder who the hell Axel Gottleib is"', he said.'[3] One might construct a hierarchy of photographs: subject pictured with the President, inscribed; ditto, uninscribed; President pictured without subject, but inscribed to him; ditto, signed but not personally inscribed; ditto, signed but without subject really being sure if President wielded the pen—or, indeed, if human hand wielded it at all.

Doris Kearns describes a comparable hierarchy of presidential gifts in the Johnson White House. It began with

certificates delivered to all those who came within the presidential presence. Each time a person flew on 'Air Force One' or on a presidential helicopter, he received a certificate attesting to that fact. If he flew with President Johnson eleven times in the course of a year, he received eleven certificates. Every person attending a White House dinner received two mementos – a place card lettered by a White House calligrapher and a printed menu, with the presidential seal in gold at the top, describing the food and the wines, the occasion and the date. To the members of his staff, Johnson personally delivered 'CARE' boxes filled with all the foods he loved the most – 10 slabs of peanut brittle, 30 ounces of fudge cake, 6 pounds of chocolate. And, of course, the countless pictures of the man himself.

In the first year of the Johnson presidency, the stock of presidential gifts more than tripled – including, bizarrely, electric toothbrushes engraved with the presidential seal, and waterproof watches inscribed 'Do unto others as you would have others do unto you.' Kearns accumulated twelve toothbrushes.[4]

Gifts, especially if there is much awareness of a pecking order, are at the boundaries of the material and the psychological. The purely non-material gifts may none the less be the most useful – for instance, the honeyed words about a big city mayor or state politician at a public function; or, unless his record has made him a liability, the President's intervention in an election campaign.

Acceptance of legitimacy. Much obedience derives simply from people acknowledging that the President legitimately seeks it of them. Routine civic duties – paying taxes and so on – can often be traced logically to this recognition (shared, in many cases, with the Congress). Congressmen themselves acknowledge, to quote the most obvious illustration, the President's constitutional authority to propose and veto legislation. In constitutional grey areas, like defence and foreign affairs, obedience may be partial or denied. One of the commonest distinctions by commentators has been between 'strong' presidents who seek to stretch the boundaries of their legitimacy and the 'weak' who let them slip. The New Deal was a continuous attempt by F. D. Roosevelt to translate popular legitimacy into governmental actions which would satisfy tests of constitutional legitimacy in the courts as well. In a similarly clear-cut example, Truman banked on his authority to take over steel-mills during a labour dispute in 1952. His authority was respected. Then came the successful challenge by the owners in the Supreme Court and the prop of legitimacy was dashed away.[5] Lyndon Johnson built the Vietnam War on the basis largely of the Gulf of

Tonkin Resolution rushed through Congress in August 1964. Among constitutional specialists it seemed a dubious justification but – the critical factor – it was an effective rationalisation in the minds of the people, and the legitimacy of the war took several years to shatter.[6]

Acceptance of expertise. Obedience based on acknowledgement of presidential expertise is similar to that based on legitimacy. Eisenhower's campaign cry in 1952 – 'I will go to Korea' – was an unusually personal and dramatic invocation of it. 'The President knows best' is an argument that can be used above all in defence and national security. Not only can he claim to know more than Congress and the public; his superior and privileged sources of information enable him to present problems and decisions in what he judges the best manner to secure public support. The claim to superior knowledge is a claim to halt argument. The President knows what you do not know: how, therefore, can you dispute on equal terms? It is difficult to withstand the crude charge of arrogance or disloyalty.

'Referent' power. The last source of power is based not on rational calculation like the others but on emotional attachment. People may obey the President because they identify with him. It is easier to illustrate this within the administration than outside. Every president has among his aides some who possess an inexhaustible commitment; who, to quote Theodore Sorensen, are 'intensely loyal, committed to our chief and determined upon his success'. Wilson had Tumulty; Roosevelt had Howe and Hopkins (among others); Kennedy had other knights beside Sorensen at his Round Table. A Johnson aide, Jack Valenti, attracted ridicule for a speech whose solemn final paragraph began, 'I sleep each night a little better, a little more confidently because Lyndon Johnson is my President.'[7] Nixon's aides, of course, carried loyalty to extreme lengths. Carter brought with him to the White House dedicated aides such as Hamilton Jordan and Jody Powell.

On a broader plane, Richard Nixon sought to achieve by executive reorganisation goals which could not be achieved by legislative means, because of congressional obstruction. His method was that 'trusted lieutenants, tied closely to Richard Nixon and without national reputations of their own, were to be placed in direct charge of the major program bureaucracies of domestic government for the second term'. 'Referent' power, in otherwords, was invoked as a substitute for the ineffective appeal to legitimacy.[8]

Outside the administration all presidents naturally have their thick-or-thin supporters in Congress and beyond. Even Nixon had Rabbi Korff's Citizens' Committee for Fairness to the Presidency in the final stages of Watergate.[9] Among the electorate, Eisenhower, of post-war presidents, has undoubtedly enjoyed the greatest referent power; and Kennedy's charisma was unique, though rooted less in achievement than in promise.

(b) Rewards and punishments: actual, stated and inferred

A distinctive and complicating feature of the reward/punishment power is that it may be effective without the reward actually being given or even offered. The feature is especially important to an analysis of communication processes in the use of power, since those processes largely account for it.

What are the possibilities? First, *A* may reward *B* in order to secure his subsequent obedience. Presidents, for example, habitually appoint to the Supreme Court judges who they hope will make decisions sympathetic to the President's own goals. (F. D. Roosevelt's court-packing plan was the extreme case.) In Britain, prime ministers often include in their cabinet a few members who are thereby bottled in the dark glass of collective responsibility for government policy, making them less troublesome than if they sat on the back benches. From the President's standpoint, giving rewards in advance is comparatively unattractive: as the history of the Supreme Court shows, appointees may not always turn out as expected.

More satisfactory for the President is a position in which he can make his reward follow obedience and thus be conditional upon it. How then does someone (for example, a senator) know he will be rewarded if he obeys? There are two alternatives. The President may deliberately indicate his intention to the senator, or the senator may infer that intention for himself. In either case the President is understood to convey a message; but only in the first does he intend to do so. Both situations are fraught with the possibility of misunderstandings, lying as they do in the swampy relationships of language, meaning and intention, and referring to hypothetical future actions. At one extreme the President may intend to offer a reward but find it goes unrecognised. At the other, an offer may be understood where none is intended.

If the nature and conditions of a reward or threat are made explicit in the offer, the danger of misunderstanding is lowest. It seems unlikely, though, that they are often spelt out plainly, even in private. For what does the President gain? If his offers are vague, whether in substance or in probability, he can pretend they were never made: he can dangle the same favour before other aspirants, multiplying the effectiveness of his patronage without challenge to his integrity. If obedience can be secured by the offer of reward, the reward itself becomes redundant and may be available for offering to other people. Since the failure to deliver the reward may reduce the chances of the aspirant obeying in the future, it is preferable that the offer should be ambiguous in the first place – unless the President is sure he has no further need of the aspirant. Most often, we can suppose, presidents offer rewards and threats obliquely: through intermediaries like congressional liaison staffs, who can be 'disowned' if necessary, and through a wide range of nods and winks. The President can make his offers as a mistress teases her lover, now rousing his expectations with a promise, now demanding new favours on the grounds that the promise is misunderstood.

The advantage to the President of making his offers ambiguous carries with it the disadvantage that they will perhaps be misunderstood in a way which actually reduces the probability of obedience. This is perhaps more true of threats than offers of reward. Explicit threats, especially if public, are notoriously counterproductive. Yet the veiled threat – intended to make acquiescence unembarrassing – may be so opaque as to be unseen. This, evidently, was what happened when Truman tried to bring General MacArthur to heel in Korea.[10]

When the President intends to secure obedience by offering rewards or threats, then, pressures inherent in this kind of power encourage him to communicate his intentions obliquely. In the second of the alternatives through which someone knows he will be rewarded for obedience, the ambiguities of communication are greater still. For here the existence of the offer or threat is a product entirely of that person's inferences. Certainly these will be based on 'messages' communicated from the President. But the messages are either unconscious or not intended as threats or offers at all. This is the well-known rule of anticipated reactions: the senator does what he believes the President wants in the expectation that the President will consequently reward him. Three kinds of source for his expectations can be distinguished. The most general is his experience of the manner in which presidents as a breed behave. If senators take the presidential line, he has observed, they tend to find federal funds, jobs, contracts and personal perks come their way. Nothing the incumbent president has done justifies the senator's obedience: the senator, even so, builds up expectations of reward. A second, more specific, source of expectations is the senator's inferences from the behaviour – not the language – of the incumbent president. Some gesture, as slight perhaps as the squeeze of a handshake, leaves in the senator the impression that the President looks favourably on him. Often such an impression might be conveyed indirectly, by the behaviour of presidential intermediaries whom the senator chooses to see as conveying conscious presidential intentions.

The third source of the senator's expectations is his assumption that the President's words mean not exactly what they say but somewhat more or less, or something else together. The President does not seem to be offering a reward or threat, but actually he is, the senator believes. So may people mislead themselves. A small example from the early months of the Carter administration illustrates the point. Carter had announced his decision to cancel nineteen water-resource projects across the country as a quick contribution to his campaign pledge of eliminating government waste. At the same time, his nominations to various senior appointments were up for Senate approval. Carter's congressional liaison aide, Frank Moore, was said to view the situation like this: 'The Senators think the President has threatened to cancel [the water projects] as a political move, to trade for their votes when he needs them later – on things like disarmament and reorganisation.' But in fact Carter had not done that at all: 'He just thinks the nineteen dams are a waste of money and harmful to the environment.' The cancellation, in other words, had no object apart from the stated one (and any incidental gain in popular support). Yet, Moore concluded, 'If the Senators figure that out, they'll begin to take [Carter] less seriously as a politician.'[11] Whether Moore's attitude was correctly reported makes little difference to the aptness of the illustration. Senators expect the President's legislative moves to have ulterior motives, to the extent that an uncalculated move may be taken as a sign of naïvety or ineptitude.

To a president, the power deriving from anticipation of his reactions must be disconcerting. It is exercised independently of his expressed wishes, perhaps even in contradiction to what he really wants. It suggests to him that nothing he says will be taken at face value. It operates regardless of his understanding of the people concerned; whereas, in his use of the reward power deliberately, information about the recipients is important. It is power exercised in ignorance; yet if those anticipating rewards are not sooner or later rewarded, the President may find himself unwittingly accumulating enemies.

Taking the different forms of reward power together, we may see how limited is the President's control over its use. He may not be short of rewards and threats that secure obedience; but his control over the circumstances in which they are effective is restricted by the pressures towards ambiguity (in those cases where he offers them) and by his complete lack of contact (in cases where the power rests on inferences about his reactions). These limitations are a product entirely of the communication processes characteristic of this source of power.

(c)   Sources of power: differences in communication

The subtle and distinctive communication processes of the reward power result from the need for two kinds of message to pass before it is effective. One conveys the desired (or inferred) action. The other conveys the power-holder's intention to offer a reward. All the other sources of power involve messages only about the desired action and not about the power-holder's future behaviour.

There are distinctive differences between these other sources too. Power based on the acceptance of legitimacy or expertise requires the power-holder to convey intrinsic qualities of the action desired – that it is indeed legitimately sought or that it falls within his area of expertise. 'Referent' power, by contrast, requires simply the unambiguous communication of the desired action: 'Who will rid me of this turbulent priest?' Loyalty does the rest. (Was this how Watergate started?)

Since these sources of power involve only one kind of message they are correspondingly less open than reward power to misunderstanding by the people expected to obey. To that extent, following the argument of the previous section, they are also less variable. Least open to misunderstanding is referent power. But although only the desired action and the fact that the power-holder desires it need conveying, drastic misunderstanding is possible on both grounds. (Through misunderstanding of King Henry II's true intentions, of course, was Thomas à Becket, the turbulent priest, killed.) Some of Nixon's most faithful supporters may have believed to the end that he did not mean the Watergate adventures to be undertaken. The same deliberate, as well as unintentional, allusions and ambiguities are open to a president here as were analysed in the use of the reward power. The crucial difference is that there they are connected to the problem of securing obedience, while in referent power no such problem exists. Deliberate ambiguity here, rather, is connected to situations like a president's doubts about whether an action is really a good idea: he can protect his own reputation by saying he did not intend an action if it turns out badly. The 'Becket syndrome' is widespread among those used to executive authority. Apparently categorical commands may be just symbolic expressions of frustration – of what the power-holder would like to do in the absence of present constraints. Kennedy's famous order to cancel White House subscriptions to the *New York Herald Tribune* was rationalised in just these terms by his press secretary, Pierre Salinger. The order was given, Salinger explained, by a minor functionary who did not understand that the President was just 'letting off steam'. Similarly Richard Nixon issued wild orders which subordinates found it prudent to ignore.[12]

In referent power, then, ambiguity attaches only to the questions, 'What is required of me?' and 'Does the President definitely want it?' None attaches to the question 'Shall I do it?'. This power is most akin to command – and to the imagery of hypodermic needles and throwing switches. Since it rests in the emotions (and often, for those close to the President, on long association in Washington or a home state) presidents may unintentionally stretch it till it breaks. F. D. Roosevelt generally dropped favourites before they dropped him. Kennedy was not in office long enough for chains to snap. Nixon's men remained remarkably loyal as his troubles grew: the voluntary resigners – law officers Elliot Richardson and William Ruckelshaus, for example – were not at all Nixon loyalists. The man who, characteristically, stretched loyalty to breaking point was Lyndon Johnson. Of the twelve top aides appointed after his election in 1964, ten failed to last out the term, including George Reedy, Jack Valenti, Horace Busby and Bill Moyers.

Power based on communicating a demand's legitimacy, or its basis in a president's expertise, involves an extra dimension of possible misunderstanding – although fewer dimensions than reward power. So great are the ambiguities about the responsibilities of the President in the American Constitution that the legitimacy of particular demands – as some of the instances in section I(b) above indicate – may depend on how they are understood. The connection is thus crucial between the presentation of a presidential action and its acceptance by people required to act in consequence. The obvious symbols of legitimacy can be powerfully invoked – the White House itself (the sense of history, the little rituals, the evidence of industry, resource and staff work), as well as small reminders such as the presidential seal of office and big ones like motor-cars and Air Force One.

The language of appeals to legitimacy and expertise is equally important. The wording of Gerald Ford's pardon of Richard Nixon, delivered in front of the TV cameras on 7 September 1974, was decked in pomp: 'Now, therefore, I, Gerald R. Ford, President of the United States, pursuant to the pardon power conferred upon me by Article II, Section 2, of the Constitution, have granted and by these presents do grant, a full, free and absolute pardon unto Richard Nixon . . . .' An altogether more spectacular example is Kennedy's painstaking broadcast justifying – literally to the world at large – the Cuban missile blockade. Parts of the speech were rhetoric and statements of resolve ('Our goal is not the victory of might, but the vindication of right', etc.), but a surprising amount, given the nature of the worldwide audience and that this was their introduction to the crisis, consisted of confusing detail about treaties infringed and missile capabilities. In his choice of language the President was invoking at once the general legitimacy of his office, its expertise in military intelligence, and a further legitimacy based on reasoned argument about a system of international law. The speech was followed up with photographic evidence supporting the charge that missiles were being transported to Cuba. The photographs did not show obviously identifiable missiles seen from the air. Their importance lay in the fact of publication, not in a naïve presidential belief that citizens could identify them. Here was confirmation that the President was determined to act reasonably and ready to show the world his evidence. On other occasions, of course, the mystifying language of strategists and the armed services has concealed dubious evidence, bad argument and crude value-judgements.

Economic affairs have a comparable language, with the added importance that by its use a president may increase or reduce the 'confidence' on which so many decisions throughout the economy rest. Foreign-exchange markets are a sensitive indicator of that confidence. In December 1977, for instance, the dollar fell sharply. The White House responded with a strong presidential statement of support, blaming the slide largely on 'a mistaken belief that the United States is not prepared to adopt an effective energy program'. The dollar promptly hardened. 'Although the President's words were not very different from those spoken by his Under-Secretary for Monetary Affairs . . . just a few weeks earlier', the London *Times* commented (23 December 1977), 'the markets attach more weight to the pronouncements of a President'.

The language of such statements will be taken as indicative, finally, not only of a president's expertise and legitimacy, but also of his determination. Given the ambiguities of the constitution, evidence of determination may itself, in turn, do much to ensure popular belief in the President's expertise and legitimacy.

(d) Sources of power: communication to the power-holder

The previous discussion should already have shown that communication processes are crucial to both sides of the power relation: *A*'s power over *B* depends on what has been communicated to *A* about *B* as well as to *B* about *A*. This factor needs further discussion before we move on to the communication implications of the scope and domain of power.

What the President knows about the people he seeks to influence will affect both the kind of thing he can expect to make them do and his chances of getting them to do it. The knowledge may be used, first, to make an estimate of the range of actions open to him. The breadth of that range is one measure of his power: how many times have presidents had the power to advance great goals but failed to act because they did not perceive it? 'Strong' presidents, to use the conventional term again, have defined their choices broadly, like Woodrow Wilson and the two Roosevelts, even if they have not always succeeded.

The connection is close between information flow to the President, his perception of his range of choices, and his exercise of power. Why did President Ford pardon Richard Nixon – a bare month after Nixon's resignation? He may have felt he really had not much choice. The time that trials would take, the distraction they would cause, the humiliation Nixon had already suffered – all these justified putting a higher priority on behaviour symbolic of healing wounds and making a new beginning. The reaction may have made Ford wonder: there was an immediate 21-point drop in his opinion-poll popularity. Perhaps after all the healing process would not have been incompatible with legal process. Indeed, within Ford's own camp the pardon produced a quick failure of authority: Jerry ter Horst, his press secretary and the first appointment to his staff, resigned on the point of principle. Obviously some people would have disapproved, whichever Ford did – pardon or not pardon. But perhaps opinion on the alternatives was more finely balanced – his range of choice was wider – than Ford let himself believe. Another example can be taken from the reflections of Theodore Sorensen. If Congress had been told the extent of the conflicting reports Kennedy was receiving about Vietnam, he argues, the effective range of choices would have been widened. The war might not have escalated.[13]

Included in the President's range of choices is 'the second face of power' – the exercise of power through 'non-decisions'. By choosing not to do things which might be within his power the President exercises power just as much as when he exerts himself to initiate change. Such 'non-decisions' are particularly relevant to ideas about the nature of presidential leadership. A relatively passive president like Eisenhower or Ford needs a smaller flow of information to him than an activist. Problems of presidential 'isolation' are acute only to the extent that his isolation is from areas in which in fact he wishes to be active.

A second product of the President's knowledge about the people he seeks to influence may be a calculation by him of the best way of getting them to do what he wants. Inaccurate information may mean miscalculation and failure – or else successful use of power on the 'wrong' basis. Rewards, for example, may be inadequate or inappropriate. Lyndon Johnson sought to woo intellectuals at one point by an elaborate White House 'Salute to the Arts'. The effort misfired. Far from seeing it as an apotheosis, some of the distinguished invitees construed it as a stratagem to associate them with Johnson's goals in Vietnam.[14] Again, coercion might be used where it was unnecessary: rough handling of anti-war demonstrators in the Johnson and Nixon administrations may have positively harmed presidential goals. A president may misjudge the power of his legitimacy or expertise to carry conviction. Richard Nixon hoped that releasing his own edited transcripts of the White House tapes would satisfy critics that he was not involved with the Watergate cover-up. He and Johnson, chief victims of a presidential 'credibility gap', both found that they could not assume that an appeal to their legitimacy or expertise would generally win support. Wrong information may equally lead to undue reliance on referent power. Johnson, we have seen, was apt to stretch the loyalty of his aides beyond breaking point.

No doubt many such calculations are rough or are not made at all. Moreover, power can obviously rest in particular cases on several bases. The base may look different, too, to some people from the way it looks to others. For example, Gerald Ford based his pardon of Richard Nixon on grounds of legitimacy – his constitutional prerogatives. Yet some observers preferred to see it as a cynical exercise of reward power: they believed it was part of a deal whereby Nixon was pardoned in return for agreeing to resign.[15]

Whatever the actual degree of calculation by presidents on the basis of their knowledge about those whom they want to influence, the important point for purposes of a communication analysis is that the President needs at least some information – unless he is going to work in the dark – and that he cannot be sure of knowing what he needs to know. Referent power illustrates the problem best of all, since it is especially liable to a 'Brutus effect'. Precisely because this power rests on loyalty or affection, that is to say, it tends to lack warning mechanisms. Other bases of power, as we have seen, may involve bargaining about rewards or argument about expertise and legitimacy: in the course of their exercise, the President can judge the probability of their future effectiveness. But the unquestioning obedience of the trusty servant can blind the master to increasing disaffection. Caesar saw a warning in Cassius's 'lean and hungry look'; but Brutus's dagger struck 'the most unkindest cut of all', because it came from the hand of a loyal friend. Winston Churchill was staggered by his resounding defeat in the British general election of 1945 because the suspension of party conflict during the war had removed the benchmarks of popular support. He did not realise how strongly the electorate wished the post-war world to be different from the 1930s. Similarly Charles de Gaulle, as President of the Fifth Republic of France from 1958, was accustomed to exert his will over politicians by resorting to popular referenda in times of crisis. In 1969 he found, to his surprise, that the device no longer worked. He staked his authority on the outcome of a referendum ostensibly about regional reform. The result was less than convincing. Shortly he retired.

There can be no clearer example of the frustration ignorance may

Wingate College Library

cause a president than the Nixon administration's wire-taps and surveillance, designed to find information that would help the President prevent people damaging the prospects of his policies by leaking secrets to the press. Perhaps the outstanding case was the burglary of the psychiatrist of former Pentagon official Daniel Ellsberg, the man who leaked the 'Pentagon papers' that laid bare the background to American involvement in Vietnam.

By denying the President information, then, people may thwart his exercise of power – whether by narrowing the range of options he perceives as available to him or by preventing him knowing how someone might be influenced.

Controlling the time at which information reaches the President, moreover, may be equally inhibiting. Bureaucracies can distort the decisions of those at the top by regulating the flow of information to them. The decision-maker cannot monitor all their activities. Kennedy remarked with feeling that the only secrets in the State Department were those kept from him. He discovered from the Russians themselves during the Cuban crisis that American missiles were still stationed on the Russian borders of Turkey. Had he known beforehand, he might well have felt the fact would affect his bargaining power.[16] Johnson was continually misinformed about the Vietnam War. He and Nixon both made decisions based on 'command power' that were strategically inadequate because they used faulty intelligence. Nixon's failure, not once but twice in succession, to secure Senate confirmation of his nominees to the Supreme Court (Carswell and Haynsworth) was generally supposed to stem from miscalculation of attitudes on Capitol Hill.

A final reflection of the fact that the President's power stems from what he is told as well as from what he says is the perennial suspicion of presidential isolation.[17] This suspicion has many sides. One of them is the fear that an ill-informed president will do good things badly and bad things all too well. Such was one of the many conclusions drawn about Watergate, the idiocy of an 'isolated' president.

II   THE SCOPE AND DOMAIN OF POWER

The scope and domain of power can be discussed together, since each involves similar questions about the significance of communication processes. 'Scope' denotes the subject areas in which power may be exercised; 'domain' denotes the number of people the power may encompass. The importance of communication lies mainly in its connection with ambiguities and uncertainties in presidential and public perceptions of the limits of scope and domain; with the consequences of the exercise of power at one time for its exercise at another; and with the implications of exercising power over one subject or group for its exercise over others.

(a) The limits of scope and domain

Who is within the President's domain? What subjects come within his scope? The answers to those questions dissolve the more one tries to fix them precisely. Much of the literature on the presidency derives from the differences between theory and practice. What the Constitution says are the scope and domain of presidential power differs from experience under any president. The incumbent is president at once of more and less than the United States of America. As leader of a global power, he has been able to affect the lives of millions beyond the United States. Close to home – Canada, the Caribbean, Central America – his influence is inescapable. Conversely, among those constitutionally within his domain are doubtless some whose alienation makes their submission minimal. Draft-avoiders, for example, effectively removed themselves from his domain during the Vietnam War by illegally leaving the country for Canada and Europe. At any time there are bound to be people who never do what the President wants, except in the most negative sense of not doing things that are illegal.

The boundaries of presidential scope and domain are a matter of perception – and hence of communication. If people do not hear the President they cannot heed his cry. Whatever the basis on which power rests in particular cases (rewards, threats, legitimacy), it can be effective only over those who perceive it to be directed at them. Draft-avoiders challenged, as a matter of conscience, the President's authority over them as commander-in-chief. Those who opposed the draft but accepted the legal consequences in effect denied that conscription for the war was within the President's scope but implicitly conceded that they remained within his domain. Those who by going abroad sought to avoid the legal consequences as well as the draft denied also that they were within his domain. In short, the President has to convince people that they are within his domain – that the exercise of his power over them is a real possibility and that it may be exercised within a certain scope. Symbolic gestures can often be understood to have just such an aim. When Carter turned down White House thermostats to 65°F in 1977 he signalled his intention to have an effective energy policy. In the event, the initiative failed; and in other fields too, notably the search for peace in the Middle East and for price and wage stabilisation at home, Carter suffered from having goals which depended upon the co-operation of people outside his domain.[18]

The other side of this coin is the President's own perception of the boundaries of his scope and domain. This includes both his own view and his understanding of the views of other people. In each case the factors discussed in the previous section are crucial. For what the President believes about the practicability of exercising power is likely to affect his decision to try and do so. American withdrawal from Vietnam was arguably based on the grounds that American power could not be made effective there – or not without paying an unacceptable cost at home. Both grounds depended on information flow to the President. The calculation of the domestic costs of the war was perhaps governed especially by impressions and imponderables. The protesters at the White House gates – whose epithets Richard Nixon could hear 'even if I had plugs in my ears' – carried a powerful message.[19]

That message, moreover, may have been inaccurate. The 'silent majority' was often invoked but never fully tested. Perhaps Lyndon Johnson and Richard Nixon could really have waged war in South East Asia until their original goals (however defined) were met. A president, that is to say, may underestimate his power as well as overestimate it. Sometimes people may be ready to obey although he does not realise it. Sometimes, perhaps, they do obey without him knowing, and certainly without his expecting it. His behaviour may have all sorts of unintended consequences. John Kennedy, to quote a trivial instance, was told that his failure to wear a hat was helping to kill the hat industry.[20] In the extreme case the President may not know he is exercising power over someone, nor may that person know it is the President whom he is obeying: both parties are the victims of misperception or incomplete communication.

Apart from the effects of feedback, the President's view of his scope and domain will also be affected by his general view of his job. An incoming president has to communicate not only his policies for specific subject areas but also which subject areas he considers to be within the scope of his power. Once in office he will continually be faced with the question whether to get involved in events. Crises provide excellent illustrations of the resulting problems. (They are discussed in detail in Chapter 2.) The record 109-day coal strike in 1977–8, for example, remained outside the President's scope for many weeks but at length he became deeply involved.

There is less room for variation in different presidents' perceptions of their domain. In one area, foreign policy, American history has, however, included in the space of fifty years a swing from isolationism to the most active foreign initiatives; and foreign relations in the nuclear age involve extreme subtleties of communication about domains. Before rocketry and nuclear weapons, a State's domain was defined by physical conditions and by limitations on the movement of armies. Domains might grow and shrink; but their boundaries were visible – if frequently contested. In a world of nuclear super-powers, where the effectiveness of weapons consists in the paradox of their not being used, States need to send messages indicating unambiguously whether territories that are unavoidably within their domain in terms of the reach of nuclear weapons are to be considered actually as sacrosanct. For the United States Cuba was the classic case in the 1960s. She was not in the United States' domain so far as internal politics were concerned: a Castroist revolution was her own affair. (Even that, of course, was a matter of dispute. The Eisenhower administration considered that her internal politics *were* in the United States' domain, and the Bay of Pigs adventure was endorsed accordingly. The new president, Kennedy, perceived Cuba as *outside* his domain; and when the adventure failed he took responsibility only in order to demonstrate his grip on his administration rather than from personal commitment to the enterprise.) So far as the military involvement of outside powers was concerned, on the other hand, Kennedy effectively communicated to Khruschev in the 1962 missile crisis his conviction that Cuba was in the American and not the Soviet domain. How far a president sees his domain extending beyond the United States, and where in particular, is a matter which each new president has to communicate.

The boundaries of the President's scope and domain are further blurred by variations in the level of commitment felt by people within the domain. People may freely perceive themselves as subject in principle to presidential power but be resistant or vague about it in practice. The power of 'moral leadership', usually claimed by presidents, provides a clear example. Who is to be led? What about?

How are we to recognise it in practice? American citizens might be willing in general to concede a measure of authority to the President to tell them what is right or wrong. The strength of feeling against Vietnam War registers was an example of it; so was the general support for Carter's boycott of the 1980 Olympic Games. But for few or none would that authority be absolute, and certainly not in every sphere of life. Other subjects of presidential power are less ephemeral. In all, however, the degree of popular commitment will depend to some extent on how the presidential goal is communicated.

(b) Timing

The implications of the exercise of power now for its exercise later have a bearing on its scope and domain just as we saw in section (a) that they have on its sources. In communication terms, the problem for a president is to know what effect upon the scope and domain of power in the middle and long run is made by his communication in the short run. Communication which effects power over particular persons and subjects at one moment may reduce the probability of compliance later – and vice versa. Calculations arising from these possibilities provide much of the stuff of Neustadt's analysis of the presidency, in which the incumbent is seen as needing to nurture his reputation and prestige and, above all, to 'guard his power prospects'. His power is the product of a bargaining process – and to strike a favourable bargain now may be at the cost of an unfavourable one later.

Given the flexibility of the presidential office, the time dimension is closely connected to questions about the boundaries of scope and domain that have already been discussed. In particular, timing is relevant to the levitational, 'dare-to-be-great' potential of the office. In some parts of its scope and domain the claim to exercise power can be self-fulfilling. Even when extending the scope of the office on a massive scale, F. D. Roosevelt got away with a lot by asserting a right to do so. Mystification and mythologising help the process. Looking back to the Kennedy years in the aftermath of Nixon, Theodore Sorensen remarks that 'Camelot-like glorifications of the Presidency are part of the problem'. By unintentionally raising public expectations of what could be achieved, he argues, the Kennedy administration made it easier for a successor-president to seek a monopoly of governmental power.[21] Similarly, congressional strictures in reaction to the excesses of Nixon, it could be argued, were likely to produce a weakened presidency. In this way, as J. M. Burns points out, the pendulum swings between 'a public opinion first calling for, and then repudiating, the heroic type of leader'.[22]

(c) Conflicts of interest with scope and domain

Much more complicated than the communication implications of the time dimension are those that arise because of the multitude of subjects and persons within the President's scope and domain. In the extreme case, a power-holder might wish to exercise power simultaneously over people who all have contradictory interests and on subjects that are incompatible. The only way he could do that would be by finding courses of action which seemed compatible even though they were not.

The American President's position is not quite as bad as that. In so far as the activities within his scope can be measured by public expenditure, he can seek to adjust incompatibilities by budgetary means. His capacity to succeed, of course, depends much on congressional relations; and his public communication is a factor both in these and in the wider endorsement of his expenditure goals. Similarly, the conflicting interests of the people within his domain (granted the uncertainties about its boundaries) are normally capable of adjustment – or at least containment – by peaceful means (with the notable exception of the Civil War).

The specific communication problem for the President here remains, even so, the possibility that a communication which effects the exercise of power in one subject or part of the domain may simultaneously prevent the exercise of power in another. Nixon's bottling-up of the Watergate scandal was effective for a time in maintaining his legitimacy and enabling him to carry on an innovative foreign policy; yet the growing hostility of Congress reduced his capacity to achieve results in domestic policy. Gerald Ford's pardon of Nixon was effective – not just over Nixon but in being widely accepted (if not approved) as a legitimate exercise of presidential power. Yet it ended the Ford honeymoon for many citizens, arguably reducing the likelihood of their supporting initiatives like Ford's anti-inflation policy. Lyndon Johnson provided a typically pithy illustration of this familiar presidential predicament. After American troops had been briefly sent to the Dominican Republic in 1965, he remarked, 'I knew that if I acted to send in the troops . . . I couldn't live in the hemisphere, and if I didn't, I couldn't live in this country.'[23]

What can a president do, faced with that predicament? Unless he is content simply to accept it as a limitation on his power he can, in sum, do two things. He may seek to minimise the conflict of interest, using his power towards the goal of compromise – if the problem permits. This involves persuading people to accept less than they want, and it may include costs in the future exercise of power. Alternatively, the President may seek to use power by communicating to the different parties in such a way as to change their perceptions: either so that they have a new perception of their own interests, no longer seeing them as in conflict with others; or else (as was suggested above) by making them believe their own interest is being served. Two fields which regularly provide illustrations of such presidential activity are congressional relations and presidential elections. Building a coalition for a bill requires a variety of forms of presidential persuasion; while techniques of voter-appeal require the definition of target audiences and the communication of specifically appropriate messages. Beyond that, public electioneering requires communications that are ambiguous enough to be understood by different people in ways which, however various, satisfy them all.

In either of those responses to his predicament, but especially in the latter, the President's task of communicating differently to different people is likely to be greatly eased if he can avoid his messages 'clashing'. The best way to avoid misunderstanding by third parties is to exclude them and make the dialogue private. Hence the great affinity not just of power and communication, but also between those and secrecy.

III POWER, COMMUNICATION AND SECRECY

Secrecy denotes the concealment of information. It is related to power because of the possibility that persons from whom information is hidden might behave differently if they knew it. To keep something secret can therefore be a means of controlling someone's behaviour. Secrecy, further, is intentional. Information unintentionally kept hidden is more accurately described as 'unknown'.

Whether a person would actually behave differently if he possessed hidden information obviously depends on a variety of factors. Only if the controller of the information has himself previously gained the right knowledge about these will he be in a position to use secrecy reliably as a means of power. Otherwise he will have to guess. His guesses might be so bad that, far from influencing the person's behaviour in the intended direction, he will have concealed the very information which, if imparted, would have secured his object. Moreover, this need of the power-holder for information about the person to be influenced provides the latter with the opportunity for the practice of secrecy too; for he in turn may be able to avoid giving the power-holder necessary knowledge. This process could in theory be infinitely regressive. (How does the person know whether the power-holder knows what the necessary knowledge is?) No doubt in the world of spies and counterspies, bluff and double-bluff, it may be so. ('He thinks that I think that he thinks that I think . . . .') Latter-day hypotheses about the murder of President Kennedy had more than a touch of such thinking too.[24] The power of concealment is thus highly conditional; and, like the matters discussed in section 1(d), it reflects the importance to the power-holder of adequate communication to himself.

The incorporation of third parties into this two-sided model complicates but does not substantially change the relation of power and secrecy. First, information may be kept secret from third parties but disclosed to the persons over whom power is exercised. If the third parties knew it, so goes the assumption, they might change their behaviour – and in a way which threatened the power-holder. Furthermore, the changed behaviour of the third parties might, if it became known to the obedient persons, render them disobedient too. Secondly, information may be kept secret from persons over whom power is exercised but *not* from third parties. In this case the third parties in effect share in the exercise of power, provided that it is true that they could themselves disclose the information to the obedient persons. Thirdly, information may be kept secret by the power-holder from third parties and obedient persons alike – the most complete kind of secrecy. The more one divides the 'third parties' and the 'obedient persons' the more complex the range of relationships becomes.

American presidents find secrecy expedient in variations of all those ways. Kennedy, for example, kept his plans in the Cuban missile crisis secret from the American public lest their knowledge (as 'third parties') constrain his ability to influence the Kremlin. 'If our deliberations had been publicized', wrote Robert Kennedy in

Thirteen Days, '. . . I believe the course that we ultimately would have taken would have been quite different and filled with far greater risks. The fact that we were able to talk, debate, argue, disagree, and then debate some more was essential in choosing our ultimate course'.[25] Good examples from the Vietnam War can be found of attempts to isolate one part of the domain – members of the armed services – from another part – anti-war members of the general public. When Lyndon Johnson made a stirring speech to American troops in Korea in 1966 and told them to forget the draft-card burners and to 'do your duty as you see it', he was, so to speak, exhorting them to self-censorship, to shut out of their minds the evil thoughts which, ideally, the President would have liked to prevent entering.[26] Anti-war protesters were a source of arguments and information – indeed, their existence was information in itself – which might reduce the President's capacity to control the troops. In time the ranks of protesters were swelled by Vietnam veterans themselves. These were a special embarrassment because they had crossed from one part of the domain into the other: anti-war information brought by people who had actually fought in the war was likely to be influential. The White House took great trouble to counter this leakage from one domain to another by its own publicity for pro-war veterans.

Secrecy may also be used to separate different subjects within the President's scope. Policies can be presented as solutions to problems without drawing attention to their implications for other problems. Nuclear energy, one may claim, was advanced for many years without its side-effects on the environment being emphasised. The Eisenhower road-building programme secured easier endorsement through the minimisation of its implications for the railway system. Kennedy's space programme seemed more attractive as (somehow) keeping the United States as world leader in science and technology than it would have done if alternative uses for the resources had been spelt out.

Obviously people want to put their case in the best light: hence the lobbying industry on Capitol Hill. Concealment of information is a commonplace in the competition for resources. Where it becomes of most significance to the President is defence and national security, areas in which he has a near-monopoly of information, in which the public right to know is weakest and his power, based on command, is strongest. The President could use secrecy about Vietnam to minimise its unattractive policy by-products, to exaggerate American success and to combat dissent at home. Secrecy enabled him to present his policy in the terms which he believed would maximise his power to implement it. As David Wise argues,

> A President can go on television, as Nixon did in 1972 to announce the mining of Haiphong harbor and other North Vietnamese ports, and rally substantial public support for military actions that may lead to war. In many such cases, the President completely controls the version of events that he chooses to tell his audience.[27]

Wise argues, indeed, that, in episodes like the Tonkin Gulf incident, which was used as the occasion for stepping up American involvement in the war in 1964, and Johnson's incursion into the Dominican Republic the next year, information was used by the administration to shape the description of events in order to conform to predetermined government policies. All events are 'shaped' by somebody: only by being 'shaped', or put in context, do they acquire meaning. The strength of the President on those and comparable occasions consists in being able to choose without challenge what information to include in his account of the event – and to insert information which is incorrect.

A clear example of the use of secrecy to maximise consent among members of the domain who would not be directly involved in carrying out a policy was Johnson's decision on 1 April 1965 to commit ground forces to combat duty in South Vietnam. The relevant National Security Council memo said that the President desired 'all possible precautions' against premature publicity. 'The actions themselves should be taken as rapidly as practicable but in ways that should minimize any appearance of sudden changes in policy. . . . The President's desire is that these movements and changes should be understood as being gradual and wholly consistent with existing policy.' By the time the change of policy became public through the action of a State Department press spokesman on 8 June, the White House was able to claim, with purely technical accuracy, that 'There has been no change in the mission of the United States ground combat units in Vietnam in recent days or weeks.'[28] Troops in Vietnam must themselves have been sharply aware of the change in their role from 'advisory' to combat. No doubt they obeyed orders for various of the reasons discussed in section I. To the 'third parties' in the case – American citizens at large – a different picture of the circumstances was presented, appropriate to securing their support by acceptance of legitimacy and expertise.

A few other variations on the theme are worth mention. For example, actions by people in one part of the domain may be concealed by the President indefinitely rather than just for a few months, like the case above. Defence and national security are the cloak for many secret doings. One of the conundrums of democratic government is how to prevent legitimate secrecy from being directed to illegitimate ends. Until activities are disclosed in the public domain their legitimacy cannot be confirmed; yet to disclose them may destroy their effectiveness.[29] The obvious illustrations are criminal detection, intelligence and counter-intelligence. The Watergate inquiries uncovered any amount of presidential power that could be exercised only because it was kept secret; and one of the common defences of the Nixon White House was that such practices as wire-tapping and the aggressive scrutiny of personal tax returns had gone on in one form or another under previous administrations. Again, presidents may exercise power without disclosing – perhaps to those at the end of the chain of command as well as to third parties – who it is that is doing so. Some of those involved in Watergate did not know that the President himself was involved. (That, at first, was Nixon's claim as well). The product of power need not be secret in such cases: President Truman, for instance, deliberately attached Secretary of State George Marshall's name, rather than his own, to the European recovery programme after the Second World War, in order to maximise its chances of acceptance by Congress. Many of the fruits of CIA activity, it seems, have first become public without any connection with that agency being plain at all. The Pentagon papers documented the connection in a number of them, including the November 1963 coup against South Vietnam's President Ngo Dinh Diem, to which President Kennedy was party.[30] The downfall of the Allende regime in Chile is another well-known case. When they happened, neither of these was publicly presented as an action within the President's scope and domain. Secrecy can also be used the other way round – to attach the President's name to exercises of power with which he has in fact had no connections (see Chapter 2) – the object being to increase his prestige and, to use Neustadt's terminology again, to 'guard his power prospects'.

Secrecy can be used, lastly, to exploit the idea of surprise. 'Surprise' consists in communicating information to people who had no previous information which prepared them to expect it. How are they to evaluate it? In the absence of other information providing benchmarks, and if they know that it comes from a person of authority and expertise like the President, people are more likely to accept the power-holder's evaluation than if the element of surprise were absent. (The likelihood remains relative: those alienated from the President may indeed be less likely to accept it, being suspicious of deception.) Provided the President retains credibility, therefore, surprise adds to his power. David Wise summarises the effect:

> Few Americans are emotionally resistant to a dramatic, sudden appearance by the President on television in the midst of a foreign policy crisis. There is a special tension in the pit of the viewer's stomach, and the adrenalin flows a bit more. . . . What is it? Are Soviet missiles on the way? Has World War III begun? It *must* be important if the President has cut into the networks in prime time. . . .[31]

Unpleasant actions are not to be turned into pleasant ones by surprise. Reactions to Nixon's announcement of the bombing of Cambodia scarcely indicated willing acceptance. It remains doubtful, however, whether the hostile reactions would have been any less if the news had been leaked out gradually.

Any new information has an element of surprise: if it were totally predictable it could not be called new. Even if he does not use it as a deliberate instrument of power in conjunction with secrecy, a president cannot avoid 'surprising' people whenever he conveys information about subjects in which he has a monopoly. In national security and foreign affairs, although his monopoly is by no means complete, there is inevitably a great amount of secrecy that may perhaps be aptly called 'bureaucratic'. That is to say, information remains unpublished for innocent reasons connected with volume, organisation and expertise, rather than for devious reasons of power and policy. The effects of this innocent secrecy, however, may be just the same as of the other. It is thus difficult for a president to avoid the appearance of deliberate concealment and deception even where none is intended. 'Unannounced presidential decisions based on unpublished information from undisclosed sources were at the heart of both Vietnam and Watergate', writes Theodore Sorensen.[32] They may equally lie at the heart of more justifiable ventures. The comment, none the less, is a powerful if ironic tribute to the contribution of secrecy to presidential power.

IV CHALLENGES TO THE POWER-HOLDER

The discussion of secrecy and much of the preceding discussion of scope and domain have both indirectly raised the question of challenges to the power-holder. Third parties, observing but not themselves submitting to power, may be able to thwart a power-holder's aims, depending on what is communicated to and by them. The obedient person has then in some sense to choose either to obey the power-holder or to interpret what is communicated in such a way as to justify obeying the third party instead – on grounds of superior threats, rewards, legitimacy or affection.

The essence of the American presidency, as intended by the founding fathers, is of course its lack of unchallenged power. The challenges come from two sides. First, people within the President's domain are able to challenge his ability to exercise power over them. Secondly, other institutions have a rival claim to exercise power over the presidential domain for some purposes, even though they are themselves within it for others. President, Congress and the Supreme Court share the same domain and, to a degree, the same scope. Failure by the President to exercise power over his domain does not necessarily mean that no one exercises power: rather, that a rival does.

The rival need not be clearly defined. Sometimes he may be an abstraction – 'public opinion', 'the silent majority' – evoked in order to rationalise disobeying the President. From the viewpoint of Johnson and Nixon, anti-war protesters were rivals: they threatened presidential policy in South East Asia. 'I knew that to get the enemy to take us seriously abroad, I had to have enough support at home', Nixon explained to David Frost in 1977.[33] That was his justification for covert operations against the White House 'enemies list' and dissidents like Daniel Ellsberg. If the protesters succeeded in convincing the enemy that domestic support was shaky, the President's power was undermined.

Sometimes the rival may be (or become) a prominent individual, like Ellsberg himself or like General MacArthur in the Korean

War.[34] MacArthur's publicity for his dissenting views forced Truman to dismiss him: otherwise MacArthur threatened to become the effective maker of the war policy – and the real commander-in-chief. One obvious set of rivals are the people aspiring to unseat a president running for a second term. If the President is low in the opinion polls, as was Carter for a year or more before the 1980 election, his present power may be reduced by popular expectations that he will lose office. For Carter, Ford and Johnson alike, the threat came from challengers not only in the rival party but also in their own.

How far the existence of rivals is, for the President himself, a matter of perception may be seen by considering that those who are the effective rivals to his power may be quite unknown to him and barely capable even of encapsulation in an opprobrious term like 'East Coast establishment' or 'middle America'. Conversely the President may perceive as a rival someone whose capacity to exert influence proves slight. Some of his advisers thought Eisenhower should have taken Senator Joe McCarthy's anti-communist excesses in the 1950s more seriously as a threat. Eisenhower judged otherwise and was not proved wrong.

Who are the rivals; what is their threat; whether they – or anybody at all – win the struggle for power over the President's domain: these things all depend upon patterns of communication and the substance of their messages.

V WHEN IS POWER SUCCESSFUL?

The more elaborate one's analysis of power relationships, the more one might expect to go on finding ways in which communication patterns affect the outcomes. But this chapter should have gone into enough detail to indicate the variety of patterns involved in the kinds of power characteristic of the American presidency. The next subject to consider, in Chapter 2, is the factors that determine the President's own communications. Before doing that, however, it is worth briefly considering the question, 'When is power successful?' Since an act of power concerns at least two people, there must be a possibility of disagreement about whether power has in fact been exercised. This is particularly true for the presidency, since its role is open to such wide interpretation and its formal powers are so limited.

How do we recognise the successful exercise of power? The question arises because the communication process integral to the exercise of power must be distinct from that which signals its success. Success cannot be recognised until the attempt to exercise power is complete; the communication involved in that recognition must logically follow the attempt. This is true even when power takes a strong form like command. An obedient person himself knows whether he has succeeded in carrying out a command only after he has attempted to do so. Until then all he can know is his own determination. The act of command may bring instantaneous obedience, but the signal of success remains separate from the signal of command. Of course, presidential power – 'the power to persuade' – does not characteristically take a command form; and in power relations resting on other bases the feedback to the power-holder may be highly ambiguous.

Two problems about recognising success are particular to presidential scope and domain. First, as textbook catalogues of the scope of the presidency all confirm, the incumbent exercises power in very fuzzy areas (Chapter 2 elaborates this point). Presidential goals are often relative: 'successful' elimination of pollution, urban decay, energy waste, unemployment or crime is a matter of opinion – and presidents devour opinion polls. 'Who knows if a government program is a "success"?', asks Jeb Magruder in his memoirs of the Nixon administration; and he gives his opinion of one programme as an illustration. 'The Peace Corps, in spite of glowing notices in its first years, actually had very serious problems. But its excellent publicity, generated by the tireless Sargent Shriver, created a climate in which the agency could grow and improve, and reflected well on the entire Kennedy administration.'[35] More cynically one might say that the best way for the United States to 'win' a war like the one in South East Asia in the 1960s would have been to declare a victory and leave. The 'fuzzier' the subject in which power is being exercised, the more will presentation of the criteria be the key to recognition of its success or failure. Different subjects within the President's scope are open in varying degrees to successful presentation.

The second problem is also connected to presentation. Whenever the President exercises power over only a part of his domain, he may be observed by other people within it but not on this occasion affected. (The public observe indirectly, for instance, his attempts to exercise power over Congress.) If they are to recognise his success, these others need it plainly demonstrated. If the President does not ram home his belief in his own success – and seek out those 'glowing notices' – he may lose out to the efforts of opponents who would prefer his exercise of power to be seen as having failed. Moreover, a general belief in the effectiveness of his power over part of his domain will, he may hope, increase the probability of his power being effective over other parts when the need arises. The assertion of success, in other words, may be thought to breed success. Even if a president does not believe that, he cannot afford to forget that his communication has a central role alike in the exercise of power and in perceptions of his success.

2 The President and Communication

Communication, we have seen in Chapter 1, is central to the exercise of power. Different kinds of power require different patterns of communication. To use power flexibly, therefore, and employ the form suitable to a particular goal, a political leader needs to control his communication.

How far does the American President have such control? This chapter considers that question by discussing a number of factors which determine the types of public communication the President can choose. Together they comprise what may be called his 'communication context'. Personality and verbal skills are not at issue here. Some presidents have been skilful orators and advocates, others awkward and uncomfortable before large audiences. Those differences may be important to their success. Franklin Roosevelt's aptitude for the fireside chat has become legend; Lyndon Johnson failed to carry conviction on television, while Kennedy, despite an unattractive delivery, was persuasive. Ford seemed to bumble and Carter was flat. These characteristics do not, in this context, need exploring. What is meant by the 'communication context' is the effect that the characteristics of his office – its formal powers and responsibilities, its corporate size and organisation, its relation to other parts of the political process – have on how the President communicates. What sort of presidential public communication to and through mass media do these factors tend to produce?

The answer, in brief, is that the President is in continuous public communication, in one sense or another. Not only is this unavoidable; it is necessary if he is to exercise power at all. Except within his spheres of command, his ability to achieve results depends on persuasion – and hence on presentation. The general theme in what follows is that, while the President has great flexibility in when, what, how and to whom he communicates, his degree of control is limited. It is a lack of control both over the consequences –

whether people will do what he wants – and over whether he is understood correctly in the first place. The latter difficulty is not simply a matter of getting the right media coverage. It is compounded by the fact that although there is only one president, large numbers of other people, in the administration, the press and outside Washington altogether, speak in his name. The real president competes, in the attempt to convey his intentions and priorities, alongside others who construe or mediate them at one or more removes – pseudo-presidents. If the President does not choose actively to manage his public communication to achieve what he hopes will be the best results, others will in effect 'make the choices' for him.

In sum, it is argued below that the circumstances of his office oblige the President to communicate; equip him to do so in ways which can tap the sources of power described in the previous chapter; but do not enable him to control his communication precisely.

I THE IMPOSSIBILITY OF SILENCE

'Can't hang you for what you don't say', remarked President Coolidge. That has not stopped historians hanging Coolidge, and even in his lifetime Coolidge's famous silences seem to have been taken as symbolic of wider attitudes than a simple dislike of talk.[1] It is impossible, surely, for a president ever to fall silent completely. His predicament has a touch of Lincoln's famous formula: he can be silent about all things some of the time and about some things all of the time. But he cannot be silent about all things all of the time. This is the most fundamental characteristic of his 'communication context'. Woodrow Wilson was totally silent after his stroke in the autumn of 1919, shielded by his wife and doctor. The very fact that they put out so little information (to Congress and the Cabinet as well as to the public) encouraged the proliferation of rumours – substitute presidential communication. Many were invented by political opponents, claiming that Wilson was insane or even dead.[2] F.D. Roosevelt would say nothing about whether he intended to run for a fourth term in 1944. In the end his silence was assumed to mean he would, and he never did announce his candidature publicly. President Truman's low key reaction to critical press statements by General Douglas MacArthur, the commander in Korea, about the conduct of the Korean War, evidently misled MacArthur into thinking that he could continue issuing them. In fact Truman was increasingly impatient and MacArthur was dismissed.[3]

Eisenhower did not practise Coolidge's kind of silence, but his habit of delegation made Jim Hagerty, his press secretary, cull the departments for things to announce from the White House, lest silence seem like idleness or ineffectiveness. When press briefings were ridiculed by the humourist Art Buchwald for their triviality, Hagerty reacted with a hostility suggesting defensiveness: Buchwald was barred from future briefings and Hagerty demanded equal space in his paper for a rebuttal.[4]

The collapse of Richard Nixon's presidency is full of illustrations of the impossibility of silence. In May 1974, at a time of exceptional rumour, Nixon's press secretary, Ron Ziegler, must have feared that continued silence would only make the rumours worse. Finally he called the *New York Times* with a statement: 'The city of Washington is full of rumours. All that have been presented to me today are false, and the one that heads the list is the one that says President Nixon intends to resign.'[5] In 'deleting expletives' from the transcripts of his White House tapes, Nixon positively accentuated instead of concealing his habits of speech. Most dramatic of all were the eighteen minutes of silence on one tape. Just as descriptions of hell gain by leaving something to imagination, so those empty minutes could encompass what awfulness the mind might conjure. To those who believed in the President's guilt it was bound to speak evil; and what message could it offer to those who believed him innocent?

As Nixon's authority seeped away, Vice-President Ford became contaminated with the impossibility of silence too. Every move he made took on significance – a factor which weighed considerably in calculations about how he should behave. His office put him in an awkward position. The more he proclaimed Nixon's innocence, the less effectively might he 'heal the nation' as a successor; yet, the more he distanced himself as Vice-President, the more he might seem ambitious for the presidency. Silence could mean as much in this situation as public activity. Ford therefore had to find the right balance of loyalty and detachment – with the latter increasing as the months passed. He refused to give advice about what Nixon should do. He was most unwilling to make contingency plans for a transition: the small team assembled by his former law partner Philip Buchen worked unknown to him. In a discussion with Senate leaders about the procedure for impeachment, a week before Nixon resigned, nice distinctions were drawn about Ford's movements in that event. He should be in Washington, not away; on Capitol Hill, not at home; in the House wing, not the Senate. He should keep well out of the way when the rules for a trial were discussed, and should not exercise his casting vote as President of the Senate if there were a tie. A few days later he reportedly walked out of a Senate Republicans' policy lunch, to a standing ovation, when the talk turned to putting pressure on the President. Altogether, a necessarily uncomfortable situation became the worse for being the object of increasing scrutiny.[6]

Jimmy Carter had a foretaste of the impossibility of silence when the sound failed for twenty-seven minutes in the first televised debate (23 September) during the 1976 presidential election. For twelve minutes both candidates stood stock still. This was natural – like a hunter 'freezing' in the presence of a lion. Any other behaviour – to continue talking, to turn aside – might have roused the lion of audience opinion through some incongruity that the candidates, lacking full knowledge of the breakdown, could not visualise. Against that argument had to be put the possibility that just standing still might strike viewers as odd. After twelve minutes Jimmy Carter sat down. Ford stood during the entire twenty-seven. But he did, like Carter, wipe his brow. From the studio audience this drew applause. The audience thereby made their own comment on the silence; and it was predictably a subject of media comment in the following days.[7]

Soon after Carter became President there was an even odder, if trivial, example of the impossibility of silence – observed by a journalist researching an article about Carter's aides Jody Powell and Hamilton Jordan. On 8 March 1977, members of a Muslim sect occupied the offices of the District of Columbia administration. Watching television in Jordan's office that evening the journalist noted, 'At 10 p.m. the local news comes on with special hour-long reports. At one point, an anchorman says that lights are burning late at the White House tonight. "It's funny," Hamilton says, "that's *us* they're talking about . . . as if we were doing something important here, and all we're doing is watching the TV."' A rounder circle could not be drawn: TV news gets a story out of the White House watching TV news – having mistakenly understood lighted windows to signify purposeful activity.[8]

The President, then, is a person from whom 'No comment' is an opinion and whose absence fills space as well as his presence. Even for him, however, the inability not to communicate is relative. He will not always be in the headlines, obviously. Nor would he be wise to try. As F. D. Roosevelt wrote to a friend in 1935, 'people tire of seeing the same name, day after day, in the important headlines of the papers, and the same voice, night after night, over the radio'.[9] Competition from events and persons at home and abroad makes him quieter at some times than at others. He can try to distract attention from one subject by focusing it on another, too. He can for a time keep 'new' subjects secret (a Cuban missile threat; the name of a new Supreme Court justice). He can do these things by the well-tried techniques of publicity and news management. But the essential point is that his freedom of choice is limited to communicating X or Y. He does not have the option to communicate nothing. With appointments to the Supreme Court, to continue the same example, he can choose to float alternative names and test reactions. Even if he does not, however, he will be understood to have done so, as the possible nominations get discussed.

Two other glosses need putting on the impossibility of presidential silence at this stage. One is the *universality* of the President's newsworthiness. George Reedy observed it as Lyndon Johnson's press secretary in 1964–5. Later he wrote,

> It is not too hard for any other high official of the Government to "make the news". But with the exception of notorious scandal, he can do so only through activities which bear a direct relationship to his official function. A secretary of state can command headlines by denouncing the Soviet Union, but no one really cares about his views on dogs.[10]

A president's views on dogs are of keen interest: indeed, Johnson became famous through informal photos as the president who picked up beagles by their ears. Gaffes and slips of the tongue will be gleefully amplified, sometimes out of all proportion. A notorious example was an impromptu remark by Richard Nixon in 1970 – headline news within hours – that the murderer Charles Manson was 'guilty directly or indirectly of eight murders without reason'; Manson's trial was still under way, even though his guilt seemed transparent.[11]

Such universality of interest stems partly from the concentration of executive authority in one man, but more from the President's position as head of state. Everything about a head of state is interesting almost by definition. A British prime minister's views on dogs are of little concern; the Queen's, on the other hand, would be as newsworthy as the President's.

Does this interest mean (which is the second gloss) that the President cannot be silent even about his private life? A distinction needs to be drawn between the private acts of the 'official' President (acts not witnessed by or reported to news media) and private acts of the personal (or human) President. Media are likely to regard all the former as fair game, except for a few activities granted the cloak of national security. A sphere of personal privacy – discussed in more detail in section IV – may be acknowledged; but competitive pressures mean that its limits will be set not by the media but by the President, at whatever place he feels he can sustain them. Although presidents vary in their desire for personal privacy, this does seem the one area where a limited degree of silence can be indefinitely maintained. Yet, as Reedy points out, the President has a monopoly of the communication of his private thoughts, 'his personal likes and dislikes, his intimate moments with his family and his associates'; and the news value of these things give him a 'trading power with individual newsmen of such magnitude that it must be seen at close quarters to be credited'.[12] The temptation to use it must be overwhelming.

Further loss of privacy is caused by the ease with which invasion can be rationalised. For it is questionable whether the behaviour of the personal President can be separated from the official President in fact. Apparently personal attributes – diet, exercise, recreation – may all have a bearing on presidential moods and hence on official activities. (Much meaning was read by some commentators into the report that Nixon twice within ten days watched the film *Patton* in the White House cinema before sending troops into Cambodia.[13]) Since Woodrow Wilson's illness this has been recognised by the White House in times of presidential incapacity. But incapacity should be distinguished from disease. Presidents often try to conceal disease, unless it is obvious, like F. D. Roosevelt's paralysis. Kennedy managed to conceal the fact that he had Addison's disease, for example. The purpose is to prevent fear or allegations of incapacity undermining the President's authority. Precisely those fears, of course, account for media interest.

Although a president can thus keep silent about aspects of his

private life, albeit with a struggle, the safest course for him to follow
is probably to assume that everything he does and every word he
utters, in whatever capacity, is potentially public, through leaks,
guesswork and accident.

A final implication of the impossibility of presidential silence is
the opportunity it gives the President to try and vary the level of
sound. Whether or not he acts calculatingly, the timing, sequence
and frequency of presidential public communication may have a
critical impact on how it is understood and the weight attached to it.
A news conference held at 1 a.m., like the conference announcing
General MacArthur's dismissal, signals a crisis.[14] To maximise its
public impact, Eisenhower's first legislative programme was her-
alded by 'six weeks of press build-up fed by meticulously staged
White House and Cabinet actions', and culminating in a live
television address to the nation on 4 January 1954. This won an
audience rating of 73.1 per cent, compared with 50.7 per cent for a
fireside chat the previous June and 52.5 per cent the following
April.[15] Such exercises have become the commonplace of presidential public relations.

Even if it were possible, it would be odd if the President chose to
be silent. If there were no other reason, he might feel that the least
he can do, since he is going to be news anyway, is turn the fact to
advantage. The Constitution, however, provides a much stronger
impulse to manage his public communication with care.

One important factor is that much presidential activity is 'soft'. It
involves little physical movement or visual interest; its consequences
may be intangible, uncertain, delayed or extenuated, and perhaps
not clearly connected to presidential behaviour at all. This is one
reason why Presidents use travel to symbolise activity (see section VII
below). F. D. Roosevelt compared dealing with the Navy to
punching a feather bed.[16] Much of the time presidents seem to
punch feather beds; less often, to split logs with the clean stroke of an
axe. In this context a revealing hazard in the day-in-the-life-of type
of book is the visual banality of the routine presidential day, unless
the chosen day includes some ritual or other for the President as
head of state or focuses on domestic detail. Very little government
anywhere involves hard, visible, activity with direct results that one
may comprehendingly watch. Indeed, one does not talk of 'doing'
government at all. Significantly, though, one can at a pinch talk of
'doing' legislation – and one can certainly watch it. Executing the
law does not involve the President even in those public verbal rituals

and interchanges of making the law – and judging it – that lend themselves so well to highly functional theatrical communication. Chief executives linked to a legislature can be seen to 'do' government in that forum, even when it is misleading to suppose their work is concentrated there. At least it provides them with the *appearance* of doing something.

Apart from his command powers in defence and the different, limited 'command' power of appointment, much of the President's work consists in seeking to convey attitudes, goals, priorities and his general view of reality. All those things are 'soft'; all connote the idea of power as persuasion not command; all, especially, require public communication for their success. Action and words are thus much the same thing for the President. Commentators who apply to him the common distinction between those two turn out usually to be distinguishing between presidential *words* and the resulting *action* of other people. George Reedy, for instance, notes that as a result of being the constant focus of attention the President 'is under the compulsion – if he is to be believed – of making his actions fit his words'.[17] From the illustrations he quotes – a stand on law and order must be followed by 'action against muggers, thieves and rapists', for example – it is obvious that the envisaged action is by other people and the President's own action is deskbound or otherwise verbal. Indeed, Reedy himself emphasises the 'soft' quality of presidential action by affirming that the job 'can be boiled down to two simple fundamentals' – resolving those policy questions that will not yield to 'quantitative, empirical analysis' and persuading 'enough of his countrymen of the rightness of his decisions so that he can carry them out without destroying the fabric of society'.[18] R. E. Neustadt, similarly, remarks that 'Events determine audience attention for a President; they also make his actions more important than his words.' Again the subsequent example – the promise and performance of F. D. Roosevelt's Hundred Days: 'work relief and a degree of real recovery' – show how far presidential action is implicitly perceived as 'results', namely the activities of other people.[19] Certainly these activities are at the bidding of the President, but they are not done by him; and Neustadt of course is chief exponent of the view that presidential power consists in persuasion and is heavily reliant on effective communication. Moreover, in analysing three cases of the use of command power (MacArthur's dismissal, Truman's seizure of the steel mills in 1952 and Eisenhower's use of troops to enforce Federal law in Little Rock in 1957), Neustadt argues that instant compliance was the product of certain conditions, including the wide publicity and un-ambiguousness of the commands, that need not necessarily have been present. 'Lacking any of them the chances are that mere command will not produce compliance.' [20] Even command power, in other words, is fairly 'soft': it too may be intangible, uncertain and delayed, and public communication may be critical to its success.

Where a command power is 'hard', with clear and certain consequences, like the veto power, its actual application may still have a 'soft' quality through being invisible or trivial. For making an impact in public the sword is far mightier than the pen. The signature or veto of a bill cannot match a public execution. To give symbolic weight to the President's bill-signing power, elaborate rose garden rituals are devised, with a generous distribution of pens that assume the magic quality of having 'signed' the bill by proximity to ones which really did. These ceremonies have their political uses and bring together legislative leaders, lobbyists and others involved in the tortuous journey to the statute book. None the less, the President's final act of consent is portentous through artifice not by its intrinsic nature. The same can be said of swearing-in ceremonies for presidential appointees.

In order to maximise the effectiveness of his 'soft' actions, then, a president will be wise to manage his public communication carefully and exploit the impossibility of silence. In some 'hard' actions too, such as the type of command cases Neustadt discusses, public communication may make the difference between success and failure. In a few others, like the veto power and those presidential appointments not requiring congressional approval, public communication will not affect the President's capacity to act, but he may still be wise to manage his public communication in order to exploit the action for purposes of some further goal.

Another key feature of the 'soft' nature of presidential activity is the relationship that results between the substance and presentation of that activity. Presentation to the public tends to become a factor in decisions about substance. The probability of achieving a presidential goal is bound to be a factor in deciding whether to try; and that probability is significantly affected by the quality of presidential public communication. Thus, in deciding what to do, a president can rarely, if ever, ignore the question of how his action is to be projected. Substance and presentation, reality and appearance, become mixed. The importance of the connection is neatly captured in the fact that Theodore Sorensen was both chief speech-writer and chief White House adviser on domestic policy under Kennedy.

A particularly good illustration both of this point and of the contribution generally of public communication of these 'soft' activities is the phenomenon of the crisis. When is something a crisis? The point is arbitrary at which inflation becomes 'rampant', cold weather an 'emergency', national security 'imperilled'. Circumstances clearly produce the situation of crisis, but the fact that a *crisis* is how the situation is perceived is a matter of reaction, even in a catastrophe. Crises are defined by the *response* to events not by the events themselves. A major plane crash or a broken dam is a crisis. The larger number of deaths caused regularly by automobiles, handguns and cigarette smoking is not: their very regularity, perhaps, conditions the response. Crisis definition, therefore, is a matter of communication – of the way events are presented and understood.[21]

Supremely placed to offer his own definition of whether and when a crisis exists and what to do about it is the President. Certainly he does not always get his definition accepted: there could be no better example of that than Watergate. But he starts out in a better position than anyone else. He speaks with one voice, unlike Congress; with the authority of a commander-in-chief and the moral force of a head of state. Who is to rival him? The Supreme Court has moral force – and played its part at critical moments in Watergate. But its sphere and its rhetoric are limited, nor need it be unanimous. There is no national church to give the leadership which can make politicians out of priests (like the Ayatollahs in Iran). The President's administration contains no rivals such as face a prime minister, who knows that most of his colleagues would seize his job if they thought their parliamentary party would stand for it. Elder statesmen are few, and the only real rivals among them – healthy ex-presidents – are rarer still. Even they do not share the fundamental advantage enjoyed by the President: his instant access to communications media. Radio and television have given him a new dimension of superiority. Speed is important in a crisis, and no one can reach more people more quickly than the President. Johnson, for instance, got the television networks to man cameras at the White House all day long, in case he wanted to go on the air without notice. Until then, it had taken six hours to make the technical arrangements for a live broadcast.[22] The only rivals of comparable stature to the President, in effect, are outside the political system: leaders of other nations.

The President's role in crisis definition is very important to his successful use of power. Crises are testing times for presidents – for the substance and for the methods of their performance and for their subsequent reputations. By definition crises concern abnormal, threatening circumstances, and presidents are often expected to resolve them. Since a crisis is in the first place a matter of perception, the resolution must be equally perceptible.

The President cannot be expected to solve every crisis. That, however, is part of the problem for him: becoming involved or keeping clear, purposely or otherwise, may be the determining factor of whether there *is* a crisis, so far as he himself is concerned. Carter, for example, studiously avoided embroiling himself in New York City's financial and social problems when these were highlighted in July 1977 by a massive power blackout, with all its side-effects of dislocation and looting. The following February, on the other hand, Carter did choose to intervene at an unexpected moment in the country's longest coal strike, already seventy-two days old. At a hastily called press conference he made a 'personal and most urgent request' to management representatives to resume negotiations with union leaders.[23] They did. But the President took a risk that his involvement might be fruitless, damaging his authority. The strike did indeed continue for another thirty-seven days, during which the President unsuccessfully tried to get the miners back to work by invoking the Taft–Hartley Act. When the strike was over, an Associated Press–National Broadcasting Company (AP–NBC) poll found that two-thirds of Americans believed Carter had done poorly, chiefly by doing too little too late.[24] Nixon sought to construe Watergate in public variously as not a crisis at all (just a 'strain', rather, on the American people – 19 October 1973); to accept it as a crisis but not one for which he himself should take blame (e.g. in a statement on 30 April 1973); and, in his resignation speech, to accept it as merely a crisis of political engineering ('it has become evident to me that I no longer have a strong enough political base in the Congress to justify continuing').[25] F. D. Roosevelt's entire New Deal rested on the assumption that the economy was in a crisis which the presidency should tackle.

The threatening nature of a crisis means that if the President fails to resolve one, having once become involved, the consequences will be correspondingly serious for him. In foreign policy ultimate failure means nuclear war – with the President's finger alone on the button. Studies of the Cuban missile crisis show how participants in the American team were conscious of the apartness of the President, caused by his exclusive responsibility for decisions. (Kennedy recognised this but was determined on a collegial approach.[26]) Carter's failure to bring home the American hostages from Iran no doubt contributed to his defeat in 1980. In domestic crises – natural disasters, civil strife, breakdown of services, economic problems – failure may affect a limited group of people but its intensity may still be deep.

The dangers of presidential failure are increased by the possibility, implicit again in the very idea of 'crisis', that no machinery yet exists for responding to a crisis. Policy-making machinery in the Cuban missile crisis, for example, had to be extemporised. Fortunately it worked.[27]

As these examples show, crises test presidents, finally, because their very qualities of conspicuousness, abnormality and threat make them touchstones of presidential performance; so much so that until he has slain his dragon it seems impossible to be adjudged 'great'. That presidents take this view themselves is reflected in small clues like the writing of Robert Kennedy's 'official' account of the Cuban missile crisis for the record and Nixon's pre-presidential autobiography, *Six Crises*. In academic literature notions of power, performance and crisis are closely linked. 'Activist and effective presidential leadership', writes Thomas E. Cronin, '. . . has been elicited almost exclusively by war, depression, or rare periods of vastly accelerating national revenues.'[28] The case studies in Richard Neustadt's book are all of crises.

The President's opportunity to guide public perception of crises and of his own involvement, should not be seen as testing him only in the sense of a threat, as the example of the New Deal may have already indicated. To create and ostentatiously solve a pseudo-crisis, for instance, is a perfectly feasible manoeuvre, the extreme case of presentation dominating substance altogether.[29] It is easiest in foreign relations since the public lack independent gauges of seriousness. A good example seems to have been the Dominican invasion ordered by President Johnson in the spring of 1965. Johnson went on television with almost no notice to announce the landing of 22,000 troops to protect American lives during an insurrection. Soon it became plain that he had greatly exaggerated the threat and that the real reason was a desire to forestall the possibility of 'another Cuba'.[30] More substantially, presidents may see crises as an exceptional opportunity for innovation: abnormal circumstances require an abnormal response. 'You must come up with a tough, well thought out and clear economic programme', the pollster Louis Harris advised Kennedy in July 1962, 'call it a crisis, and rally the people'.[31] Discussing the fate of his energy policy in Congress, President Ford told *Newsweek* in 1974, 'There are just roadblocks up there that are apparently unbreakable until we get a real crisis. . . . I do not think you are going to get a breakthrough in legislation in the field of energy until you get a brownout or a blackout.' [32] If a president can manage to create a sense of crisis new machinery and new policy may follow.

Energy policy in the 1970s is an excellent example, however, of the uphill task a president can have. Carter, for all the assistance he had from the blizzards of 1976–7 and his honeymoon with the electorate, was no more able than Ford to convince Americans that their energy problems were the kind of crisis requiring treatment in a new dimension. His own legislative proposals in 1977 were cut to pieces. It is thus important to distinguish further between types of crisis in which the President can successfully impose his definition from those in which he may fail because his primacy is only relative – even though no one else is actually better placed than he. The long-run and fuzzy crises, of which energy is a classic case, are the most difficult. The fuzzier the circumstances, the less easily can they be exploited to jolt opinion. F. D. Roosevelt had great difficulty in awakening Americans to a security threat before the USA entered the Second World War. In that tragic sense the Japanese attack on Pearl Harbor was a godsend. Hitler's un-expected declaration of war in December 1941 saved Roosevelt even more embarrassment by legitimating at a stroke what had until then been a more or less unacknowledged war against Germany. The same problem of a moment of crisis justifying war was never really solved in Vietnam: the Gulf of Tonkin resolution seemed an increasingly threadbare pretext, the response to a pseudo-crisis, not a real threat. In matters of security and military confrontation, of course, it is axiomatic that circumstances may seem different later from how they seemed at the time; but this ought surely to make it easier not more difficult for presidents to vary the extent to which those events are construed as crises. To define energy needs as a crisis, Americans were helped by the huge OPEC oil price rise of 1973. The speed with which that crisis was 'defined away', leaving little visible beyond a 55-miles-per-hour speed limit and a lot of thermal insulation, shows how difficult it is for a president to maintain a sense of crisis for long in the absence of pressing physical conditions. One of the recurring criticisms of Eisenhower as president is that he did not even try to articulate and highlight what became major 'fuzzy' domestic crises of the 1960s – urban decay, environmental pollution and race relations.

The other difficulty about long-run, fuzzy crises, equally connected with matters of presentation, is adequacy of response. If the nature of a crisis is blurred, the adequacy of response must be too. A bullseye is defined by the edges of the target: blurred edges mean an uncertain centre. Moreover, in such crises the President may succeed in imposing his own definition but the power to respond may lie elsewhere. Defence and foreign-policy crises, barring total war, normally require response only from specialists in a 'command relation' with the President – the State Department and the Pentagon. Go outside them and the response may be imperfect, as Johnson found with draft resisters. In 'fuzzy' domestic crises the nature of the American political system obviously makes the range of people involved in a response much wider, especially if legislation is considered appropriate.

Narrow, short-run crises are generally easier for the President to dominate, for the reasons earlier indicated – executive authority, access to news media, etc. In the face of a sudden external threat, Congress has shown itself ready to give the President latitude and presidents have anyway been able to get by with *faits accomplis*. The specialised and often secret processes of foreign relations give the President latitude too. Eisenhower and the State Department sought initially to define the U2 spy plane incident in 1960 emphatically not as crisis: the plane had strayed into Soviet territory; it was on a 'weather' mission. The definition was rudely contradicted when the Russians produced both plane and pilot.[33] By cancelling the carefully arranged Paris summit meeting Khruschev proved an effective rival and successfully defined the incident as a crisis. Kennedy had better fortune in the Cuban missile crisis. That was defined as a crisis by him publicly at a point when his decision about how to react to it – by a blockade (tactfully described as a 'quarantine') – had already been taken, with careful weighing of alternatives and consequences. The 'real' moment of crisis for

Kennedy came with his initial, private decision to regard missile bases on the island as an intolerable threat and with the resulting need immediately to construct both an appropriate policy-making instrument and an appropriate policy. By the time he presented the situation as a crisis to the public, after six days, the danger of major confrontation with the USSR through miscalculation had been lessened.[34] The secret element in security affairs, again, enabled Johnson to take the significant step of committing ground troops to Vietnam in April 1965 without construing it as a crisis and a new commitment of principle (see above, Chapter 1, section III).

From this discussion the relation of crises to presidential power should be clear. They can provide exceptional opportunities for leadership and the definition and achievement of presidential goals. They are used publicly in the evaluation of presidential performance and potential. The presentation and substance of crises are closely connected. A president has unequalled opportunities to define the existence and nature of a crisis and its relevance to himself, especially in defence and foreign policy and in short-run crises. Not to try and use those opportunities but to stay silent and let other voices define the crises and responses would, in the United States of the 1980s, be odd indeed.

A second constitutional factor likely to encourage a president to exploit the impossibility of silence is the provision (for all practical purposes) of direct election. This gives the office its populist potential. It cannot be gained without an appeal to the people. In contrast a British prime minister, say, may sometimes be said to *retain* office by a successful appeal in a general election, but he may first gain office through succeeding a predecessor of the same party in the House of Commons between elections. (James Callaghan succeeded Harold Wilson in this way when Wilson retired in 1976, for example.) Direct election and fixed tenure distance the President from the Congress and give him an instrument of moral pressure – the rival mandate – and a role as 'Voice of the People' (in the textbook phrase). All presidents piously confirm that without the people they are nothing. 'Unless the President goes to the people, unless he visits and talks with them, unless he senses how they respond as he discusses issues with them, he cannot do the President's job': thus Lyndon Johnson, but the words could come from any president.[35] Many have sought by the most direct appeal to bolster their power against Congress or a foreign leader. Wilson wore himself out trying to mobilise the country behind the Versailles Treaty. F. D. Roosevelt's initiatives rested on his confidence in popular support. Johnson stood down when he realised he could no longer carry the country in the Vietnam War. Nixon persistently used the TV address to the nation to try and maintain his authority. Carter began his term with all manner of populist magic: a nationwide phone-in; a visit to a New England town meeting; endorsement of a scheme to make presidential elections truly popular by eliminating the electoral college. The direct line to the people is so obvious a source of presidential power that presidents vary more in the means and occasions of using it than in their willingness to do so at all.

Presidents are further encouraged to exploit the impossibility of silence out of recognition of the fact that democratic values make communication an end in itself. No one can be against 'openness' in the presidency, any more than against freedom and justice. The arguments, as with them, are about how to recognise and achieve it. They are epitomised by the controversy over publication of the Pentagon papers and over Nixon's use of executive privilege and national security to deny information to Congress. One of Gerald Ford's first presidential statements was a commitment to restore openness.[36] Yet some commentators were sceptical whether he did so; and Nixon himself had been as clear as anyone in his original commitment to the principle. Criticism of its abandonment runs through the three articles of impeachment agreed by the House Judiciary Committee in July 1974.[37] It was this background, of course, that enabled Carter to run in 1976 on the slogan 'I'll never lie to you' and to elevate the virtue of an open presidency to a major place in the campaign.[38]

Similar to openness as a democratic value is 'moral leadership'. F. D. Roosevelt is a prime exponent of the idea. The presidency is 'pre-eminently a place of moral leadership', he told a magazine interviewer in a famous phrase during his 1932 campaign; 'All of our great Presidents were leaders of thought at times when certain historic ideas in the life of the nation had to be clarified.' Eisenhower wrote of his 'deep belief' that all presidents have 'one profound duty to the nation: to exert moral leadership'. Kennedy used comparable rhetoric in the 1960 campaign; and Johnson saw the presidency as 'a clear beacon of national purpose'. Gerald Ford, at his first televised conference nineteen days after taking office, replied to a question about a code of ethics for the executive branch, 'The code of ethics that will be followed will be the example that I set.' [39] Jimmy Carter geared his general strategy in 1976 to the idea that he would provide a new set of values in the White House.

Whether or not such claims are empty, 'moral leadership' could not thrive on silence but requires intensive public communication; and the claim to exercise it shows a self-awareness by presidents of their communication needs. What differs widely, on the other hand, is the kind of communication required by varying interpretations of the phrase. Roosevelt and Eisenhower make a good comparison. Roosevelt, after talking of the need to clarify historic ideas, went on to describe the presidency as a superb opportunity for *reapplying* 'the simple rules of human conduct we always go back to'. Eisenhower, in contrast, wrote of *standing* 'for what is right and decent'. The one chose an active word, the other a static. Roosevelt had a dynamic concept of moral leadership, Eisenhower a passive. The passive concept is easier to effect, since it allows everyone to decide for himself what 'right and decent' mean, regardless of what Eisenhower might intend. Roosevelt set himself a more difficult task: 'clarifying historic ideas' would inevitably involve dispute, with a chance that people would misunderstand what he meant. Moreover, clarification would also involve what that earlier activist moral leader, Woodrow Wilson, called 'the sort of action that makes for enlightenment';[40] and in the process of dispelling darkness the innovative leader is bound to meet misunderstanding. Richard Nixon expressed much the same view in a TV interview on 22 March 1971. Asked about press hostility and problems in communicating with the people, he argued, in the context of the Vietnam War, that any president who avoided 'that very, very inviting but dangerous road of peace at any price, sort of instant peace, so to speak', and who insisted instead on giving the kind of leadership implicit in taking 'the long view', 'is going to have problems with communicating'.[41] One may be sceptical about what presidents say in TV interviews and still find acceptable the proposition that a moral leader trying to set new standards or new ways of looking at things will need to manage his public communication more deliberately than the leader seeking merely to confirm or restore familiar values.

That example illustrates two of the commonest themes in analysis of the presidency – the flexibility inherent in the office and the resulting distinction between 'strong' and 'weak' presidents. Presidents may choose whether to be conscious 'moral leaders'.

According to their choice, their communication needs will vary. The strong/weak distinction declined as circumstances after 1945 seemed to call for any president to be strong by pre-war standards. Recent presidents, rather, have been 'strong' or 'less strong' and their efforts to manage their public communication effectively have simply varied in scale. No recent president has ignored a public communication strategy altogether. The flexibility of the office has been more evident in the goals presidents have tried to achieve and the means they have preferred than in whether they have had policy goals at all. Public-communication needs and strategies have varied accordingly.

Differing goals themselves have differing communication consequences. An emphasis on foreign and not domestic policy involves different assumptions about public concern, knowledge and predispositions.[42] A massive legislative programme like Lyndon Johnson's impinges on the wider public more closely than Nixon's attempt to gain policy goals through executive reorganisation.[43] An attempt to educate the nation – to the threat of a rival ideology, or to new attitudes towards ethnic minorities or energy use – in turn needs more public impact than a primarily legislative operation. Different subjects, again, pose different communication problems.

In many such ways the flexibility of the office presents the President with communication choices and reduces the likelihood that he would be content to fall silent or let his public communication 'drift'. Even routine constitutional duties are open to varying exploitation. Woodrow Wilson revived the practice of delivering the State of the Union message to Congress in person to give it extra weight. The publicity attached to vetoes varies greatly with the President's desire for attention: one of the conventional reasons for using a pocket veto is to reduce publicity.

The phases of the presidential life-cycle also have changing communication implications. The initial honeymoon period gives way to controversy: every action the President takes will annoy somebody. Foreign affairs come to absorb more of his time. In his fourth year he must go electioneering. After re-election he will make a big legislative push. In his last two years, he will gradually lose the attention of the media as they focus on possible successors. Then, as Stephen Hess puts it, he 'will continue to hold the nation's attention if there is a serious international crisis; otherwise he must try to manufacture interest through summit meetings, foreign travel (the more exotic the better), and by attaching himself to major events, such as space exploits, disaster relief, or even athletic achievements that involve his countrymen'.[44]

A final consequence of the flexibility of the presidency is that observers continually look for signs of how an incumbent is interpreting it. This will happen whether he intends to give signs or not, and therefore he risks being misunderstood if he gives no thought to his performance. A good example is the presidential press conference. Part of the value of these has always been the opportunity to read signs, especially when conferences are off the record. Both the flexibility of the job and the 'softness' of so much presidential action make thinking out loud an extremely important presidential activity for journalists to observe. The charm of F. D. Roosevelt's press conferences was due to this in no small measure. Truman, by contrast, did little speculation: the usefulness of his conferences lay more in his unpredictability and occasional indiscretions.[45]

All this discussion should show that the impossibility of silence is simply the condition in which the President has to start his communication behaviour. The nature of presidential action, the method of election to the office, the democratic value of openness, the flexibility in interpreting the duties, scope and limits of the office and the changing priorities of policy all make it inconceivable that a modern president should pay no heed to the manner of his public communication and wish that he was less the focus of attention. Instead he is impelled to try and *steer* his public communication. Just how limited may be his control of the consequences of his communication choices may be seen next from a consideration of the different levels of his communication.

II THREE LEVELS OF PRESIDENTIAL PUBLIC COMMUNICATION

The range of communication choices open to the President and the different problems of control they pose are well illustrated by dividing his public communication into three levels (summarised in Figure 1). Control becomes progressively more difficult.

Primary communication
Presidential activity carried on for the purpose of communicating with the public either directly (public speeches, etc.) or through news media (TV addresses, press conferences).

Secondary communication
Presidential activity reported by news media but not undertaken for the purpose of public communication.

Tertiary communication
Speculation, comment, interpretation etc. by news media, or reported in news media, attributing opinions, motives, intentions, feelings, etc. to the President.

FIGURE 1   Levels of Presidential Public Communication: Summary

Primary communication. This itself can be divided into two kinds: communication directly to members of the public and communication to or through mass media. The former includes personal contact – necessarily with a minuscule proportion of the population, though it may take up quite a lot of the President's time. The commonest form may be the speech to a live audience; and many people can see the President casually as bystanders to a motorcade or at an airport. There is a hierarchy of personal contact, which is nicely exemplified in the domain of party relationships by the varying scale of dollars-per-plate at fund-raising dinners. Access to the President's handshake and dinner-table no doubt follows rules of political competition.[46] Presidents can break out of the hierarchy by such expedients as Lyndon Johnson's garden-gate ploy. Four times during two weeks in the spring of 1964 Johnson stunned tourists outside the White House by inviting them in for a walk. 'He trooped everybody around the black-topped drive which circles the South Lawn. C. L. Prashar from India, an architecture student at Howard University, found himself strolling beside the President. "Is Mr Nehru getting any better?" Lyndon Johnson asked. Mr Prashar said he believed the Indian Prime Minister was improving.'[47] A classic case of spontaneous personal contact, referred to in the introduction to this book, was Richard Nixon's nocturnal expedition to the Lincoln Memorial during the 1970 anti-war vigil.

Not all contact is person-to-person. Thousands of letters go every year over the President's signature to members of the public; few,

obviously, are drafted or signed by him. Photographs go in their
thousands too. Presidential phone calls to the public have been
rarer: when Jimmy Carter agreed in March 1977 to talk to a
hijacker who made this a condition for surrendering a hostage,
officials worried that a precedent might be set.[48] As part of his
campaign to stay close to the people, Carter conducted the first
presidential radio phone-in on 5 March 1977, and spoke to forty-
two out of 9 million hopeful callers.

Primary communication to or through mass media is presidential
behaviour which would not otherwise take place but is deliberately
intended for media consumption. It includes a variety of television
programmes. The 'purest', in the sense that contact between
President and audience is least diluted by intermediaries, is the face-
to-camera address. Eisenhower first developed this, transferring to
television the fireside chat tradition started by F. D. Roosevelt on
radio. Lyndon Johnson and Richard Nixon both set great store by it
as a means of securing public support. Nixon's resignation
broadcast, as he pointed out in its very first words, was the thirty-
seventh time he had spoken to the nation from the Oval Office – an
average of once every couple of months. Different degrees of
'dilution' by intermediaries are discussed in the section below on
presidential platforms. But all kinds of television programme share
the characteristic – not necessarily advantageous – that they frequently provide extra coverage for the President by being reported subsequently in the press. When the broadcast is successfully billed by the President as of major importance, reports are
verbatim in papers like the *New York Times*; and the verbatim
report, like the face-to-camera address, avoids loss of control by
intermediary editing.

Presidents meet the press in a wide range of circumstances
beyond the formal on-the-record press conferences. Provided that
the meeting is intentionally for the purpose of public
communication, all such occasions count as primary presidential communication. So too do the telephone calls to
journalists, which Kennedy and Johnson made so assiduously in
person and which Nixon delegated to his staff, all with the aim of
changing or reinforcing journalists' behaviour. The diversity of
contacts between the White House and the press reached its height
in the Nixon administration. Paradoxically, fewer of them involved
Nixon directly (television addresses and press conferences apart)
than in any post-1945 presidency except Eisenhower's. 'News

operations' communicated the President to the mass media, but through a large communications staff.

Secondary communication. The essential distinction between primary and secondary presidential public communication is in their purposes. Secondary communication consists in media reporting of *'non-media'* presidential activity; that is, of activity which has a purpose independent of public communication and which would take place without it. Primary communication, in contrast, is activity which the President would not undertake if the media did not exist or if he did not intend to communicate directly with the public (in the case of direct personal contact). Thus media reporting of direct presidential contact with the public counts as secondary communication, unless that contact is made with consequential media coverage in mind.

This distinction shows up the loss of control by the President in secondary communication. So long as public communication is the primary or sole purpose of contact with the public or the media, he can govern his behaviour by reference exclusively to his communication goals. But whenever he is involved in secondary communication other goals obtrude and communication criteria take second place. In the extreme he may have to do something which is bad from the point of view of public communication but unavoidable on other grounds. For example, it was disastrous for Richard Nixon to make public transcripts of his White House tapes: his authority crumbled. Yet he had no option. The alternative was to flout a subpoena and make impeachment even more likely. Besides, 'the public burning of the tapes would have been a confession of guilt, and guilt is one thing Nixon never admitted'.[49]

Presidents are probably not often faced with such a contradiction between the demands of public communication and other goals. Often, indeed, their behaviour can be a happy combination of the two, given the extent to which the President's leadership role consists in conveying attitudes, intentions and priorities. Obvious examples can be found among normal presidential duties. As the discussion of the flexibility of the office showed in section 1, presidents can use State of the Union addresses, vetos of bills and messages to Congress with the aim of greater or less publicity. 'Give me a Bill that I can veto', F. D. Roosevelt is alleged to have said on occasion to his aides – so that he could remind Congress that 'they had the President to reckon with'.[50] Sponsors of such bills must have despaired if they knew they were frustrated simply to make a point about presidential power. Richard Nixon, receptive to staff advice that he should veto an extravagant appropriations bill 'with a very loud noise indeed', became in January 1970 the first president to veto a bill in front of the television cameras.[51] Again, while a 'message to Congress' is ostensibly just that, in practice it is addressed as much or more to the wider audience who will read or see reports of it as secondary communication. If the message is delivered in person, as happens with State of the Union addresses, it may be relayed on to the public just like a television address and become a piece of primary communication. Presidents themselves perhaps draw little distinction between the Congress which they are addressing in person and the attentive nation beyond. Similarly, Lyndon Johnson knew that his garden-gate encounters with the public would be followed up by the media. So did Richard Nixon in his foray to the Lincoln Memorial and Carter in his occasional visits – sometimes at very short notice – to the homes of ordinary citizens.

The distinction between primary and secondary communication becomes blurred, then, whenever the President raises considerations of public communication above an activity's explicit purpose. In the routines of the presidential day, however, considerations of media coverage, though managed diligently by the President's publicity advisers, take second place. Much secondary presidential communication thus consists in media reports of activities that are private – not necessarily confidential, but private in the sense that they are not observed by journalists nor geared to their timetables. Such activities include the regular round of meetings with Cabinet members, White House and Executive Office aides, congressional leaders and foreign statesmen; and the domestic routines and recreations of the presidential family. Also, of course, there is a vast amount of secondary communication in the President's name but reporting activities with which he has been connected only in a formal constitutional sense as chief executive. The communication problems concerned with who and what is meant by 'the President' and who speaks in the President's name are explored in sections IV and V.

Tertiary communication. The President's name is used with abandon in tertiary communication. This consists in public discussion and comment about reported presidential behaviour and primary or secondary communication. American news media – and those of other countries – contain enormous quantities of speculation, interpretation and guesswork about the President's feelings, opinions, motives and intentions, including no doubt many he has never felt or expressed. The fact that this is public communication *about* the President not *by* him is unimportant. The feelings and opinions are alleged to be *his*, just as though he had communicated them in a primary sense himself. Certainly the weight placed upon them may be less if the public read about them in a newspaper column than if they hear them from the President's own lips. They are all none the less 'news about the President' and apt to make a contribution to his exercise of power.[52]

Woodward and Bernstein's second Watergate book, *The Final Days*, is a tertiary communication on an epic scale. Again and again Richard Nixon's state of mind is described. Conversations are reported in direct quotation. To quote an instance near the end of the book, Woodward and Bernstein report this exchange between Nixon and his chief of staff, General Alexander Haig:

> 'You fellows, in your business,' the President began, meaning the Army, which he always seemed to consider Haig's real business, 'you have a way of handling problems like this. Somebody leaves a pistol in the drawer.' Haig waited. 'I don't have a pistol,' the President said sadly, as if it were one more deprivation in a long history of under-privilege. As if he were half asking to be given one . . . .[53]

Only two people evidently were at that meeting: Nixon and Haig. Whether it is an accurate account of Nixon's feelings (including such details as his view of Haig's 'real business') makes little difference from Nixon's point of view. It is on public record and the process of getting there was entirely outside his control.

This lack of control must be the most distinctive and frustrating feature of tertiary communication for a president, more especially because this is probably also his commonest form of communication. Nixon showed his frustration in scathing allusions to Woodward and Bernstein during one of his long television interviews with David Frost in 1977: 'for those who write history as fiction on third-hand knowledge, I have nothing but utter contempt. And, I will never forgive them. Never.'[54] Kennedy, in very different circumstances, remarked to Arthur Schlesinger Jr, apropos the familiar game of president-ranking, 'How the hell can you tell? Only the President himself can know what his real pressures and his real alternatives are. If you don't know that, how can you judge performance?' All leaders are in a position where people look to them for signs and messages, so the frustration is not peculiar to presidents. But the characteristics which make a president's silence impossible make his tertiary communication particularly inescapable. One small measure of it is that Eisenhower, and then Nixon, took steps to isolate the press corps in the White House by the erection of barriers and then the provision of a separate entrance. 'You cannot see who is coming and going to see the President', commented one journalist. 'The whole purpose is to cut the press off from the flow of visitors to the White House.' Observation of this traffic, even if it did not involve direct contact, had sometimes yielded useful 'messages'.[55]

The President's tertiary communication can be highly ambiguous as a result of his lack of control (and the fact that he might sometimes benefit from being misunderstood would not in general reduce his frustration). Among all the speculation, the nudges and the winks, lie statements about presidential attitudes and intentions that are indeed accurate – and are sometimes learnt by the writer from the President himself. How much then should the reader believe? How is he to know? The problem was discussed by the London *Economist* after Jimmy Carter had been in office some six months. A formal White House statement on 2 May 1977, ruling out any reform of the welfare system that involved an initial cost to the federal treasury, was apparently qualified by stories in July in the *Washington Post* and *Wall Street Journal*. 'It was learned yesterday', said the former; it 'is understood', said the latter. But from whom? 'As a matter of fact', *The Economist* explained, 'it was President Carter'; and went on to describe techniques the President was exploring in order to keep in touch with journalists outside the public news conference format. Being on 'deep background' these encounters meant that, to quote the present case, 'Mr Carter's formal statement about the financial limit on welfare reform gets retracted, or qualified, by an unattributable remark in indirect speech amounting to not much more than a wink or a nod.'[56] In this case, then, the tertiary communication could be believed. But there were few clues to guide the ordinary reader, other than the papers' reputations.

New administrations bring new styles of communication. In the summer of 1977 President and president-watchers alike were learning new rules of language and meaning. As the pattern became set – and unless it was jolted by some confidence-sapping episode on either side – watchers would learn to differentiate the reliable from the unreliable tertiary communication by matching stories against performance.

The best illustration of this process is the status of syndicated columnists. Those with good access to the President quickly become identified and are closely followed in Washington and across the nation. Too-close access brings the risk of being perceived as in the President's pocket – perhaps wrongly. For example, George Reedy suggests that William S. White was the unfortunate victim of such misperception in the Johnson years. White's circulation, Reedy claims, 'actually picked up when Johnson left the White House because people started to read him for what *he* was saying rather than for what they thought the president was saying'.[57]

A further problem about the ambiguity of the President's tertiary communication is its indiscriminate quality. The more distant a reader is from the President, literally or figuratively, the fewer criteria he possesses by which to sort the nuggets from the rocks. 'Washingtonians' – Neustadt's term for those on Capitol Hill, in the lobbies and in the bureaucracy – have the best means to do so. But the President obviously wants (however unwisely) to communicate accurately to the wider public; and that public has little on which to judge apart from the status attached to columnists by their newspapers.

Columnists have been discussed so far as reporters – passing on information, usually unattributed, as though it were the President's. Of course, they are far more than that. They pass judgement on the President in a straightforward-enough manner. More subtly they offer in addition descriptions of presidential attitudes and behaviour that may differ from the President's self-descriptions yet may plausibly be claimed to be as accurate. (This again is not a predicament unique to Presidents.) To take a generalised example, presidents prosecuting the Vietnam War described themselves as promoting peace. Critics described them as promoting war. Columnists, further, rank the President's priorities, either explicitly or by their choice of subjects to write about.

Columnists and editorial-writers thus present to the public a continually updated image of the President's style and goals, in the guise of interpretation and comment on his primary and secondary communication. They have in their gift, collectively, the only regular, coherent exposition of his style and goals in the mass media – a view of the White House which at the same time purports to be a view *from* the White House. The narrowness of the boundary between 'of' and 'from' is exemplified in the press-conference convention that, if the President answers 'yes' to a journalist's question, the journalist's own words may be quoted as those of the President himself. Thus, in a trice, is tertiary communication translated into primary communication. Truman, notoriously, was a victim of the practice. Several of his public gaffes – for example, about the possibility of using the atom bomb in Korea – were phrases coined and put into his mouth by journalists.[58]

The columnist's position, including his very visibility as a 'name', makes him an obvious target for a president's exasperation at the impossibility of controlling tertiary communication. All presidents are wary of columnists. Some let their hostility flare; others hide it behind a simulated disregard or contempt. Franklin Roosevelt said, 'In most cases their columns are based either on the pure imagination of the writer or on untrue gossip . . . .' Truman wrote privately to a columnist, 'I have never seen the irritable, petulant and angry President – you probably have been reading certain columnists – they are not really reliable reporters, you know.' Eisenhower in his memoirs noted, 'There were journalists whose work I read regularly. . . . But when I found that the writings of any newsman or columnist consistently strayed too far from the facts, I thereafter ignored his column.' Nixon enjoined his Cabinet appointees, 'Always remember, the men and women of the news media approach this as an adversary relationship. The time will come when they will run lies about you, when the columnists and editorial writers will make you seem scoundrels or fools or both . . . .'[59] This edginess or resentment is increased by presidents' awareness of the advantages of having sympathetic columnists, not least as people with an element of detachment and with whom to talk over the course of events.

A last, almost pathetic, reflection of the President's predicament, faced with such limited control over all but his primary public communication, is the hope presidents place in history. The presidential library has become an institution if not an industry, the ultimate example of a general presidential tactic – publish your own version to forestall or counter other people's versions.[60] Presidents itch to set the record straight. Truman, Eisenhower and Nixon all sanctioned 'official' biographies while still in office. Kennedy was fortunate to be the subject of one even before he reached the White

House. Later, Theodore Sorensen's *Decision-making in the White House* bore the stamp of official approval in the form of an introduction by Kennedy himself. Johnson may have seen Doris Kearns as his best bet for a sympathetic biography: certainly she was licensed as few biographers are. Most of these books, it should be added, have been warmly received: pitfalls of 'the official version' have been largely avoided.

A variation of setting the record straight is 'telling it like it is'. Presidents like 'day-in-the-life-of' books. An early example was John Hersey's account of Truman in action.[61] Another was Jim Bishop's *A Day in the Life of President Kennedy*. Such books are easy to monitor: Kennedy followed Bishop's work closely, expressing concern to Ben Bradlee about questions asked of Jackie and of his valet.[62] Reading and approving Bishop's manuscript was one of the last things Kennedy did.[63] Nixon and Carter agreed also to 'day-in-the-life-of' TV programmes. A switch on his tie-clip microphone gave Carter control over what was recorded.[64]

The most ironic illustration of the appeal to history is Richard Nixon. Why, oh why, did he set up his taping system? The answer in his memoirs, from the vantage point of 1978, is this:

> The existence of the tapes was never meant to be made public – at least not during my presidency. I thought that afterward I could consult the tapes in preparing whatever books or memoirs I might write. Such an objective record might also be useful to the extent that any President feels vulnerable to revisionist histories – whether from within or without his administration – and particularly so when the issues are as controversial and the personalities as volatile as they were in my first term.

The system was not introduced until February 1971 and the decision seems to have been little premeditated – though Nixon had an obvious later interest in giving that impression. Certainly 'from the very beginning I had decided that my administration would be the best chronicled in history'; but at first he relied on stenographic records.[65]

Should one take the memoirs at face value? The question reflects the communication problem of a discredited president. Before the memoirs appeared, his ex-chief of staff H. R. Haldeman offered another version. The system 'was not to provide tapes for historians to peruse, but for the President's use alone'. To be sure, Nixon might have had history-writing in mind too; but 'the main driving force', Haldeman insists, '. . . was [Nixon's] desire for an accurate record of everything that was said in meetings with foreign guests, government officials and his own staff. He recognised the problem of either intentional or unintentional distortion or misunderstanding and became more and more concerned about the absence of such a record'.[66]

'Putting the record straight', or 'keeping a grip on policy and administration'? Nixon's motives for taping may not have been wholly explicit. Haldeman's account, of course, is tertiary communication. The difficulty of discerning the truth is a final illustration of the nuances and ambiguities typical of tertiary communication and of the President's inability to be sure that the version of truth which prevails is his own.

III HEAD OF STATE AND CHIEF EXECUTIVE

The President's public communication is complicated by his dual role as head of state and chief executive. The two tend to work in opposite directions. The rules of communication in one role – the kind of things a president is expected to communicate and how; the weight attached to them and how they will be understood – are not quite the same as in the other. The democratic principle requires the closest contact between President and people: yet the head of state benefits from the haze of distance. The chief executive is elected on a sectional basis and cannot disregard specific constituencies; yet the head of state feels a compulsion to speak for the whole nation.

These contrasts produce tensions, while the overlap of roles produces ambiguity. What is to be done about illness, for example? The head of state loses by publicity for his bowel movements (Eisenhower) or by thrusting abdominal scars at the television cameras (Johnson): yet the democratic principle requires public communication of the causes of incapacity (if the incapacity itself is public – which may not be to the President's advantage). The controversy surrounding publicity for serious presidential illness reflects these contrasting needs. 'A President's heart attack is the property of the people', said Eisenhower's press secretary, Jim Hagerty, defending himself for being more candid about that than a later illness. 'But we did not consider the ileitis something that endangered the President's life.'[67]

In areas where these two presidential roles overlap, the opportunities for unsuccessful public communication are bound to be greater than otherwise. The President has to make a choice about which rules of communication to adopt – the head of state's or the chief executive's – and his choice may not be the same as that of journalists or audience. A president seeking re-election, for instance, likes to emphasise his incumbency – whether on a limited scale, by the lavish use of Air Force One, or by a total strategy of playing the statesman who is above all this, successfully followed by Nixon in 1972. Journalists, to judge by the atmosphere at daily press briefings once the campaign starts, are keener to think of the President as 'the candidate' again.

Where the two roles do not overlap, that particular communication problem may not arise. But precisely because the head-of-state role has little political importance, the President's ability to communicate in it as he wishes is great. The more he can associate that role with his political goals, the more likely he is to achieve them. He may thus willingly run the risk that journalists will use the rules of communication appropriate to the chief executive.

The head-of-state role confers upon presidential communication an 'expletives deleted' quality. This is associated with the dignity of office. George Reedy has evoked well the court atmosphere at the White House, with functionaries alert to the King/President's every whim. One might assume this would increase the number of expletives, since people accustomed to instant satisfaction become impatient of deprivation and are under no constraint. Expletives certainly punctuated White House discourse under Eisenhower, Kennedy and Johnson before Nixon, to go back no further. (Johnson wanted a paper-shredder for his presidential archive so that the expletives would not go down in history.[68]) Yet the same quality of kingship deletes expletives when the discourse is published outside the court, in the interests of the dignity and symbolism of the role.

One good illustration of the 'deletion effect' on presidential communication is the embarrassment felt when old associates address a new president. What do you call him? What will he call you? What are the new rules? On Eisenhower's first day in office General Omar Bradley phoned. 'For years we had been "Ike" and "Brad" to each other', Eisenhower reflected later. 'But now, in the course of our conversation, he addressed me as "Mr President". Somehow this little incident rocked me back on my heels.'[69] Nixon found that journalists who normally called him 'Dick' started calling him 'Mr Vice-President' after Eisenhower's heart attack.[70] 'Jordan, Jack Watson and the other young White House aides are obviously having a little trouble about how to address the new skipper', reported James Reston during the Carter transition. ' "Mr President" seems too formal. "The Governor" is out of date and a little confusing. And "Jimmy" sounds disrespectful if not downright cheeky.'[71]

Taken further the dignity of office reaches mythic heights. Presidents are credited with superhuman qualities of stamina, energy, intellect, judgement, reading speed, dispatch, management of time, capacity to grasp essentials. An enduring cliché is the belief (by no means unchallenged, obviously, even before Watergate) that 'the office elevates the man'. Eisenhower had mythic qualities as a military hero – exemplified in his high presidential poll ratings. He needed no elevation. Kennedy and his extended family were quickly elevated in the Camelot myth, which his triumphant joust with Khrushchev in the Cuban missile crisis and his tragic assassination have fixed for generations. Johnson, in a number of engaging incidents, showed a sense of the mythic, though he never achieved mythic qualities himself. 'Why, Lyndon, you know you were born in a much better house closer to town', his mother protested, when Johnson showed journalists a ramshackle cabin on his Texas ranch. 'I know, Mama, but everybody has to have a birthplace', Johnson replied.[72] In a morale-boosting speech to troops in Korea in 1966, Johnson referred to his great-great-grandfather dying in the battle of the Alamo. Journalists, their curiosity aroused, quickly established that this was nonsense.[73]

The importance of dignity and myth to presidential public communication is the latitude they give the President in two directions. 'Deleting expletives' enables him in effect to censor some kinds of communication. The mythic tendency, by contrast, enables him to exaggerate or add weight to communication. Whenever he plays the head of state, he can speak (not quite) the truth, (not quite) the whole truth and (not quite) nothing but the truth. He benefits from the little lies made possible for that office by the willing suspension of journalistic disbelief.

Disbelief is not always suspended. The credibility gap that troubled Johnson and Nixon can trouble any president. But he has to stretch suspension till it snaps for that to happen. Up to that point he benefits from certain values held by journalists as a result of their commitment to the political system. As one commentator, William E. Porter, puts it,

> newsmen in this country have seldom reported personal scandal relating to politicians; drunks and womanisers and even homosexuals have been widely known as such within the press corps without ever being reported. . . . There traditionally has been a commitment of the political journalist [in the USA] to the belief that the system works; there may be occasional highly particularistic aberrations, but basically it works, and he feels a certain obligation to ignore many things which he feels are essentially irrelevant but might undermine public confidence.[74]

Public confidence, the polar opposite of the credibility gap, is of course the very basis of most presidential power. The journalist David Wise refers casually in the same way to the fact that 'newsmen cannot report certain details for one reason or another – a presidential remark not suitable for a family newspaper, for example' – and this in a book, *The Politics of Lying*, devoted to the thesis that government secrecy and deception should be reduced.[75] The literal deletion of expletives is insignificant. But the attitude William Porter describes, though it may have been modified by the Nixon presidency, has enabled presidents to get away with much of the secrecy and deception practised in the name (for instance) of national security.

An important part of the latitude given to the President's communication by dignity and myth is semantic. 'I'll never lie to you', promised Jimmy Carter. No doubt he meant it. But of course he *would* lie to us. Presidents promise things which they turn out not to achieve, or which they may think are achieved but others may not (e.g. those 'improving' and 'eliminating' kinds of goal, which are necessarily relative). New information makes presidents change their minds. 'National security' looms. Bureaucrats dilute programmes. Statements such as 'I'll never lie to you' are honest only in a context of meaning which takes account of those and other factors. They are statements of a president's aspirations and good faith – and, like many of his statements, of his priorities. Put in a different context of meaning they seem cynical and self-serving: hence the frequent scepticism among non-politicians about the genuineness of politicians' promises. Porter's point credits journalists with a traditional willingness to take the President (especially, it is argued here, as head of state) on his own terms.

The dangers of Carter's 'never lie' pledge were neatly illustrated in the area of communications policy by the agonies supposedly suffered about the presidential letter-writing machine – a contrivance the whole purpose of which is a mechanical lie. The system was set up in the Eisenhower administration. 10,000 'autopen' signatures per year under Johnson had become 191,578 in Ford's last year. Twelve magnetic-tape selective typewriters chattered out standard replies to incoming letters coded by twenty White House mail analysts. 'Chatty letters from children' got reply no. P-814; sick citizens whose relatives solicited a presidential get-well message had PR-70; widows of policemen killed on duty, PD. Each took its turn on the signature-writing machine. Even senators were thanked in this way for their votes on key issues (letter no. P-15). Carter at once ordered the system dismantled. After only a few days, however, he changed his mind and asked instead that it just be scaled down.[76]

The President's combination of the roles of head of state and chief executive, then, works to his advantage in controlling his public communication. The possibilities of misunderstanding and confusion are unavoidable too. But respect for the office of head of state seems to legitimise communication practices that the office of chief executive alone would not legitimise. The main risk to a president is that journalists and voters will separate the office from the man and keep their respect only for the former. From the viewpoint of his reputation, Kennedy's presidency perhaps ended at a good time. Critics have worried away at the Camelot myth since 1963, and especially at Kennedy's faithfulness to his wife.[77] The sweetness of Eisenhower's character – the truth behind the grin – is questioned. Even he emerged in biographies of the 1970s as having had a less than perfect marriage and a wartime affair with his English secretary. Roosevelt's long association with Lucy Mercer eventually came to light, sullying the image of his partnership with Eleanor. None of these associations was on public record during each man's incumbency. But they raise the question whether the mood of disillusion after the mid-1960s broke the deference William Porter discerns, so that future presidents (in the near future at least) would not be able to exploit their communication advantages as head of state so well. Alternatively one might see the tide of revelations about the essential humanity of presidents not as demystification of the office but rather as a shift. Perhaps a new ideal of the head of state was evolving, suited to changing views of marriage (most of the revelations were about sexual relations) and where presidential dignity would consist in admitting honestly to *Playboy* magazine that one had lusted after other women (to quote Jimmy Carter) and not in managing to prevent that idea from entering anyone's mind. The role of head of state has ample flexibility to accommodate such changes of social values. In the immediate post-Watergate era integrity seemed a more estimable ideal than Happy Families.

IV VERSIONS OF THE PRESIDENT: PERSONALITY AND OFFICE-HOLDER

The possibility of dissociating the office of president from the man, mentioned at the end of the previous section, extends far beyond the context in which it has just been discussed. Several different 'versions' of the President can be communicated. The President has considerable choice of which to offer, though his version will not necessarily be the one that is understood. The versions can be seen as falling within two ranges:

President as personality _____ (Ronald Reagan)	President as office-holder (Mr President)
President as individual _____ (Ronald Reagan/ Mr President)	President as institution (the presidency)

As with the President's different offices, these versions may involve different rules of language and understanding. The President can control his communication more successfully in some versions than in others. But these may not be the most appropriate versions for the goals he is seeking at the time, so he would not be wise simply to try and communicate consistently the versions he can best control. The more complex range of versions is the individual–institution range examined in the next section. This section deals with the personality/office-holder distinction.

The interplay of personality and office-holder in communications about the President as individual is very subtle. The weight of authority lies with the office. Yet its flexibility means that much of what presidents seek to achieve depends upon what they bring personally to the job and that watchers look for idiosyncrasies of presidential style. The office-holder commands attention, one might say; but often it is the personality who engineers compliance. Moral leadership, for instance, cannot be exerted merely by citing the authority of the office: it depends as well on confidence in the personality. A man with Eisenhower's reputation scarcely needed the extra halo of the presidency. When he promised to 'go to Korea' to end the war, the attraction for voters was Ike the general not Ike the aspiring president. In contrast, when Eisenhower decided to send Federal troops to Little Rock in 1957 to enforce desegregation laws, he flew home to the White House to broadcast the announcement. That was the fit place for a *presidential* (office-holder's) announcement, rather than the New England resort where the (personal) President was holidaying when the crisis blew up.[78] Eisenhower made the same distinction, no doubt unconsciously, when he developed the habit of referring to himself in press conferences in the third person – 'the President feels', or 'it seems to the President'. The personality was answering for the office-holder. (See the section on Eisenhower in Chapter 3 below.)

Harry Truman is perhaps the president to whom the personality-office-holder distinction applies most naturally, since Truman himself drew such a sharp distinction between his ordinariness as a person and the responsibility of the office. His well-known remark that there were probably a million people who could have done the job better than he came near the end of his term (at a press conference on 17 April 1952) but it epitomised his style. To Neustadt, 'Truman's image of the Presidency and of himself as President kept job and man distinct to a degree unknown in Roosevelt's case or Eisenhower's.'[79]

Some of the disillusion with Richard Nixon was that a president who had preached law and order turned out to be personally corrupt. Watergate, indeed, provides the extreme case of a president needing to fuse personality and office-holder, if his authority was to survive. If impeachment could be construed for the people as hurting the office of president, not just Richard Nixon, it might more likely be avoided. Watergate was harming the office holder's capacity to fulfil his constitutional obligations – particularly foreign policy: therefore it should be finished with.[80] To accept that a man might without damage to constitutional process *resign* the office of president would be to separate the incumbent from the office: therefore resignation must never become known as an option accepted in the White House.

One might suggest a rule of thumb for presidents: when things go wrong, stress yourself as office-holder; when they go well, stress your own personality. It is difficult to visualise circumstances where it would be a positive disadvantage for a president to stress his incumbency. The point is a comparative one. It may well be desirable sometimes that a president stress his personality *more*, compared with his office, than at other times – the object being to increase his reputation and hence the likelihood of people doing what he wants in the future; and perhaps to strengthen his appeal as a candidate if he seeks re-election.

A rather special case of 'things going wrong' is a president's death in office. The emptiness of the vice-presidency, the lack of collective responsibility, the individuality of each President's White House machine, the short notice (if any) and the size of the presidential burden are ample excuse for the consternation successors feel. Truman expressed it graphically in his famous remark to journalists: 'Boys, if you ever pray, pray for me now. . . . I felt like the moon, the stars and all the planets had fallen on me.'[81] At such a time a new president badly wants to communicate reassurance and continuity and thus to stress himself as office-holder and head of state, not as a human being whom the American electoral process, through the balanced ticket, tends ironically to cast in a different mould from the deceased president. Johnson dramatised continuity by taking the oath of office on the aeroplane back from Dallas, recorded in a memorable photograph, Kennedy's widow, still in bloodstained clothes, at his side. Johnson let his own personality (and his own associates) emerge slowly. Only after his massive electoral victory in 1964 did he subordinate the Kennedy legacy completely.[82] Ford, not even elected as vice-president, had to emphasise the office-holder. His personality too emerged but gradually – apart, obviously, from an initial stress on its differences from Richard Nixon's.

A good indicator of the subtleties involved routinely in the personality–office-holder range is the question of presidential privacy. This has been discussed previously in the section on presidential silence but also needs analysis here. Its significance is that the successful assertion of privacy gives the President what amounts to a power of censorship – the capacity to remove certain features from the portrait presented to the public. The personality/

office-holder distinction is crucial, for the personal President may be conceded privacy by the mass media *as a right*. The office-holder, by contrast, is entirely in the public domain: his privacy then is construed by journalists as secrecy and is liable to challenge. The more a president associates problems or people with his personality, the greater his chances of controlling communication about them through the imposition of secrecy legitimised as privacy. One way of making this association is geographical. Presidents often take knotty problems to their private homes: F. D. Roosevelt to Hyde Park, Eisenhower to Gettysburg, Johnson to Texas, Nixon to San Clemente. Journalists are then at a practical and psychological disadvantage. Compared with the White House, these homes have worse technical facilities. Physical access is more difficult. When invited into the home, newsmen are subject more literally to the constraint of 'enjoying hospitality' than at the White House. Camp David has become the official residence for the personal President; and its common description as a 'retreat' connotes nicely the idea of legitimate withdrawal.

The problem posed by the concession of legitimate privacy to the personal President is how far away to put the fence round Camp David and how high to build it.[83] The personal President and the office-holder are the same man. News media persistently probe for the 'real' President, the roots of his personality and his style. Hence the competition for seats on the presidential plane and contemptuous names like 'the zoo plane' for separate press planes.[84] Hence too the fascination with background briefings and other opportunities to observe the President first-hand, even when no hard news results. The formal presidential press conferences too have been justified in terms of seeing the 'real' President: 'the President reveals not only his policies but himself', writes David Wise: '. . . and the press conference, more than any other institution, permits voters to glimpse the human being who occupies the Presidency'.[85]

The boundaries of privacy are thus a common source of friction between news media and the White House. Hagerty's strict protection of Eisenhower, for example, resulted in a 'very narrow, self-serving definition' of presidential news and caused resentment among journalists – especially, no doubt, because Eisenhower did so much work in holiday surroundings.[86] Eisenhower's heart attack – manifestly imperilling the office-holder as well as the personality – eventually made a policy of total frankness expedient. The intimate friendship of Kennedy (as personality) with Ben

Bradlee of *Newsweek* was jeopardised by Bradlee using Kennedy as a news source (about the office-holder). Ironically, Kennedy used Bradlee as a news source too; but, of course, his bargaining position enabled him to dictate the relationship. After some five months of ostracism Bradlee was back into the fold.[87] Lyndon Johnson, Evans and Novak claim, was concerned to find that the White House press corps would not be so discreet in their treatment of his private foibles – the racy language, the mimicry of politicians, the fast driving – as the Senate correspondents had been.[88] Nixon (as personality) relaxed in the company of successful entrepreneurs like Bebe Rebozo and Robert Abplanalp. Newspaper investigations of the affairs of Rebozo seem to have been resented as an attack on Nixon (as office-holder) and to have provoked White House harrassment of the journalists concerned. The circumstances of Kennedy's assassination led the White House to agree that the news media should be allowed at least to know where the President (as office-holder) was at any hour of the day. Even this practice, however, caused problems in the early days of the Carter incumbency.[89]

The example of Rebozo raises a further question. How far does privacy extend to the presidential family and friends? The answer is linked to a factor explored in detail below: the institutionalised presidency. Some presidents deliberately involve their family in the work of the office; indeed, it is difficult to avoid involvement in the head-of-state role. How far the family are involved in the other political and governmental roles is a matter of choice, even in the goldfish bowl of the TV age. Woodrow Wilson was outraged when the press, daring to write about 'the ladies of my household', speculated about the engagement of his daughter.[90] Truman crossed swords with the press about treatment of his daughter too.[91] Johnson and Nixon daughters, on the other hand, had fairy-tale public weddings. Julie Nixon was a spokesman for her father in the later stages of Watergate. Tricia preferred a private life and on the whole was granted one. Amy Carter – nine when her father took office – was part and parcel of the Carter populist style. Symbolic points were made about the arrangements for her attendance at the local school and her informality at official meals. Caroline Kennedy, equally, was included in the general Camelot saga.[92]

Sons have perhaps had a harder time maintaining privacy. Even though they are not heirs apparent, their father's status obliges them, so to speak, to be in the front line of every war. 'I had heartily concurred in his determination to go to a front-line batallion', wrote Eisenhower of his son John's service in Korea.[93] Some sons have had the personality problems typically faced by sons of famous men, and these may have increased the interest of news media. Some – like James Roosevelt, John Eisenhower and Chip Carter – have been used by their fathers as aides.

Wives too have enjoyed privacy varying with their involvement in presidential duties. Woodrow Wilson could not have foreseen, in his indignation about his 'ladies', that within a few years his wife would be the prime focus of publicity in his illness. Eleanor Roosevelt remains the extreme case of a wife sharing her husband's work and experiencing as little privacy – indeed, perhaps less, since we now know of his long, secret liaison with Lucy Mercer. Jackie Kennedy and Rosalynn Carter made diplomatic visits abroad by themselves; and Pat Nixon prominently accompanied her husband to China in 1972. Betty Ford's success led to 'Yes to Betty, No to Gerry' stickers in the 1976 election. Presidents' wives have had their own press secretary since the 1930s. But, if a wife has chosen to remain in the background like Bess Truman or to restrict herself, like Mamie Eisenhower and Jackie Kennedy, to the (then) traditional women's concerns, the press has not complained.

The choice whether to involve his family in duties beyond those of head of state is the President's, but the potentiality of exploiting the 'first family' role for political purposes, especially at election times, means that news media may believe the family are involved to a greater degree than the President in fact intends. (Billy Carter was a particular liability in this way.) Family privacy may thus be challenged. Further, the amount of publicity reasonably expected of a 'first family' can always be a matter of argument: how far does being head of state involve offering one's family as a model? Both possibilities reduce the President's discretion. The ambiguities are made plain by comparison with systems that separate head of state and chief executive. The families of heads of state are unquestionably involved in publicity. In Britain the Royal Family is in the public domain as well as the Queen herself. (Though just what degree of cousinage is included is unclear.) Chief executives, in contrast, have no difficulty in maintaining their families' privacy. A British prime minister's spouse, even in an age when his own publicity outfaces his colleagues', remains neither a strong political asset nor a liability. A wife who played Eleanor Roosevelt – to the extent even of writing a newspaper column that strayed into political matters –

would quickly become a liability. Her status as wife carries no delegated authority. The prime minister's authority is shared – but with his cabinet. His wife, politically, is 'irresponsible'. Prime Minister Heath's public image was sometimes said to suffer from bachelordom; but any wife, so to speak, would have been better than none. Prime ministers' children can lead almost entirely private lives.

The non-governmental head of state is deeply entrenched in Britain. In many other countries, no doubt, the chief executive assumes some head-of-state characteristics even though a separate office exists. In Canada and Australia, for example, publicity attaches to prime ministers' families in a way which is absent in Britain. Australian Prime Minister Gough Whitlam's wife did become a public figure in her own right in the early 1970s. In Canada, Prime Minister Trudeau's marriage was a source of constant publicity and political exploitation. Its breakdown in 1977 would perhaps have been papered over if he were formal head of state and rather less publicised if he were prime minister in the British mould.

The subtle interplay of personality and office-holder in communications about the President as individual thus takes on extra ambiguities when the involvement of his family is considered. The family belongs to the 'personal' President and therefore qualifies for legitimate privacy at his discretion. Yet the inclusion of his wife in the office-holder role of head of state, plus the opportunities to include other family members both in that and more political roles, all reduce the President's control over what is communicated about them.

V VERSIONS OF THE PRESIDENT: INDIVIDUAL AND INSTITUTION

Who exactly is the President? Far wider than the personality – office-holder range is the second range of presidential 'versions' mentioned at the start of the last section – that of the President as individual or as institution. As individual he is 'Ronald Reagan' or '*Mr* President' (a personal prefix); as institution, '*the* President' (an impersonal prefix), if not an abstraction – 'the presidency'. The difference between institution and individual is reflected in the fact that one may as sensibly ask 'what is the President?' as who he is.

The possible meanings of 'the President' have grown in proportion to the institutionalisation of the office since the New Deal.[94]
This prompts two main questions. First, when the President's name
is invoked, what does 'the President' mean? 'I stand before you
representing the President of the United States and I say to you
today that we shall stand by Israel always', Vice-President Mondale
told a pro-Israeli pressure group in 1977.[95] 'Representing' in what
sense? What 'President'? Which 'we'? Second is a mechanical
question: who speaks for the President? Who, that is to say, has the
opportunity to invoke his name and define the version in particular
cases? 'There has absolutely got to be an end to the confusion over
who speaks for you', urged Cyrus Vance after resigning as Secretary
of State over Carter's decision to attempt a military rescue of the
American hostages in Iran in April 1980.[96]

In relation to both questions the President can make choices. In
neither does he enjoy a monopoly, nor can he always make his
choice effective; even so, he is almost bound to try and impose his
choice, since the outcome may be crucial to his exercise of power.
The more the President as individual is believed to be engaged in a
matter, the greater will be the public expectations of success and the
costs of failure. Following Neustadt's type of analysis, failure will
reduce the President's individual prestige and public reputation
and hence his chances of success in the future.

(a)　What does 'the President' mean?

The institutionalisation of the President has created a situation
where in principle 'the President' may mean anyone from
the person himself to the uttermost bureaucrat acting legally in the
President's name. In public communications, statements about the
President will commonly describe things actually said or done, for
instance, by the President's wife and family, White House staff
members (such as press secretaries and legislative aides), Cabinet
members, the Vice-President, Executive Office and departmental
officials, as well as the President himself.

Two kinds of ambiguity are produced by this proliferation. On
the one hand the President's name may be attached to views or
actions which in fact he knows nothing about. The 'Eisenhower
doctrine' for defence of the Middle East was announced as such at
the end of 1956 without Eisenhower's having had anything to do

with it at all.[97] Similarly, speaking as an individual at routine press conferences, how far is the President really just a spokesman for the institutional presidency, talking to a brief? One of the intentions of journalists at the conferences is to probe the depths of presidential knowledge, seeking the degree of engagement of the individual President in particular subjects in order to discover which version of the President is talking.

The President may, on the other hand, be involved with something to which his name is not attached. The Marshall Plan for European recovery after the Second World War was fostered by Truman, but he deliberately named it after his Secretary of State, so as to reduce controversy.[98] During the passage of his civil-rights bill through the Senate in 1964, claimed Lyndon Johnson, 'I deliberately tried to tone down my personal involvement in the daily struggle so that my colleagues on the Hill could take tactical responsibility – and credit.'[99] Vice-President Agnew's polemics against the press and broadcast networks in 1969 were made in his own name yet widely and rightly regarded as expressing Nixon's views.[100] According to Nixon's memoirs, the most notorious Agnew speech was initially sketched out by the President's speech-writer Pat Buchanan, toned down by Nixon, further moderated after discussions with Agnew and then edited by Agnew 'so that the final version would be his words'.[101] In contrast, an order from President Truman in December 1950, specifically intended to curb General MacArthur's discretion in Korea, was misunderstood by the General to be of no significance.

> The order was expressed in terms more easily construed as the concoction of press attachés to hush Assistant Secretaries than as Truman's word to his Supreme Commander. . . . But how was the General to know? The order's widespread application and routine appearance were meant to spare him personal embarrassment. . . . Their effect was to minimise its impact and to blur its source.[102]

The incident contributed to Truman's growing dissatisfaction with the General.

These ambiguities reflect the range of choices open to the President. There is the basic choice whether to attach his personal name to a communication or let it be presented as information from the institutional presidency. Hagerty, for instance, busily attached Eisenhower's name to announcements actually originating in the departments. There is a comparable choice of behaviour towards senior appointees. They may be folded in the presidential embrace, so that their work is seen to be his work (by indicating the regularity of consultation and the like). Or it may suit the President to distance himself from an unpopular or ineffective appointee. Immediately Carter's budget director, Bert Lance, became the subject of critical newspaper columns about his financial practices, Carter distanced himself. When Lance seemed to have been officially cleared, Carter endorsed him again, on television – but prematurely, as it turned out, since twenty-four days later Lance felt obliged to resign.[103] Another option is to leave vague the extent to which the President himself is personally involved. Part of the job of the Council of Economic Advisers under Kennedy was 'to venture out ahead of policy', as Arthur Schlesinger puts it. 'The President would say to Heller [the Chairman], "I can't say that yet, but you can." '[104] Kennedy could thus conceal or delay his own commitment to a policy. Yet another option is to communicate with two voices: to leak out a private message qualifying a public version. Kennedy concealed as institutional President the dissatisfaction he felt personally with full sessions of his cabinet. But he took care to make plain his dissatisfaction privately to journalists, who relayed it appropriately to the public.

The wider the choices, the more scope there is for public misunderstanding. 'Versions of the President' are one more area where the President has great flexibility but no equivalent control. The institutionalisation of the office has long since removed from him the capacity to know everything communicated in his name, even by his appointees. The facts of secondary and tertiary communication mean that he has little control anyway over many of those, like columnists, who use his name. 'Washingtonians', Neustadt's term for those who, in effect, do not rely solely on mass media for information about the presidency and some of whom are sources for the media, may be offering a rival version of the President as appropriate to a particular case. Was the President as individual involved in Watergate, or the presidency as institution? Richard Nixon obviously did not manage to defeat the challenge to his own version and prevent others entering public circulation. Even in the field of foreign policy, Henry Kissinger noted that Nixon's associates grew unhappy, 'and not without reason, that some journalists were giving me perhaps excessive credit for the more appealing aspects of our foreign policy while blaming Nixon for the unpopular moves'.[105]

Notwithstanding the possibility of failure, the President is obliged to choose versions of himself, it was argued previously, because the implications of different versions for his future power may be so great. Several factors seem to affect his calculations. One, obviously, is his assessment whether his personality will make a positive contribution to public acceptance of his goals. Eisenhower, Ford and (at first) Carter all had public personalities that were advantageous, partly in reaction to their predecessors' (counting Nixon as Carter's predecessor as well as Ford's). Carter's concern about the ethics of his letter-writing machine illustrate well (if somewhat trivially) his general desire to stress the personal President. If anything is institutional communication it is a letter-writing machine.

Johnson, in contrast to those three, was repeatedly anxious about the harmful public effects of his personality. At one level he felt convinced – and resentful – that the press despised him for not being an Ivy League man and that he was therefore treated unfairly.[106] His attitude to those involved in secondary and tertiary communication about him was suspicious if not hostile. At the public level he was the unhappy president for whom, in his disastrous Vietnam policy, the phrase 'credibility gap' was coined.[107] The characteristics that struck so many close observers – delight in deviousness; secretiveness; fast-and-loose treatment of facts; manipulation of news stories – were conveyed eventually to the wider public, despite his attempts to bypass intermediaries by frequent use of television and to polish his image with public-relations advisers. Johnson knew only too well, then, as his Great Society successes gave way to his Vietnam difficulties, that to stress the personal rather than the institutional presidency would not further his goals.

Nixon too was dogged by personal unpopularity, over a much longer period than Johnson. White House aides were conscious that his personality was a liability. 'We felt we faced special problems in selling the Nixon program', wrote Jeb Magruder. 'Our man lacked the warmth of an Eisenhower, the charisma of a Kennedy, or the flamboyance of a Johnson . . . .'[108]

A more complex factor in the decision which version of the President to try and project is the calculation of credit and blame, or benefit and cost. In theory, of course, the President cannot delegate responsibility, nor therefore guilt. In practice up to a point he can. Where that point is requires nice judgement. The same problem is all too familiar to parliamentary governments operating the principle of ministerial responsibility. In Britain, for example, a Cabinet minister is responsible, by constitutional convention, for every act carried out in his department. He cannot know every decision taken in his name. What then does 'responsibility' mean? A simple obligation to behave uncorruptly? A duty to be answerable to Parliament? Or a liability to accept personal blame for the incompetence of officials? Despite the fine distinctions periodically redrawn by constitutional lawyers, the answer in particular cases is determined by political expediency – a minister's standing with his prime minister, his colleagues and his party, and perhaps the government's standing in the Commons and the country.

The precise considerations are different for an American president but the need for nice judgement is the same. In deciding how far he can dissociate himself personally – with his reputation and his prospects – from a problem within the ambit of the institutional presidency, the President must correctly answer the question, 'Is this a matter the public will think the President personally ought to handle?' To deny personal knowledge of activities within the institutionalised presidency will be damaging in some circumstances; to admit it, in others. The occupational hazard for Eisenhower, for example, was of seeming to have delegated too much and to have lost control. Carter, in contrast, was occasionally criticised early in his presidency for not delegating administrative chores enough.

Sometimes the President cannot avoid blame attaching to him personally because he did not know enough of the circumstances – or know them in time. Carter's poll ratings dropped as details of his budget director Bert Lance's banking practices emerged, though Carter personally was not involved. Truman may not have known anything of the small-time corruption of several of his aides. But his steadfast loyalty to them was taken as a sign that he did: it was grist to the Republican mill in the 1952 election campaign.

If a President does have foreknowledge of events within the institutional presidency that may damage him, at least he has the opportunity to try and detach himself personally. Bradlee's memoirs again provide an anecdotal example:

Kennedy was enthusiastic about a story *Newsweek* had done about the liberals who were criticising him, wondered who had written it, but was worried about how Arthur Schlesinger would take the paragraph that quoted Kennedy as saying 'boy, when those liberals start mixing into policy, it's murder'. He asked me 'with your well-known tact', to let Arthur know the quote was from someone else, not the president . . . .[109]

Johnson, somewhat more seriously, worked hard to dissociate himself from Bobby Baker, his former assistant as Senate Majority Leader, when Baker was the subject of a Senate investigation for corrupt practice in 1964. Baker had in fact been so clearly his protegé that newsmen simply found the effort funny.[110]

Infinitely more serious than either of those examples, of course, is the Watergate case. At first Nixon sought to construe it as a misdeed of the institutional presidency, apparently hoping that he could accept responsibility but not blame.[111] The previous section has shown how he took refuge in his office – figuratively and literally – as his personal involvement became more widely known. For his supporters in the country a disjunction between the individual and institutional presidencies was the only basis for maintaining faith. For them the key question was: when did Nixon learn about the cover-up? The articles of impeachment, on the other hand, included all versions of the President. They alleged that he 'engaged personally and through his subordinates and agents' in various malpractices. In some places they said he 'knew *or had reason to know*' (author's emphasis) certain things.[112]

If presidents cannot always detach themselves personally from wrongdoings within the institutional presidency, the opposite seems simple. There are excellent examples of presidents moving personally into nasty situations in which the institutional presidency might readily have soaked up the criticism. An obvious case is the U2 incident in 1960. Allen Dulles, Director of the CIA, volunteered to take full responsibility for the shooting down of the spy plane over Soviet Russia and to resign – thus giving the President-as-individual protection. Khruschev himself made that course even smoother by stating, 'I am quite willing to grant that the President knew nothing.'[113] Eisenhower, however, felt that to have denied knowledge personally would have been an intolerable admission of failure to control national security. He took personal responsibility and thus ensured the humiliating collapse of the imminent Paris summit meeting. The long-run benefit of maintaining confidence in the presidency was presumably considered greater than the cost to international diplomacy.

Kennedy had to make a similar calculation after the Bay of Pigs fiasco a few years later. Although he had been told of the planned assault after his election and could no doubt have sloughed off responsibility onto the previous administration, he willingly took responsibility upon himself.[114] In 1980, on the other hand, Carter had little choice when the attempt to rescue American hostages in Iran was abandoned because of aircraft failure. However little he may have shared in the actual planning or the decision on the ground to withdraw, it was natural that he should publicly accept responsibility with as much dignity as possible: 'It was my responsibility as President to launch this mission. It was my responsibility to terminate the mission when it ended . . . .'[115]

A third, more straightforward factor in a president's decision about what version of himself to project is his set of priorities. The indication of personal involvement in a problem provides a simple public measure of presidential concerns. The more things are left to agents within the institutional presidency, the less will they be presumed to matter. The earlier discussion of the President's relationship to crises is adequate illustration of the point.

Two other factors deserve mention briefly. First is presidential character. Some presidents just like to hog credit, on the assumption no doubt that it all helps to bolster their prestige. Franklin Roosevelt and Lyndon Johnson were notorious for this. Truman and Kennedy, on the other hand, did not mind aides and cabinet members taking due credit. Where credit and blame are not at issue, presidents vary also in their desire to show themselves well informed about the institutional presidency. Kennedy and Johnson, for instance, worked hard to leave the impression of having an overall grasp of the work of the administration – seeking, as it were, to minimise the gap between the President as individual and as institution. Eisenhower was most extreme in the other direction. At press conferences he cheerfully admitted ignorance of matters that newsmen expected him to know.

The second point is the general significance of presidents' administrative styles. Variations in these affect the point and extent to which the President-as-individual becomes involved with something. Delegating presidents like Eisenhower and Nixon became personally involved in different ways from 'open door' presidents such as F. D. Roosevelt and Kennedy. Again, with

Kennedy's presidency came the practice of White House aides' giving instructions to the subordinates of cabinet members. The White House office – grown from thirty-seven to 600 over the forty years up to Nixon's resignation – has similarly tended to usurp functions of other branches of the Executive Office.[116] His administrative style is one of the President's most basic choices, and different styles carry different implications for public communication – including differences in the projection of the President as individual or as institution.

In conclusion, the President's greatest discretion in the communication of versions of himself probably lies in his freedom to try and identify himself personally with whatever he chooses in the ambit of the institutional presidency. 'You are the personification of problems and when you address a problem even successfully you become identified', Carter remarked to a TV interviewer in 1978.[117] Extracting himself from situations is more difficult if news media and the public are disposed to perceive him as involved – even if he has not been. That is an unavoidable hazard of his constitutional position. The advantages of projecting himself as personally involved lie in the accrual of prestige, if he is successful (in legislation, for instance); and also in the appearance of expertise and grasp and in the opportunities for setting public priorities and playing the moral leadership role. The costs to the President-as-individual are correspondingly great if the project fails. There is much to be said, as the chapter on power and communication has shown, for a president keeping his personal involvement ambiguous, at least until he can see which way the tide is flowing. The benefits of projecting an institutional president lie in muffling or sharing the blame for incompetence and in taking advantage of public respect for the office when respect for the personal President is weak. Finally, the more a president seeks to project himself as an individual, the more control he is likely to have over the process of communication, since he is more likely to communicate in person.

(b) Who speaks for the President?

The question 'Who speaks for the President?' overlaps with the question, 'What does "the President" mean?' The President himself may communicate the 'personal President', just as staff members may attach his name to decisions and opinions of their own. In either case, spokesman and version then coincide. Equally, however, they may differ: information about the 'personal President', for example, may be communicated by a press secretary. The question of who uses the President's name thus needs separate discussion – though some of the considerations echo the previous section.

Who does speak for the President? In one sense anybody may do so. 'The President is not going to let X happen.' 'The President knows that.' 'What the President is trying to do is . . . .' Such remarks are the currency of citizens' everyday discussion of politics. When published by mass media they were described in section II as *tertiary communication* – messages about the President with which he himself has had no direct connection. Even a tree seemed to speak for President Nixon. FROSTBITE KILLS TREE PLANTED FOR NIXON was the *New York Times* headline over a little two-inch story on 13 May 1977: 'A tree planted in honour of former President Richard M. Nixon has died of frostbite, according to the director of Cincinnati's city parks.' The tree, a bald cypress, had been chosen by Mr Nixon for planting in 1968 in the President's Grove in a Cincinnati park. Though scarcely 'the tree that died of shame', the point of the item, published when Nixon's career was being extensively raked over in a series of long TV interviews with David Frost, could certainly evoke the idea of poetic justice.

In general, then, the answer to the question 'Who speaks for the President?' reflects the range of communication levels outlined previously. At one end the President speaks for himself (as in his primary communication). At the other end the President is totally passive or inaccessible, and those who use his name (perhaps attaching it to inanimate objects like trees) can do so without any direct connection with him (tertiary communication). In between come 'spokesmen', who use the President's name with varying degrees of authority or presidential contact or both. As with the different levels of presidential communication, the further away those who use his name are from the President himself, the less is his personal control over how they use it.

The forms of a president's own personal public communication have already been noted above in section II. So too have the problems faced by presidents wishing to fall silent. Personal inaccessibility is no guarantee at all against other people's invoking the President's name, but it can certainly enable a president not to use it himself. By imposing rules of confidentiality on journalists, a president can also be his own spokesman while appearing to be inaccessible. The earliest president consistently to hide behind the device of 'a White House spokesman' – actually himself – seems to have been Calvin Coolidge, who regularly allowed reporters to quote him under that label.[118] Through this subterfuge what is actually primary communication (behaviour designed for media consumption) takes on the appearance of secondary or tertiary communication (reporting or speculating about non-media presidential behaviour). At other times the subterfuge works in reverse. The President appears to use his own name when making a formal speech, for example; but the words and thoughts are those of speech-writers.

Presidents obviously vary in how much they like to speak for themselves. Some of the variations are indicated later in this section when discussing what determines the choice of spokesmen. Others are analysed in the chapter on individual presidents' perceptions of public communication as a factor in their power. Presidents who like to devolve the use of their name upon subordinates rely heavily on spokesmen, and it is upon this middle range between the President-as-spokesman and the inaccessible President that this section will concentrate.

No one could chart all the eddies of communication in the President's name. They are too complex; and too many people use the President's name privily in source relationships with journalists. What can be done, though, is to categorise spokesmen according to their places on three dimensions:

$$\left.\begin{array}{l} \text{routine/non-routine} \\ \text{authorised/unauthorised} \\ \text{specialist/non-specialist} \end{array}\right\} \text{spokesman}$$

These embody key features of presidential public communication: first, torrents of routine news; second, the potentiality for leaks in a system where legitimate authority rests in one man but where its exercise requires delegation to (often competing) subordinates; third, differences of administrative style between presidents.

A few of the possible combinations of these dimensions do not work. For instance, the idea of communication specialists using the President's name routinely but *without* authorisation is self-contradictory. Of the other combinations, the easiest to observe are the *routine authorised specialists*. Most visible of all is the presidential press secretary. From informal beginnings this office has grown into

a specialised institution. Early secretaries had few staff and, like
Coolidge's secretary C. Bascom Slemp, combined press relations
with other work.[119] By the end of F. D. Roosevelt's presidency the
staff was specialised but the press secretary himself was not.
Roosevelt compartmentalised none of his aides, as a matter of
principle. Truman's press secretaries were probably more
specialised; even so, he was apt to delegate to Charlie Ross
unpleasant tasks like firing people. Eisenhower's Jim Hagerty was
the first clearly compartmentalised press secretary – but, intentionally or not, he 'broke out', speaking up regularly at cabinet meetings
(by which Eisenhower set much store) and playing an influential
part in Eisenhower's world-tour diplomacy after the death of
Dulles.[120] Neither Kennedy's nor Johnson's aides were rigidly
divided by function either. Reedy played a role in labour relations;
Moyers carried on some of his earlier activities after becoming press
secretary. Powell had general advisory functions under Carter.

It is thus the secretary's staff and the conduct of his press relations
that have become specialised, rather than press relations becoming
the exclusive substance of the job. There has always been a tendency
for the press secretary to get sucked into a role of giving general
policy advice. Jody Powell was no exception. Compared with
Wilson's Jo Tumulty sixty years earlier, however, his professional
staff was huge – about forty-five, and one of the largest in the Carter
White House.[121] These responsibilities differed in detail from
his immediate predecessors', but the general scope of the press
secretary's office has been much the same since Kennedy's presidency if not Eisenhower's.

Much of the confidence with which the press secretary can
speak – and hence much of the weight attached to him by
journalists – depends upon the nature of his access to the President.
Access, especially as perceived by the press corps, may mean two
things. First, it means having, and being known to have, literal
access to the Oval Office at will – the secretary's will. In a subtler
form it consists of being thought to have a special empathy with, or
understanding of, the President's mind – a valuable asset, given the
propensity of presidents to communicate in symbols. The two are
certainly not contradictory; but there is a paradox in the fact that,
the greater his empathy with the President, the less a secretary may
need literal access.

Some secretaries have enjoyed both forms of access, some one
form and some not much of either. Clearly both are not necessary in

order for the secretary to speak confidently for the President. Empathy has often been a product of long as well as close association; and it is reflected in the sacrifices of money and family life that secretaries have willingly made. Charlie Ross was hauled to Washington from the *St Louis Post–Dispatch* by a pleading call from Truman in 1945. Johnson summoned George Reedy from hospital when Salinger abruptly resigned in 1964. Ter Horst had two days' notice from Ford. A few others (Tumulty and Salinger, for instance) have coveted the job and worried that they might not get it – a sign of the 'referent' nature of the President's power over them and of the lack of any power base or constituency linked to the job.[122]

F. D. Roosevelt's Stephen Early was a classic example of 'empathy' access, though he enjoyed the other kind too. Clear examples since then are Ross (a boyhood friend of Truman's), Reedy (a Johnson aide from 1951), Moyers (for a time regarded as Johnson's surrogate son), ter Horst (a friend since Ford's first congressional campaign) and Powell (with Carter since 1966). Some of these, however, suffered from a lack of literal access. Reedy, for instance, was said to have 'trouble keeping the press informed about the President's thinking or plans because in many instances he simply did not know'.[123] Ter Horst made literal access a condition of accepting the job: he wanted – and got – a daily slot in Ford's schedule and the right of *entrée* to the Oval Office whenever he wanted.[124] Ford's failure to keep him informed about plans to pardon Nixon was a reason, together with the principle of the pardon, for his resignation after one month.

The obvious case of lack of empathy was Salinger under Johnson – a Kennedy man staying with the ship in an emergency. Under Kennedy, Salinger had benefited, like all Kennedy aides, from the President's open-door policy. Ziegler, in contrast, suffered from Nixon's closed-door policy; and Ron Nessen was not thought to be close to Ford.

The confidence with which the press secretary speaks for the President depends on the character of their relationship as well as upon the secretary's access. Four types can be distinguished. Some secretaries, first, have been, so to speak, in the President's image – sharing his attitudes and qualities. This is different from 'empathy': the distinction is between knowing what something is like and being like it oneself. Salinger, for example, shared some of Kennedy's own communications style, particularly his brand of wit. Ter Horst seems to have been thought of as rather the same type as Ford and was mistaken for a Republican partisan. Other secretaries, secondly, have been presidential confidants; a good indicator, possibly, being their ability to answer with the word 'Yes' the question 'Does he argue with the President?' Reedy and Moyers, for example, argued with Johnson; George Christian, Moyers's successor, did not. Nessen certainly was not in a position to argue with Ford, though ter Horst probably would have been. Nor was Ziegler with Nixon, unless their relationship matured to that degree during the aftermath of Watergate in 1974. Nixon, indeed, took office determined not to have a secretary with the discretion of a Hagerty – Hagerty being the single example of the third category, a secretary who enjoyed much delegated authority. Eisenhower 'disliked the cajolery, the deception, the self-promotion of press relations, and he was happy to delegate it all to Hagerty, as he delegated political affairs to Adams'.[125] Johnson's reluctance to delegate even the details of such things as press-conference scheduling was clearly one of the frustrating aspects of working for him.[126] Lastly, press secretaries can become established as personalities in their own right. Early, Hagerty, Salinger, Reedy, Moyers and Powell all seem to have become so. Even Ziegler, in sad circumstances, took on a certain style through episodes like his remark that certain previous statements were now 'inoperative' (i.e. untrue) (a phrase initially put into his mouth by a press man).

Although press secretaries have thus spoken for the President with a variety of voices, they are the clearest, most prominent example of the routine, authorised, specialist spokesman. Other examples are plentiful but less institutionalised. They have been particular to individual presidents, or their role has been more loosely or less explicitly defined. Eisenhower, for example, innovated by appointing the actor Robert Montgomery as adviser on television appearances. Johnson charged one of his loyalest aides, Jack Valenti, with the job of 'news creator', which for a time he seems to have done very well; and Reedy talks of 'a long succession of PR specialists', most of whom departed in disillusion or frustration.[127] There is traditionally an official White House photographer, whose access can be surprisingly intimate – as witness the revealing photographs of the Nixon entourage in the final days of Nixon's presidency.

Many of these authorised specialists are advisers to the President more than spokesmen for him themselves. They are concerned with optimising his own primary communication (e.g. Montgomery) or the secondary and tertiary communication conveyed by reporters and columnists from information provided by spokesmen who *do* speak in the President's name. Undoubtedly the most elaborate set of authorised specialists of this kind worked for Richard Nixon (see the section on Nixon in Chapter 3). Carter, after eighteen months in office, appointed an 'Assistant for Communications', Jerry Rafshoon, an advertising man who had campaigned with him since 1966. The object was to counter Carter's image of weak leadership. Rafshoon gave general strategic advice as well as orchestrating, for Cabinet members and White House aides as well as the President, news conferences, television appearances and hospitality for news executives.[128]

A second common category of spokesman for the President is the *routine authorised non-specialist*. These are people inside the administration who have regular contact with news media and wittingly or unwittingly pass on information. Some presidents try to make their administration leak-proof. 'Breaking round Hagerty' was considered an achievement in Eisenhower's time, so effective was the centralisation of news.[129] Richard Nixon curbed his aides' contacts with the press. 'Responding to what we viewed as the daily attacks of television news commentators, the *New York Times* and the *Washington Post*,' Charles Colson has noted, 'cryptic memoranda were circulated containing, as one did in 1971, the blanket order: "No one on the staff is to see any reporter from the *New York Times* for any purpose whatever." '[130] On their side, reporters found that contacts with aides got back to the press office. 'It is all highly organised', a White House correspondent of the *New York Times* remarked; 'I've very rarely seen anyone in this administration without Ron [Ziegler] knowing about it.'

Attempts at leak-proofing are foredoomed. Nixon, the great sealer, came unstuck with the loudest rip of all. It need not be true that there will be more unauthorised presidential 'spokesmen' (i.e. leakers) when the rules against leaking are tight. There may indeed be fewer. Woodward and Bernstein, after all, relied heavily on one source, 'Deep Throat'. What does seem a likely axiom is: 'the stricter the rules, the deeper the throat'. Those willing to pass information will not be deterred by rules against it: they will simply take more care. Those who do so unwittingly – by gossip or innocent remarks that take on significance when fitted to information a journalist has already – do not know they are breaking the rules anyway. Leaking can always be rationalised: by a loyalty to country that transcends, in the last resort, one's loyalty to a president; by a loyalty to the President which claims that leaking will actually serve his interests better than his policy of non-leaking (in general, or on the principle of particular exceptions to general rules); or by a calculation of self-interest by the leaker, technically disloyal but capable also of rationalisation as in the President's interest ('he will be better served by my getting what I want than by X getting what X wants').

Why do some presidents work so hard to stop leaks? The answer has once more to do with control. Presidents believe in their policies. This belief may be a sufficient reason for them to feel that failure to gain public acceptance is (at least partly) a failure of presentation. Presentation and substance, it has already been argued, are inseparable. The will to silence unauthorised spokesmen is an expression of the fear – or recognition – of lack of control over presidential communication. When things are going badly for the President, therefore, concern about leaks will be greater than otherwise. In October 1979 even Carter, lately champion of an open administration, was said to be so angry over a leak to the *Washington Post* that senior officials, including the Secretary of State, Director of the CIA and several deputy secretaries, signed sworn statements denying responsibility.[131] Presidents are always keen on an 'open administration' before they have had a chance to fail. Those who continue not to worry about unauthorised spokesmen seem to have had particular self-confidence in public communication, like F. D. Roosevelt and Kennedy.

The fact that some presidents worry little about unauthorised spokesmen blurs the distinction between this and the next category: *routine authorised (or at worst, tolerated) non-specialists*. F. D. Roosevelt, we have seen, did not compartmentalise his staff, though Steve Early was his main press-relations aide and he himself liked to hog the headlines. Eisenhower, according to his chief of staff, Sherman Adams, disliked doing business on the phone, so 'I and a few other staff members would speak for him on the telephone on many matters that required his personal attention.'[132] Kennedy, as was mentioned, saw profit in letting his aides have their headlines. The Johnson White House was 'one vast sieve', in the words of Eric Goldman, a sometime strand in the mesh. This was despite, not because of, Johnson's wishes: he aspired to a leak-proof administration ('He, not others, was to determine the news, and if an assistant talked to reporters, it was to be at his instruction'), but he does not seem to have worried enough about it to try and control it with the rigour of Richard Nixon.[133] The Ford and Carter attitudes were closer to the Kennedy tradition again. Carter certainly suffered from the multiplicity of voices with which the White House seemed to speak: in February 1979, for example, his Energy and Treasury secretaries gave conflicting accounts of the likely impact of the Iran crisis on the dollar, with resulting confusion and loss of confidence on the money markets.[134]

Among spokesmen in this category are members of the President's family. The publicity role of the President's wife is reflected in the fact that she has a press secretary of her own. The more political wives – Edith Wilson (in the President's illness), Eleanor Roosevelt, Lady Bird Johnson, Betty Ford – have spoken directly for the President in presidential areas. The less political – Bess Truman, Mamie Eisenhower, Jackie Kennedy – have of course communicated presidential symbols in the head-of-state role. On trips abroad, like Jackie's to India in 1962 and Rosalynn Carter's to Latin America in 1977, political and ceremonial objectives have mingled. Whenever they speak, presidential wives are likely to be understood as speaking for the President. Pat Nixon, inevitably, found that whenever she met the press during the Watergate investigations Watergate cropped up. Her defence was to become 'more and more reclusive', as Woodward and Bernstein describe it. The potential significance of any remarks by her, moreover, meant that 'Ziegler and the President concerned themselves with the slightest details of [her] few public appearances', and her own press secretary was disregarded.[135]

Other family members come into this category more rarely. The Kennedy and Carter families provide the most common modern examples. A few have had jobs in the administration – Bobby Kennedy being the most prominent – which gives an ambiguity to the status of anything they say to newsmen. ('Has the President put him up to this?') The rest are more properly thought of as having non-routine contact.

Non-routine, non-specialist spokesmen provide the last two categories. The non-routine element gives them a casual, catch-all quality. *Authorised* spokesmen include anybody who has had contact with the President, including the garden-gate variety, and who publicly uses his name without disapproval. Younger members of the President's family often provide examples. Johnson, Nixon, Ford and Carter all had children of an age and sophistication to speak publicly on occasion for their father.

Reticent presidential aides on occasion emerge as spokesmen. H. R. Haldeman, for example, went on television's *Today* show in 1970 (and called anti-war critics 'traitors'). That was a rare appearance. Commenting in retrospect, Jeb Magruder, who had publicity responsibilities in the White House at the time, reflected that, 'if Haldeman had talked more to our critics, and seen that they weren't all radicals or revolutionaries, it might have made a difference'. Magruder wrote memos urging that the younger members of the administration should be deliberately publicised. But he made little impact.[136]

To take one example like that, risks making the role of 'authorised non-routine, non-specialist spokesmen' seem exceptional. In fact, the number and diversity of such spokesmen must be greater than those of any other kind. Congressional leaders conventionally report on their encounters with the President. Cabinet members, White House aides – anybody within the ambit of the President – may at some time speak in his name.

No doubt administration members and White House aides act also as *unauthorised* non-routine, non-specialist spokesmen on occasion. 'Deep Throat' may serve as their symbol (assuming he/she/they were not among the specialist communication staff).

What, finally, determines a president's choice of the kind of spokesman to speak for him on specific occasions – to the extent that the decision is in his hands? As with the question what kind of president to communicate, much depends upon the incumbent's administrative style and attitude to media. Does he trust and get on with journalists, like F. D. Roosevelt and Kennedy? Is he suspicious of the media collectively, like Johnson and Nixon? Does he fancy himself as a populist communicator, like Carter? What does he think of his aides as media performers? 'Nixon and Haldeman had made a judgement, early in the administration, that Kissinger should not appear on television because of his thick German accent', claims Jeb Magruder; 'his Dr Strangelove accent, we called it'.[137] These are questions touched on above and in sections about individual presidents in Chapter 3. Some presidents, again, have the common touch and insist on 'pressing the flesh'. The conditions of twentieth-century politics have made this more and more difficult. Johnson in the Vietnam years found his public experiences increasingly limited to safe territory like army bases. Richard

Nixon, with less of a common touch anyway, was in a worse position and campaigned in 1972 largely through television film.

The development of television has given presidents a powerful instrument for bypassing intermediaries. 'I always said that when we don't have to go through you bastards, we can really get our story over to the American people.' Thus John Kennedy on the phone to Ben Bradlee after a live television interview with three network White House correspondents (two of them personal friends of Kennedy). Bradlee's own reaction had been equally pointed: 'I watched it at home, and felt professionally threatened as a man who was trying to make a living by the written word. The programme was exceptionally good . . . and I felt that a written account would have paled by comparison.'[138] At the least, presidents can use broadcasting to complement press coverage. If they feel at logger-heads with the press, television provides a bypass – and a possibly spurious feeling that they can make themselves properly understood.

Presidents have varied too in their use of the formal public press conference, and in their private contact with journalists individually and in groups. In contrast with F. D. Roosevelt's easy informality, Nixon, for instance, appeared to take pride in assuring a television interviewer in 1971 that he had 'never called a publisher or editor to complain of anything since he had been President'. (Notwithstanding that claim, William Safire lists thirty-three phone calls by Nixon to media people between 21 January 1970 and 7 March 1971, including several publishers.[139]) Johnson seems hardly to have been off the phone, not to mention inviting journalists to his home to impromptu press conferences and to private *têtes-à-têtes*.[140] Eisenhower was remote, apart from some stilted dinners with journalists near the end of his second term.[141] Kennedy wooed publishers to great effect in a series of White House dinners and enjoyed relaxing in the company of Washington journalists. 'It is unbelievable to an outsider how interested Kennedy was in journalists,' remarks Bradlee, 'and how clued in he was to their characters, their office politics, their petty rivalries.'[142] Many presidents, like Kennedy, have had favourites – though, in George Reedy's view, every such president has suffered in the long run.[143]

A crucial factor in the President's choice of spokesmen is the significance of ambiguity. Sometimes, as we have already seen, a president may not wish to attach his own person firmly to an opinion or decision. In the categories of spokesman outlined above there is a hierarchy of ambiguity. Next to the President's own public communication, that of routine authorised specialists like his press secretary is most unambiguously in his own name (though journalists quickly spurn a secretary if they think he has lost the President's ear). Routine authorised non-specialists – White House aides, for example – may also speak unambiguously for the President. But non-routine spokesmen – family members, congressmen, industrialists, state politicians, interest-group leaders – must by virtue of their very irregularity be far less reliable as reporters of the President's mind than of their own; ambiguity surrounds their remarks, whether the President likes it or not. Once one reaches the unauthorised spokesmen (the leakers), the President has altogether lost control; and, for its part, the public is entangled with the problems of evaluating anonymous sources – including the possibility of a deliberate presidential plant (i.e. an authorised spokesman posing as unauthorised). The least unsure way for a president to speak unambiguously is to speak himself.

A comparable consideration for the President is how loudly he wishes to speak. Generally the same sort of hierarchy applies: the more certainly a communication comes from the President, the more attention it will receive, and if the President wants maximum publicity he talks direct to the public. This rule is qualified, however, in several ways that do not apply to the ambiguity factor. That factor operates once public attention is caught: the actual catching of attention involves a far wider range of factors, including the complexities of news values. What the President wants to say and the context of events in which he says it are of key importance. Who 'speaks for him' is but one of many variables. Conceivably a rather 'distant' spokesman – a non-routine, unauthorised non-specialist, for example – might attract enormous attention because of the significance of what he said. Rumour, indeed, by its very ambiguity and rootlessness, can grip the imagination better than a solidly grounded story. As so often, Watergate provides an illustration: some of the most significant sources were unauthorised and, for the public, anonymous. Unauthorised spokesmen are by definition beyond the President's control. But he should remember that the best way to maximise public attention is not always to speak for himself. Further, the existence of a hierarchy of spokesmen means that the President could not expect always to get maximum media exposure if he always used the most direct form – personal communication. He cannot indicate loudness unless occasionally he indicates softness. Overexposure is a real threat to a president. The non-routine can quickly become the routine.

The conclusion to which these considerations point, once again, is that the President's freedom of choice is not matched by his ability to control the consequences. He has a range of constructive opportunities to decide who speaks in his name, but even this is nullified to some degree by the activity of unauthorised spokesmen (however well meaning). Beyond that, the factors that might make one or another kind of spokesman suitable to a particular occasion are imponderable. Successful outcomes appear to owe as much to luck as to design.

VI PRESIDENTIAL PLATFORMS

The separation of powers obliges the President to make his own opportunities for public communication. His ease of doing so – the impossibility of silence – increases rather than reduces the necessity of choice; and, once again, choice does not imply control over the consequences. Congress and the Supreme Court are their own forum. Each in its way is a talking shop; business is conducted openly on the shop floor. The essence of making and judging the law is argument and exposition. In a society that values governmental responsiveness these bodies have a fundamental purpose of communication. This is not enough to guarantee them headlines. Legislators and justices also make news beyond their halls. But the Capitol Building and the Court provide a central, consistent focus of communication to which there is no equivalent in the White House; for the executive process, as was seen in section 1, does not involve 'doing' anything in the way that legislation and judgement do. Presidents, of course, do have opportunities to address Congress; but their very rarity commands public attention, and in communication terms they are hardly distinguishable from direct presidential television addresses.

In general, then, whenever the President wishes to communicate publicly, nice calculations have to be made about audiences and occasions. As Murray Edelman puts it in a discussion of 'Political Settings as Symbolism', 'Witnesses of political acts are likely to be sensitive to settings and to judge them as appropriate or inappropriate.'[144] Is it a case for the television studio? For a speech to an audience, with television eavesdropping? For a press conference? For a statement put out through a spokesman? Often there cannot be time for much calculation; and about routine news little can be needed. On other occasions speeches are made before incongruous audiences. The convenience of the university as (usually) neutral territory makes American campuses thick with sites marking the delivery of some historic address. The Marshall Aid plan for post-war European recovery was unveiled at Harvard (not, in fact, by Truman but by Marshall himself). Johnson chose Glassboro State College, New Jersey, for talks with the Soviet leader Kosygin in 1967; it was not far from New York and Washington, near the Philadelphia International Airport, and quiet – Kosygin did not want a highly public visit.[145] Carter gave a 'world review' of America's defence responsibilities, widely reported overseas, to an audience at Wake Forest University, North Carolina, in March 1978. One of the 1976 election television debates was located at William and Mary College, Williamsburg, Virginia.

The kinds of forum available to the President have been discussed in previous sections. James E. Pollard's list of 'the more obvious channels and devices' (in his painstaking study *The Presidents and the Press*) tots up to twenty-five.[146] Differences in the size of such lists are a matter of degrees of sub-categorisation (for example, between different kinds of published 'letter'). From the standpoint of the President's ability to control the communication process in each case, either personally or through a spokesman, six important factors can be distinguished.

Reciprocity. Is the communication all one way, by the President? Or is there a free exchange between him and an interviewer or audience? The face-to-face address to the nation and the set-piece speech to a conference give the President most control. Jimmy Carter, at the opposite extreme, moved to a new level of risk in having a nationwide live phone-in. A seven-second delay in transmission provided a fig-leaf against embarrassment; and callers were vetted in advance by computer for 'geographical balance'.[147] Even so, the potential for being caught on the hop was real. Between these extremes is a wide range of reciprocity: President and interviewer; and panel of interviewers; and questioners at press conferences; with aide(s) and interviewer(s), etc. But ultimately the difference between reciprocal and non-reciprocal communication is one of degree. For presidential public communication always provokes reaction – in editorial pages or the comments and counter-statements of others concerned in the matter at issue. The narrowness of the distinction is well exemplified in the television networks' habit of commenting on presidential face-to-camera addresses immediately they end. Not surprisingly this habit quickly caused resentment. The President found the non-reciprocal, completely controlled character of his communication challenged by an analysis that was equally non-reciprocal and controlled (by someone else) and that followed his own so swiftly as to be virtually part of the same process – an exchange in which he did not have the last word. These analyses so angered Richard Nixon that, encouraged by popular reaction to a television address about the Vietnam War on 3 November 1969, he decided to 'take on the television network news organisations'. 'Unless the practice were challenged,' he wrote later, 'it would make it impossible for a President to appeal directly to the people, something which I considered to be the essence of democracy.' Vice-President Agnew thus 'tore into the unaccountable power in the hands of the "unelected elite" of network newsmen'.[148]

Choice of subject. Who chooses what the President is to communicate about? In the extreme case of a solo performance, again, the subject is at the President's discretion. In interviews he may ask for questions or lay down the topics in advance, or steer them by his handling of discussion. The larger the number of interviewers, unless they all want to talk about the same thing, the more easily can he deflect or dampen the tiresome. Presidential press conferences supply regular examples of this – reinforced by the limitations on supplementaries. If a subject cannot be dodged completely, a president who controls the terms of exchange can seek refuge in irrelevancies. Or he can try to forestall questioning by reading a prepared statement in advance and limiting questions to its contents. The encounter then is a mixture of one-way communication and exchange.

Preparation. Does the President know what he is talking about? The adequacy of presidential preparation is appropriately measured against the preparation of others taking part in an encounter. If no one else takes part, the President must try to calculate what preparation is needed to carry conviction with those who will react afterwards. Reaction to a speech or television address is delayed and diffuse; the President is free to explain and expound as he wishes. Reaction in a news conference or television interview, on the other hand, is immediate and conditioned by the format: the mode is dialogue, the relationship adversary. There will still be the delayed and diffused reaction from press and politicians; but the President has the more immediate reactions of those in the dialogue to cope with – and the delayed reactions will partly be to how well he copes. Adequate preparation for, say, a scheduled press conference thus involves both intrinsically vague calculations about the reactions of wider audiences and the more definite drill necessary to make the President at least as quick on his feet as the newsmen are on theirs. Hesitations, slowness to grasp the point, vagueness about details, prolix answers: such habits mark a president down. Eisenhower, who had them all, was criticised and sometimes mocked. The fact that his delegating style made lack of detailed knowledge defensible did not save him: at best the criticism just shifted to his delegating style. Kennedy, who had none of those habits, was correspondingly applauded.

Unscheduled interviews and press conferences, of course, increase a president's advantage, since newsmen have had no chance to do their homework; though a president might suffer if he lost control of the subject-matter. Exchanges that are spontaneous on both sides give the President only the natural advantages of his office.

Audience. Who chooses the audience for presidential communication? Some audiences cannot be avoided. The requirements of American political life impose geographical, sectional and partisan obligations, as well as constitutional ones like the State of the Union message. The President can try to match subjects to audiences. But the impossibility of silence means that most of his primary communication to the public is reported also in some form through mass media, which are likely to provide a wider audience. He can calculate, too, about the varying audiences for primary communication through media (televised press conferences, interviews, etc.).

Length of communication. How long does a speech, interview or press conference last? Who decides? Presidential press conferences conventionally end with the senior Wire Service reporter calling out, 'Thank you, Mr President.' Face-to-camera addresses are determined by the President himself. TV interviews are more convenient if fitted into a routine slot. Spontaneous exchanges with newsmen at airports, on planes, after bill-signing ceremonies, are controlled by the President. The President is rarely in a position where he cannot terminate an exchange. If he cannot do so literally, he can become evasive. His problem must surely more often be to extend his communication in order to make points which he feels have not emerged from questioning or which need further emphasis.

An even greater problem is who decides when a communication shall begin. While the President cannot fall silent he cannot always get the kind of attention he wants just when he wants it. Many of the occasions he makes are routine: the daily press conferences of his press secretary; the regular press conferences of his own. Generating the right communication at the right time, however, is a far more fundamental problem.

Control over use. The President's primary communication – direct to the public or through mass media – is by definition in the public domain. If his communication is secondary, through inter-mediaries, the question of the *terms of exchange* arises. Are remarks on or off the record? On 'deep background' or for use without attribution? F. D. Roosevelt expertly manipulated the flow of news through White House correspondents by switching between different rules. Eisenhower's televised press conferences were in effect off the record, since they were checked by Jim Hagerty for 'mistakes' before being released.

The ideal forum for a president is one in which he has maximum control over all six of those factors. This is one reason for the attraction of the televised address – though a president may be unwise to choose that forum, since his own self-interest might be better served if other people had some control. In general, we may conclude, the President has to offset the desire for control against other factors affecting the purpose for which he is communicating. Frequent televised addresses, as has been argued, risk being counter-productive. In a 'national security' issue or in sensitive diplomacy, control over use is crucial: in both of Kennedy's Cuban episodes, the media bowed to pressure not to publish premature information. When expounding a new programme or setting priorities, control over the details or length of a communication may seem most important. In communication about Watergate, control over 'preparation' must often have been crucial, in the sense at least that showing up newsmen as ill-informed seemed a good tactic. For a routine press conference, preparation matters most; for spontaneous conferences, control over subject and length matter more. When demonstrating public accountability, as Ford and Carter sought to do, minimising control of any kind may seem the best policy. In a crisis, by contrast, total control will seem best, since crises represent in their nature a threat to control. Non-routine events demand non-routine communication. Crisis communication is typified by eccentric timing, breaking into programmes, preparing audiences in advance for a major address later on – eventualities best dealt with if the President has total discretion. Even so, different crises suit different forms of communication. A domestic disaster may suit an on-the-spot interview; a foreign crisis may require an address to the nation. In some crises, as suggested in section I, the President should perhaps stay remote and communicate through intermediaries; in others, speed of reaction may rule out anything but broadcast communication, with details relegated to later occasions.

VII SYMBOLIC COMMUNICATION

The last aspect of the President's communication context which needs comment is his tendency to use symbolic communication. That is to say, the President may intend his words and actions to be understood as representing something different from, and often larger than, their apparent content. Small gestures signal big ideas; manifest content is taken to imply significant latent meaning. In turning down White House thermostats to 65° F in 1977 Carter signalled the need for national energy conservation. In swearing the presidential oath as 'Jimmy' instead of 'James Earl' Carter, the new president presented himself as an ordinary American not puffed up by office.

Examples of this tendency, and some of its causes, can be found in the previous sections. Any chief executive who doubles as head of state, for instance, is bound to deal in symbols. As head of state he gives life to an abstraction. His office embodies the ideals and rituals inherent in constitutional government. Again, the particular clutch of formal presidential powers, lacking opportunities for command and the sure implementation of a legislative programme, favours leadership that deploys symbols. The President's role in crisis definition provides good examples: he can indicate symbolically the seriousness of a crisis and how far he expects to be involved. The responsibility to give 'moral leadership' provides others. So does the habit of adopting labels – New Deal, Fair Deal, New Frontier, Great Society. These denote presidential aspirations. The fact that presidents cannot guarantee results arguably makes them more important. Prime ministers with secure parliamentary majorities, by comparison, can detail their programmes in advance and rely on them to convey their own meaning. The labels that stay in the mind from British politics since 1945 have been retrospective ('the Welfare State'), or allusive ('You've never had it so good' – a hustings comment of Prime Minister Macmillan that came to epitomise Conservative government in the 1959 election).

The impossibility of presidential silence, too, entails a great deal of symbolic communication, much of it in the form of tertiary communication. President-watchers look for meaning in silence itself. If the President is understood willy-nilly as intending to convey a message in his most trivial or 'non-political' actions, it will not be surprising if he does indeed seek to manage them with such intentions in mind. The different versions of 'the President' and the choices of public platform, finally, provide obvious scope for the manipulation of symbols in the pursuit of presidential goals.

The President's use of symbols can be seen, against this background, as having two objects. The first is to communicate himself *as* a symbol. This is most evident in the head-of-state role but extends beyond it. Where power is the 'power to persuade', the respect of those who must be persuaded is an important quality. A president's 'prestige' and 'professional reputation', two of the key terms in Neustadt's analysis of the constituents of presidential power, lend themselves well to symbolic communication. A president will therefore try to project himself as standing for certain values and attitudes of which he hopes the public will approve and which may therefore increase the weight of his authority over special interests. Eisenhower is the clearest case of this kind of symbol since 1945. He seemed to reign rather than rule – an approach in tune with the America of the 1950s. George Reedy makes a representative evaluation:

> In Dwight D. Eisenhower, the American people found an answer to their deep yearning for a presiding officer over their affairs. They did not care about his lack of expertise because they recognised instinctively that expertise can always be hired. They were looking for a symbol of legitimacy, continuity, and morality . . . .[149]

Three presidents since 1945 have had to symbolise continuity strongly – Truman, Johnson and Ford – since they took office surrounded by crisis. The most important function Ford could fulfil, obviously, was to convey by every means possible those qualities of

personal integrity and constitutional propriety that the Nixon
presidency had been shown to lack. 'Continuity' in his case meant
confirmation of the dominant values in American government,
from which Nixon had been merely a lapse.

Every president, however, whatever the circumstances of his
accession, will project himself as symbolic of certain values.
Kennedy and Carter, both of whom worked hard at manipulating
symbols, provide clear and contrasting illustrations. Both invited
public respect; but Kennedy sought for respect for excellence,
Carter for a respect appealing to citizens' self-respect. Kennedy's
style involved the arts and achievements of Camelot, the display of
the exceptional in every sphere, from first-rate intellects in the
administration to first-rate wallpaper in the White House. Here was
a model to which Americans might aspire or at any rate admire.
Carter, with his informality, his insistence on putting his daughter
in the local school, his constant gestures offering himself as an
ordinary man called to do an extraordinary job, gave the public a
populist president, one whom they should respect because he was
fundamentally like themselves.

The presidential office, then, obliges the incumbent to project
himself as a symbol. The process starts even before he has taken
office. The existence of television confronts candidates with the
possibility of prime-time debates. These will not happen unless both
candidates see advantage in them – or think the electoral risks are
less than in dodging them. But the refusal to debate is unavoidably
defensive, for presidential debates represent the purest symbol of
electoral democracy. The candidates face each other and the
electorate in person, without institutional props and intermediaries.
Unlike other campaign communications, the debates are outside
the control of the candidates themselves, spontaneous and thus
uniquely real. Television is the medium which most approximates
to personal contact and provides the largest possible hustings. The
'debate' format stresses reason, argument, issues, not the electioneering of stickers, handshakes and smiles. It maximises
'fairness': Carter and Ford in 1976 had fair shares of everything –
camera angles, close-ups and minutes – so that the voter's judgement could be totally free. It mitigates the vice of the candidate
appearing alone – that of a 'monologue in public' not a 'dialogue
with the public'.[150] Popular feedback is direct, decisive and quick,
through the ballot. The whole process is exalted by the press and
dignified by minute academic analysis.[151]

The reality of the debates is different. The Kennedy–Nixon and Carter–Ford exchanges were not debates at all but question-and-answer sessions, necessarily compressed, in which the candidates sidestepped the questioners as well as each other. Spontaneity was qualified by the predictability of the topics and the Olympic training with which the participants prepared themselves. Personal contact remains illusory, even if television is better at the pretence than other media. The most spontaneous element in the Ford–Carter debates was the 27-minute breakdown of sound, which left the participants stunned, since they did not know what to do. The most obvious analogy is to see the debates as pure mediaeval ordeal, in which electorate and candidates share the belief that treading hot coals barefoot reveals virtue. They were symbols, not substance.

The second object of the President's symbolic communication is the advancement of his goals: communicating *in* symbols, as distinct from communicating himself *as* a symbol.[152] To take the examples of the first paragraph, swearing the presidential oath as 'Jimmy' conveyed a symbol of the sort of president Carter wished to be; while turning down the thermostats, though contributing to the same image, was designed to promote the goal of energy conservation. The former was an end in itself; the latter, the means to an end. (The former too, as has been pointed out, could be used in a general way as the means to a further end.) The President's lack of command powers means that in routine matters like management of the economy, as well as the more visionary roles, like 'moral leadership', his actions frequently consist in trying to communicate to mass or sectional publics his desires, intentions, definition of problems, priorities and determination. Information, reasons, arguments – the substance of such matters – are displaced or complemented by symbols. Any of his formal powers, indeed, can be used for this purpose in addition to their manifest purposes. Franklin Roosevelt's use of the veto power – to show Congress they had a President to reckon with – has already been quoted. Another sphere rife with examples is the power of appointment. British journalists, working with a parliamentary system, ask *why* particular appointments are made. Less often do they ask (the test of symbolic communication) what an appointment is supposed to *mean*. The latter, however, is a preoccupation of those speculating about presidential appointments.

This preoccupation is understandable. To continue the British comparison, the existence there of a career civil service from top to

bottom of the administration defines the field from which bureaucratic appointees can be drawn and reduces almost to nil the
number to be appointed by an incoming prime minister. At the
same time, the ranks from which the Prime Minister can draw his
colleagues in the Cabinet are limited to those with a seat in the
House of Commons or, in a few cases, the Lords; and, within the
legislature, to senior or rising members of the governing party. The
relations of Cabinet, Parliament and Civil Service are also well
defined, if not always open to scrutiny. The details differ, but in
many other parliamentary systems the same considerations, with
their advantages and disadvantages, apply.

The President, by contrast, has to shape his administration – to
determine the relative weight of the White House, the different
branches of the Executive Office, the Cabinet members and
departments. Posts have to be filled within the bureaucracy as well
as at the most senior and 'visible' levels. The definition of 'talent'
and the margins of the pool are unconstrained by any particular
field or institution, nor even by a strong programmatic ideology.
When a new president makes his appointments, therefore, it is
natural to wonder what he is trying to 'say'.[153] When, like Carter,
the newcomer has no congressional experience and thus no tally of
votes on key issues over the years, the search for meaning in the
appointments is all the greater.

Day-to-day actions also provide good illustrations of symbolic
communication. For instance, presidents use travel far more often
than British prime ministers do in order to convey a message – as
well as to go somewhere. (The Queen, more than the Prime
Minister, says things a good deal by travelling. But, then, she is not
allowed to talk very much in public.) Eisenhower's press secretary,
Hagerty, once persuaded the President unnecessarily to attend a
conference of the Organisation of American States in Panama three
weeks after his operation for ileitis in 1956, to show that he was fit
and in control. When Eisenhower was beginning to recover from his
heart attack of 24 September 1955, Hagerty organised a procession
of government officials to his hospital bedside in Denver, Colorado,
to convey a (completely symbolic) public impression that the
President was taking up the reins of power.[154] Nixon undertook
foreign trips of doubtful purpose to the Middle East and Russia
when he wanted to distract attention from Watergate in 1974.
Carter's decision to visit Israel and Egypt in March 1979, in
furtherance of the elusive goal of a Middle East peace treaty,

seemed partly based on a desire to distract attention from domestic gloom. As *Time* put it, 'Having been stung by his decline in the opinion polls, Carter was reaching for a dramatic foreign venture. By going to Cairo and Jerusalem on short notice, he might satisfy those critics who have been clamoring for him to "do something somewhere".'[155] Later, Carter was judged to have made an error in failing to travel to Yugoslavia in 1980 for the funeral of President Tito. Routinely, presidents indicate their concern at natural disasters by visiting afflicted areas. All such travel has a more substantial purpose than travel aimed simply at capturing headlines, such as Johnson was wont to undertake.

Communication in symbols can be very potent. By definition, it is directed at the emotions, since its persuasiveness does not rest on facts and arguments. It is thus linked to 'referent' power. If the symbols carry conviction, as the lasting popularity of Eisenhower and the endurance of the Kennedy magic show, facts and argument do not easily dislodge them.

Yet communication in symbols is perilous: more so than less allusive forms. Symbols are a substitute for substance. Their success depends on the receiver's willingness to take the substance on trust. They are therefore brittle: if the symbols once ring hollow, a president's goals will seem but an empty shell. Credibility and public respect shatter and fall, as Johnson, Nixon and Carter found. The symbols in which the President deals are 'promissory': they indicate his intention to deliver substantive results later on, and if the results are not witnessed, disillusion will follow. What makes this possibility so perilous is that, again by definition, the meaning attached to symbols is at the discretion of those receiving them. Since the meaning is latent, the President has less control over how it will be understood than when the weight of communication is on the manifest content. There is a high risk that people will attach the wrong meaning, or the right meaning but the wrong emphasis. 'Perhaps the black's exaggerated expectations of the Great Society,' observes Robert E. Goodin, 'were more fuelled by symbolic gestures – appointment of Thurgood Marshall to the Supreme Court, the Voting Rights Act, and the like – than by any proposal for welfare legislation contained in any of President Johnson's speeches.'[156] As to unintended symbols, Nixon's 'lazy shave' appearance in his TV debates with Kennedy in 1960 bedevilled his attempts to slough off the 'tricky Dick' image; while 'Ford the stumbler' was an image the White House did not quite succeed in defusing even with humour, despite President Ford's obvious athleticism. A few chance stumbles caught by the camera symbolised too well a lack of intellectual surefootedness (see Chapter 3). Lyndon Johnson, we have seen, believed Americans would never accept him as they had Kennedy, because he had no prestigious education.

Even the President's press secretary finds the interpretation of symbolic communication fraught with problems. He cannot just be a reporter, relaying what the President says and does, for this may all be understood to mean something beyond its manifest content; and if he says 'no comment' his words themselves are a comment. Interpretation, however, shades into the dangers of 'management' and deception. Hagerty's management of Eisenhower's public communication after his heart attack in 1955 was a classic of skilful publicity, for it was done without jeopardising Hagerty's integrity. The (often adjustable) timing of a communication can make a big difference to its symbolic meaning; and the decision what to say and what not to say can lead to 'deception'. Gerald Ford's press secretary, Ron Nessen, did not like to interpolate into his press conferences items about which he had been briefed but no one asked, for fear that they would be thought 'plants': some legitimate news was therefore missed.[157]

Once again, in sum, the President is faced with wide-ranging opportunities for communication when he does so through symbols, but without much control over the outcome. If he does not have an eye to the possible symbolic meanings of his actions, he may find himself misrepresented. When he does exploit his advantages of public attention, he still cannot be sure that he will be understood as he wishes or that he is not giving hostages to fortune and raising expectations that he cannot satisfy.

3 The President, Power and Communication

Chapter 1 of this book has argued that communication is a crucial influence on the nature and outcome of power relationships and has examined the different communication processes involved in different kinds of power. Chapter 2 has sought to show that the President is obliged by his position continually to communicate and to make certain kinds of choice, with varying but often slight control over the outcome, about how to try and make himself publicly understood.

Taking these two propositions together, the central question of this third chapter must be: how far does the President's public communication help or hinder his use of power? The implication of the previous chapters, clearly, is that the two are intricately connected. Indeed, one might expect that explanations of presidential power in the academic literature would have much to say about communication processes – perhaps even to use a methodology of communication concepts and categories.

On the whole, however, they do not; and the omission is sufficiently puzzling to justify devoting the first section of this chapter to an inevitably abbreviated discussion of it and of the manner in which the literature has in fact generally treated presidential communication. Following this the chapter suggests, through a study of some particular presidents, the sort of judgements that an analysis might reach which did place more weight on communication as a factor. Since a study of this length cannot look at every post-1945 president in detail, the perspectives of two strongly contrasting presidents are first explored. One, Eisenhower, had limited power goals and an apparently slight awareness of communication as an instrument of power – yet, overall, a communication strategy that fitted his needs and was successfully implemented. The other, Nixon, had ambitious goals for the presidency and an aggressive communication strategy which, though triumphant in the 1972 election, at length collapsed. Those two serve to draw out and illustrate the connections between presidents' views of the proper uses of their power, of its nature, and of the importance of their public communication as an element in it. They provide us with the basis, finally, for a judgement about whether their communication behaviour was in fact appropriate to what they tried to achieve. These two cases are supplemented by a similar but somewhat briefer discussion of other presidents since 1945.

I   ACADEMIC PERSPECTIVES ON PRESIDENTIAL POWER AND COMMUNICATION

Any broad comment on so voluminous a literature as the general works about presidential power is necessarily sweeping and perhaps more informative about its author than about its subject. Two claims, none the less, are made here. One, which is made quite often, is that the works typically adopt a 'roles' or 'functions' approach. The other is that they tend to be imprecise about the notion of power. Each of these leads to an under-emphasis on the President's public communication as a factor in his power. The first does so, obviously, by encouraging the conclusion that there is a distinct communication role for the President ('Voice of the People'). This may be a power in the sense of a goal or duty; or else a means to other goals, in which case it is often described as 'the power of publicity'. In either case discussion falls naturally into institutional categories like presidential press conferences and broadcasts. Imprecision in the notion of power contributes to the under-emphasis, because treatment of factors bearing upon a vague notion will itself be uncertain. Where power is loosely assimilated to 'powers' or 'roles', factors which differentiate them, like communication, are disregarded. In sum, the 'roles' approach and its conceptual imprecision hive off presidential communication and discourage its systematic treatment as a factor in the exercise of every kind of presidential power (in terms of the categories of Chapter 1). They treat it, rather, as an isolated topic.

The dominance of the 'roles' approach owes much to the ambiguities of the Constitution. Powers in the sense of the duties of the President (for example, Article II, Section 3, the 'take care' clause) exist alongside powers in the sense of instruments for executing his duties (the veto power, the commander-in-chief power). Moreover, the separation of powers, compounded by the checks and balances on their use, leave the constitutional powers of the President open to flexible interpretation – epitomised in the familiar 'strong' and 'weak' theories often illustrated from the words of Theodore Roosevelt and William Howard Taft.[1] The Constitution thus gets the analyst of presidential power off to a bad start with its own imprecision of concepts. The flexibility of interpretation, further, provides a powerful incentive to prescription. In studying how a president has interpreted his powers, the question whether he has done so wisely for his times is almost intrinsic to the discussion. For example, an analysis of F. D. Roosevelt's disputes with the Supreme Court over the constitutionality of his New Deal legislation is a matter both of the boundaries of presidential power and of the propriety of its goals.

These explanations help to account also for a similar lack of discussion about presidential power in specialised literature on presidential communication. One sort tends to be descriptive, or related to the theoretical tangle about press freedom and the Fourth Estate, or both. Other kinds are limited by their techniques to presidential campaign communications, to attitude formation or to content analyses. Even so pioneering a study as Elmer E. Cornwell Jr's *Presidential Leadership of Public Opinion* has only a few paragraphs about the relationship of his subject (broadly, presidential news operations) to presidential power.[2]

The roles approach has been so prevalent that it ought not to be passed over without some further discussion of its implications for the treatment of presidential communication. In a survey of the literature in 1970 David Paletz judged the approach 'the most prevalent and academically respectable way of viewing the presidency'; and the five other approaches he described – stressing obligations, constraints, statecraft, 'anti-aggrandisement' and 'power elites' – are all more or less role-related too, with heavy prescriptive overtones.[3] In Paletz's survey the prize for roles goes to Thomas A. Bailey: his book *Presidential Greatness* (1966) listed forty-three. The classic study, however, remained at that time Clinton Rossiter's *The American Presidency*. The powers of the presidency are listed there in a chapter with that name as: 'Chief of State', 'Chief Executive', 'Commander-in-Chief', 'Chief Diplomat' and 'Chief

Legislator' – the five making up the 'strictly constitutional burden' (p. 28).[4] On top Rossiter added 'Chief of Party', 'Voice of the People', 'Protector of the Peace', 'Manager of Prosperity' and 'World Leader'. Besides hiving off public communication, the list illustrates both the confusion of concepts and the prescriptive bias. Sometimes Rossiter refers to the list as 'roles' (pp. 28, 36); as 'functions' (pp. 28, 38); as 'duties' (pp. 26, 35); as 'responsibilities' (pp. 19, 36), as well as 'powers' (pp. 16, 17). Only in the discussion of the President as chief executive are 'power' and 'powers' explicitly differentiated; and then the distinction is confused by Rossiter using the plural and differentiating 'powers' from 'responsibilities'. Distinctions throughout the book between what the President can, may, must and ought to do are largely unaccentuated. Public communication, which (together with other factors) crucially separates the 'can' from the others, remains in a functional cubby-hole.

The prescriptive character is exemplified in the second half of Rossiter's list. The roles here cut across both the first half and each other and constitute a mixture of means and ends. 'Chief of Party' refers to an important electoral institution and instrument of political cohesion; 'Peace' and 'Prosperity' to valued governmental goals. 'Voice of the People', according to Rossiter, means acting, in Woodrow Wilson's words, as 'the spokesman for the real sentiment and purpose of the country' (p. 30); defining a goal and in the process presumably abetting its achievement. 'World Leader' is marked out as a 'duty' (p. 36). Many of these powers, of course, might be affected by the President's other powers, as commander-in-chief, chief legislator and so on.

A more modern example of the 'roles' approach, but with the same implication for the treatment of presidential communication, is Louis W. Koenig's *The Chief Executive*. To Rossiter's substantive roles ('Manager of Prosperity', etc.) Koenig added a 'social justice' role: 'The strong Presidency of the future will need to be continuously and deeply involved in furthering social justice.'[5] In this he simply reflected some of the major policy concerns of the 1960s and 1970s and was in the company of other authors. By its third edition the book had been enlarged to include chapters with a less specifically functional focus (presidential personality, decision-making, conflict management). But there is no consistent or rigorous analysis of the nature of power. One chapter begins with the words 'Tenure is power' (p. 63); yet there is no such dramatic focus on the situational power of other aspects of the presidency. The distinction between 'real' and 'imagined' power is clear throughout; but Koenig's attitude to presidential communication as a factor in the difference between them is illustrated by his analysis of the constituents of 'practical politics' that make up 'actual power'. These, the 'means that exist nowhere else in the political structure' and make the President 'the major unifying force in a diffuse political system and pluralistic society', are 'his power of publicity, his veto, his power over budget and expenditure, his power of appointment . . .' (p. 14). Publicity is given its due – and rates a chapter to itself – but what the analysis ignores is that the other powers require, for most effective exercise, a crucial publicity element as well. Once again communication has been hived off into a self-contained and comparatively brief discussion of 'The Mass Media', 'Communication Experts', 'The News Conference', and 'The Art of News Management' (Chapter 5).

Prescriptively, Koenig's book originally advocated 'a strong Presidency as a source of good works, as a force for betterment in domestic society and in the world at large' (p. v). That was in 1964. Watergate and Vietnam shifted the focus in the third edition, ten years later, to the traditional American preoccupation with checks and balances. This shift was typical of what came to be known as the 'revisionist model' of the presidency; and it was substantial enough to mean that Paletz's categories of 'anti-aggrandisement' and 'power elite' would now be appropriately renamed and much swollen. But the shift seriously affected neither the 'roles' orientation nor its prescriptive quality. On the contrary, the mood was a reaction both against what the 'imperial presidency' of Richard Nixon for a time did with and for the office, and against the excessive optimism in the literature of the 1950s and early 1960s about what the 'New Deal' presidency, as Thomas Cronin describes it, could and should achieve.

The main feature of the literature from the middle of the 1970s was thus an exploration of forms of accountability. Constitutional procedures (votes of no confidence, popular referenda, a single six-year term); institutional tinkering (a collective presidency, stronger parties, a parliamentary model); popular education (demystifying the presidency) and other socio-cultural changes (including a more intense watch-dog role for mass media): these suggestions and many others entered the market-place or, if they had been there before, were pushed to the front of the stalls.[6] They had no constant relationship, one should add, to opinions about presidential strength; though Koenig was not unrepresentative in believing that a strong president – but an accountable one – is required for the most effective working of American government.

The revisionist model left unaffected the previous tendency to see presidential public communication in the context of media institutions and of a 'Voice of the People' role. The tendency was, if anything, accentuated by the concern that mass media should strengthen their 'Fourth Estate' watchdog role. The literature on political communication, especially by journalists in the scissors-and-paste tradition and by academics in journalism schools, was overwhelmingly preoccupied after Watergate with chronicling presidential excesses of news management and anti-media operations, and with defending media rights of access and scrutiny.[7]

The other element in the revisionist model was a recognition that analysts of the 'New Deal' presidency had exaggerated its potential in the process of extrapolating an idealised image of presidential leadership into the postwar world. Possible reasons for this, ranging from the commercial goals of textbook authors to the massive expansion of the institutional presidency, are discussed by Cronin in his *The State of the Presidency*, in the course of a dissection of the 'New Deal' model based on thirty-five texts. The exaggeration is crucial in an explanation of the failure of the literature to give proper attention to presidential communication as an instrument of power; for the belief that in meeting the challenges of the nation and the world after 1945 the presidency *ought* to be a powerful office blurred yet again the distinction between powers and power. Provided the constitutional checks on presidential action were intact, the distinction was of secondary importance: the President had vital roles to perform, and he should get on with them. His actual capacity to do so, distinct from his authority and his obligation, was neglected and, in the light of the New Deal experience, exaggerated.

Neustadt's *Presidential Power* is one of the two best known exceptions to the 'roles' approach.[8] The other is James David Barber's *The Presidential Character*, the most original study to appear in the 1970s. *Presidential Power*, a seminal essay first published in 1960, has been updated, in the manner of essays, by the addition of forewords and afterwords, not revision of the text. The book has come to resemble a great Gothic cathedral: the core stands firm, but aisles and side

chapels are added. First, an 'Afterword: JFK' was stuck on the end
(1968). Next, 'An Introduction: Reflections on Johnson and Nixon'
was put on the front (1976). Later this new fabric was rearranged as
two concluding chapters called 'Later Reflections'. A third chapter
joined them, 'Hazards of Transition' (1980), including – but not
confined to – Ford and Carter. The whole, by its consistency of
approach, successfully retains, like Gothic cathedrals, a sense of
balance, proportion, strength and lightness.

A third book, George E. Reedy's *The Twilight of the Presidency*
(1970), deserves inclusion with these two for its sensitiveness to
presidential communication and its insistence on viewing the
institution in human terms. The book, indeed, is both prescient of
the destructiveness of the office in the hands of an all-too-human
incumbent like Richard Nixon and 'revisionist' in its scepticism
about presidential overwork, the effectiveness of the staff system and
the President's capacity to achieve his goals. Like the revisionist
academics, Reedy found the literature inadequate in that 'it is
virtually taken for granted that the proper objective of a study of the
chief executive is to identify those inhibiting factors which frustrate
his efforts to resolve national problems and to devise mechanisms
which will remove those frustrations' (p. x). What was missing from
the literature was 'the impact of the institution on individuals'. For
Reedy the key question was 'whether the structures have created an
environment in which men cannot function in any kind of decent
and humane relationship to the people whom they are supposed to
lead' (ibid.). His answer – vindicated in the Nixon White House a
few years after he gave it – was that they had.

The essence of Reedy's argument was distilled during fourteen
years as an assistant to Lyndon Johnson, two of them spent as press
secretary. The contrast between the collegial style of the Senate and
the hierarchy of the institutionalised presidency led him immediately to a monarchical metaphor. His distinctive contribution
is his emphasis upon a theme recognised briefly by previous
authors – the isolation of the President. Isolation weakens the
President; and the chief antidote is the mass media. 'Of the few
social institutions which tend to keep a president in touch with
reality, the most effective – and the most resented by the chief
beneficiary – is the press.' To Reedy the reasons are clear:

It is entirely possible within the walls of 1600 Pennsylvania
Avenue to create a universe that is utterly to the liking of the

principal occupant. He will not go so far as to alter all facts. But he can be certain that the facts will be brought to him in the most sympathetic of forms and with the harshest blows softened. Within this atmosphere, the only grating note comes from the newspapers and the electronics media which are produced on the outside and which are not subject to rewriting.[9]

Reedy's discussion of presidential public communication in this context is full of shrewd insights rooted in his own experience as press secretary. But it is part only of his book, and the book itself was not intended as a general study of the nature of presidential power. The communication factor is therefore not explored in many dimensions.

Barber's book similarly does not confront presidential power directly. Like Reedy's (which was published a couple of years earlier) the book is concerned 'to see the man whole . . . as a human being like the rest of us, a person trying to cope with a difficult environment' (pp. 3–4). Barber's analysis starts with the proposition that 'A President's personality is an important shaper of his presidential behaviour on non-trivial matters' (p. 6). His personality is patterned by his particular character, world view and style. This pattern interacts with two other factors – 'the power situation he faces and the national "climate of expectations" dominant at the time he serves'. Together, the five factors 'set in motion the dynamic of [a] Presidency'. The results are categorised by Barber on two dimensions: (a) how active a president is, and (b) 'whether or not he gives the impression he enjoys his political life'. These provide four presidential types round which the book is structured: active–positive, active–negative, passive–positive, and passive–negative. If one knows a president's personality, which means seeing how his character, world view and style were 'put together in the first place', then, Barber argues, one can predict which presidential type an incumbent will be (p. 6).

Barber allows particular attention to style, since it is the most visible determinant of the personality pattern. Style, 'not to be confused with "stylishness", charisma or appearance', is defined as the President's 'habitual way of performing his three political roles: rhetoric, personal relations and homework' (p. 7). This puts communication at the heart of the analysis, and the discussions of particular presidents treat in detail their approaches to public communication. But Barber's focus avoids the specific analysis of power – of how far and why presidents achieved or failed in their objects. Significantly, the subtitle to *The Presidential Character* is 'Predicting *Performance* in the White House' (my emphasis). The phrase connotes a view of the presidency as theatre or display. Barber's classification of presidential types has more to do with communication as a factor in the determination of presidential attitudes and intentions than of their results.

Neustadt's *Presidential Power* comes close to being, uniquely, a 'communication analysis' of its subject. By making a simple identity – 'presidential power is the power to persuade' (p. 10) – he makes communication integral to his discussion. The excitement of his approach was its distinction between the President's formal powers and his actual personal power – an obvious distinction but novel in 1960 (as Neustadt himself remarks in the preface to the 1976 edition of his book) and one which, so it has just been argued, remained unmarked hitherto because of the literature's particular prescriptive bias. By making power and persuasion identical, however, Neustadt removed the need for a discussion of the varying communication characteristics of the different sources of power. In a subtle and complex set of relationships (teased out in a notable article by Peter W. Sperlich)[10] Neustadt sees the President's power to persuade as determined by his bargaining prospects. These in turn are a product of successful 'guarding of his power prospects' and are themselves determined by a number of factors. The President has, for instance, to 'make the right choices'. Much will depend, too, on his professional reputation among 'Washingtonians': this community assesses the 'skill and will' with which he puts his formal powers to use (p. 164) and they look, as his term of office proceeds, for 'signs of pattern in the things he says and does' (p. 62). Much depends, again, upon the President's public prestige with Americans at large – and upon Washingtonians' estimates and anticipations of it. In sum Neustadt argues,

> Effective influence for the man in the White House stems from three related sources: first are the bargaining advantages inherent in his job with which to persuade other men that what he wants of them is what their own reponsibilities require them to do. Second are the expectations of these other men regarding his ability and will to use the various advantages they think he has. Third are those men's estimates of how his public views him and of how their public may view them if they do what he wants. In

short, his power is the product of his vantage point in government, together with his reputation in the Washington community and his prestige outside. (p. 131)

How does the President use those sources?

He makes his personal impact by the things he says and does. Accordingly, his choices of what he should say and do, and how and when, are his means to conserve and tap the sources of his power. Alternatively, choices are the means by which he dissipates his power. The outcome, case by case, will often turn on whether he perceives his risk in power terms and takes account of what he sees before he makes his choice. (Ibid.)

Neustadt's later reflections did not change this model but dwelt on the 'hazards of transition' and detailed factors which have tended to change the President's bargaining position – for example, changes in Congress, the parties, electoral politics and mass communications (especially the phenomenon of the credibility gap).

The problem for the analyst of presidential public communication as a factor in presidential power is that Neustadt's analysis (save for part of the chapter on public prestige) contains no explicit nor systematic discussion of how all the elements in his model may be affected by the President's public communication. Presidential communication continually crops up as an important factor in the case studies that provide much of the stuff of the book (for example, in the fate of Eisenhower's budget for 1958). But, as Neustadt says in the 1980 edition (p. 235), television came of age after the bulk of the book was written. Account of it could therefore be taken only in the addenda: the 1980 edition includes, for instance, a few pages on different presidents' communication styles and on the impact of their use of television upon their public prestige (and, indirectly, upon their professional reputation among Washingtonians). In Neustadt's basic model, the President's public communication is not treated as a separate variable. It is construed, because of the initial axiom that presidential power is the power to persuade, as part of what is being explained and not as a factor in the explanation.

'There is an extraordinary dearth of students of the Presidency,' remarked Aaron Wildavsky in the introduction to a book of readings in 1969; 'although scholars ritually swear that the Presidency is where the action is before they go somewhere else to do their research.'[11] This section has suggested that the dominant characteristics of what does exist are to be explained partly by the ambiguities and flexibility of the Constitution. Some other explanations should perhaps be added. One, in the words of Emmet John Hughes, is that

> the search of the 'scientist' of politics tends to be a quest for indisputable data, measurable forces, and provable judgements. This very demand for precision essentially explains his 'shyness' of the Presidency: the office refuses to qualify as an object of such fine scrutiny. Instead it defies neat analysis in the most varied ways: by the character of its origins, its annals, its standards, its crises and its decisions.[12]

Academic political science has tended to leave the presidency to lawyers, historians and biographers.

Another side to the difficulty is access. Compared with legislatures, whose nature as representative institutions requires them to be open to scrutiny, chief executives are private, if not always secretive, and prefer publicity on their own terms. Even parliamentary executives who share collective responsibility with a cabinet are difficult to study – except in the legislative forum. Collective responsibility breeds secretiveness as an instrument of party and government cohesion. But, without that spur, prime ministers would still be less open to scholarly access than parliaments, because of the nature of their work. Surely part of the attractiveness of John F. Kennedy to academic observers was his unusual openness to academic observers and his apparent willingness to take them seriously on their own terms.

One result of this difficulty is that many studies of the presidency are by in-and-outers. A few of these, Neustadt and Emmet Hughes among them, have attempted general studies for an academic audience (and theirs were emphatically for consumption also by Washingtonians). More often, they have written memoirs or fairly specialised studies. Many in-and-outers have not been academics anyway. Their books have been, so to speak, part of the evidence for academic studies rather than academic studies in themselves. Journalists in particular tend to write rambling accounts which leave the reader feeling he has breathed briefly on the window panes of power but which do not pretend to disciplinary rigour. All who wish may dally in Camelot with the Schlesingers and Sorensens or play Redford and Hoffman playing Woodward and Bernstein.[13] The student of the presidency is bound to be struck by the enormous number – and length – of such studies and their variations in quality.

For such reasons, then, there are many books about the presidency which may be called without disparagement ephemera or epiphenomena. They are often fascinating to the academics. The very reasons which explain their number help to explain also the relative dearth of books by political scientists.

Simply to enumerate these points is enough to confirm that this particular essay can have no ambitions to succeed in explaining presidential power through a model giving a central place to communication factors. But the essay has sought to show why such a model ought to be constructed and to guess at the sort of judgements to which it might lead. To put the question differently, if one eschews a 'roles' approach and does give a central place to presidential communication, what does presidential power look like? How far does a president's public communication equip him with the right kind and amount of power to achieve his goals?

The rest of this chapter will approach those questions through the answers that some presidents themselves have apparently given.

II EISENHOWER'S PERSPECTIVE

(a) On the proper uses of presidential power

Eisenhower was 'handed the presidential sword only to spend much of his time trying to get it back in the scabbard'. He was 'the unadventurous President who held on one term too long in the new age of adventure'; who 'loved office but not power'; who 'came to crown a reputation, not to make one'; who led 'a life in politics' not 'a political life'.[14] It is no accident that such pithy phrases – typical of judgements on the Eisenhower presidency – make frequent use of counterpoint. For Eisenhower's view of the office made a strong contrast with the previous twenty years of New Deal activism – and was all the more ironic because the enormous popularity he had earned as a military hero seemed to arm him for mighty presidential conquests. Instead, to quote Clinton Rossiter, 'he never really saw himself, neither in his proudest moments nor in his most humble, as the steady focus of the American system of government'.[15] Far from exploring the boundaries of presidential power, he deferred to the other branches of government. He surprised even the House Speaker by his willingness to consult over the problem of Formosa in 1953. He kept out of congressional leadership choices and delegated mid-term electioneering to Vice-President Nixon. He persistently refused to get involved in the controversy about Senator Joe McCarthy's anti-Communist crusade. Partly, no doubt, for that very reason, there were more questions about McCarthy at Eisenhower's press conferences in his first term than about any other subject. More than once he indicated to Congress that he himself did not support every detail of his own legislative proposals – the famous case being the budget presented in January 1957.

To many commentators, Eisenhower's passivity was exasperating because many of the problems which beset the United States in the 1960s – civil rights, urban decay, the environment – might have been articulated in the 1950s; and their resolution might have been eased, in so far as it required changes of heart not legislation and material resources, by the kind of moral suasion that Eisenhower might have exerted through his hold on the people. In this failure the extra element of poignancy – to use Rossiter's word – comes from the fact that Eisenhower did indeed earnestly believe that all presidents have 'one profound duty to the nation: to exert moral leadership'.[16] Implicitly, however, this was in his conception a static function. He would be unifier of the nation 'not by assertion of power', as Erwin Hargrove puts it (in another exercise of counterpoint), 'but by proclamation of virtue'.[17] He wanted to lead by example rather than rally people to a standard. To him the presidency, his aide and biographer Emmet J. Hughes wrote, 'should be sought and occupied less as an exercise of political power than as a test of personal virtue.'[18]

The constructive side of this tendency to reign not rule should not be ignored – and after Watergate it seemed more attractive still. Even in the context of 'the mess in Washington' at the end of the Truman administration, there was something to be said for elevating presidential purity to a policy. Consistent with this, Eisenhower came to admit in retirement that his 'greatest regret' as president was 'the lie we told about the U2. I didn't realise how high a price we were going to have to pay for that lie . . . .'[19] If Eisenhower could not stay out of the kitchen altogether, he could at least aspire to a more *haute cuisine* than Truman. Similarly the argument that the nation needed a 'breathing space' after the hectic years of domestic change and the Second World War is justifiable at the very least on the ground that Eisenhower legitimated for Republicans the acceptance of the New Deal reforms and interventionism. He confirmed a new definition of normality. In this sense reigning *was* ruling. In foreign relations too his passivity amounted to a policy of consolidation: he ' "kept the shop", faithfully but unimaginatively, which was set up before him by Harry S. Truman in pursuit of the general directions of Franklin D. Roosevelt'.[20]

What bothers critics is the corollary of Eisenhower's passivity. By settling for eggs he turned down omelettes. His conception of the presidency left vacant 'the energizing, initiating, stimulating possibilities of the role'. Such a president is a responder, David Barber remarks; 'issues are "brought to his attention" – and there are too damned many of them'.[21]

(b) On the nature of presidential power

The more modest a president's goals, the simpler may be the power he needs to achieve them. Eisenhower allegedly came to the office 'with practically no thoughts of his own about its powers and purposes'.[22] Moreover, he had arrived at the age of 62, by which time professional administrators are in or near retirement and few men can be expected to have flexible minds. His experience of power was in the military bureaucracy. His view of the nature of power was shaped there and is exemplified in the administrative style he brought thence to the presidency.

Eisenhower's administration was characterised by a pyramidal structure, delegation of authority and functional specialisation. He strongly preferred to solve problems by conciliation and compromise ('I don't know any other way to lead')[23] – the qualities that made him so successful a war leader. But he vacillated in making hard decisions, and, compared with some others, his system did not provide for much deliberation of policy options.

The details of Eisenhower's system have often been described. An extreme beneficiary of delegation was John Foster Dulles, who as Secretary of State not only dominated foreign policy but was quick to stamp out signs of anyone else having the President's ear in that field. Dulles was also the only officer entitled to talk with

Eisenhower alone. George Humphrey was given great latitude at the Treasury; and Ezra Taft Benson went his own way at Agriculture. All Cabinet members, indeed, were expected to get on with their jobs without bothering the President more than absolutely necessary. Even their appointments to office in the first place were made by Eisenhower's old friend General Lucius D. Clay. The final decisions on three-quarters of other personnel seem to have been made by Eisenhower's chief of staff, Sherman Adams, with the rest made by Eisenhower from lists prepared by Adams.[24] Adams himself enjoyed formidable delegated authority. Eisenhower's cry, 'I need him', when Adams resigned after an indiscretion in the receipt of gifts, takes on thrice the significance when one realises how close Adams was to the top of the pyramid. As Stephen Hess has summarised his job,

> All activities except those relating to foreign relations came under Adams. These included appointments and scheduling, patronage and personnel, press, speech writing, Cabinet liaison, congressional relations and special projects. A newly created staff secretariat . . . kept track of the status of all pending presidential business and assured the proper clearances on all papers that reached the Oval Office. A two-man operation within the secretariat prepared daily staff notes for the President giving him advance notice of actions that were to be taken by the departments and agencies. Adams coordinated White House work through frequent early morning staff meetings, generally three times a week. These sessions also were used for briefings by the CIA and to prepare suggested answers to questions that might be asked at presidential press conferences.[25]

As that account may suggest, activities in the Eisenhower administration were carefully compartmentalised. Hagerty, for example, was the first compartmentalised press secretary, though inevitably and increasingly he became drawn into matters affecting the substance of policy. Such a practice in turn required efficient coordination. What Adams did at the staff level, Eisenhower used cabinet meetings for higher up. More than any modern president he used his cabinet for collective discussion and to maintain his overall perspective on events. For defence matters he similarly developed the National Security Council.

The charge that this system, by its very orderliness and

delegation, reduced the amount of policy deliberation by the President throws clear light on the system's assumptions about the nature of power. From one viewpoint on power the practice of maximising compromise and decision-taking low down the pyramid *reduces* the power of the man at the top. The very process of increasing the time available to the President for pondering choices reduces the number of choices for him to ponder. The fewer a president's choices, the less is his power – in the sense of his flexibility and his opportunity to choose widely from a range of alternatives. Eisenhower's system, in contrast, was particularly appropriate to a view of power as command. The emphasis was on sorting out the 'facts', keeping lines of authority clear, defining the options plainly, taking the little decisions at the lower levels. All these practices certainly have a bearing on the execution as well as the taking of decisions, but power is implicitly a push-button concept. Securing obedience is a matter of effective organisation; and if a decision is not executed – even through misunderstanding – faulty organisation is the reason. The exercise of power, in other words, concerns problems of mechanics not of persuasion or bargaining.

Such a view of power as command involves fairly simple notions of communication (though the actual communication networks could be prodigious). The President merely needs to convey his desires to someone for those desires to be met. The possibilities of misunderstanding are presumed slight. The situation about sanctions and rewards is presumed unambiguous; or the President's legitimacy or expertise or both are presumed to be unquestioned; or else the 'referent' loyalty of the person is presumed secure. In the Eisenhower White House the President's dislike of 'politicking' removed sanctions and rewards as a substitute for the military basis of 'command' power. He was left heavily reliant instead on the others. For this reason it was important, for example, that the members of his cabinet were selected to make a homogeneous group – and were so much in tune with his own personality. They were more likely, left to their own devices, to do things in a way he would approve. Again, he was more comfortable with executive politicians than with legislator politicians. Five ex-state governors served on his White House staff (Adams was one), and the only elected senator to whom he gave cabinet status was Henry Cabot Lodge, his earliest supporter.

The communication process, in this system, was like the simple job of the signpost, whose function is to point the way – not to urge the traveller to go there, still less to go there itself. Such an uncomplicated idea of the contribution of communication to power was consistent both with the 'communication needs' of Eisenhower's goals and with his personal attitude towards public communication. Perhaps it explains, too, the note of frustration or despair in remarks which the President – the military man, used to the habit of command – once made when labouring at speechwriting, the craft of the politician: 'You know, it is *so* difficult. You come up to face these terrible issues, and you know that what is in everyone's heart is a wish for peace, and you want so much to do *something*. And then you wonder . . . if there really *is* anything you can do . . . by words and promises . . . . You wonder and you wonder.'[26]

(c) Communication implications

Eisenhower's approach to the presidency required little communication at all – comparatively speaking. He did not seek to educate the public to new ideas, like a Roosevelt, and set the agenda of government for a decade; nor did he use his popular support to galvanise interest groups or Congress. His bent for foreign affairs made some such omissions all the more natural. His attitude to keeping in touch with the people was that of a responsible elected official – informing them of what they should know and recognising the right of intermediaries, the press, to put questions.

The 'reigning' side of Eisenhower's presidency required little effort in communication. 'Gentlemen,' he said at the swearing-in of his staff in 1953, 'I want the White House to be an example to the nation.'[27] 'Being an example' (even less active than setting one) places responsibility on others to follow from a sense of duty or desire – in either case, through self-discipline. For the President it was a matter of 'persuading by being'. His very presence in the White House was the result of a desire to do his duty: going there at all was setting an example. Hargrove's phrase, unifying the nation 'by proclamation of virtue', is nicely coined. Eisenhower's communication needed only to be proclamatory. To 'reign', he just had to demonstrate his continuing qualities of character and charm. After his illness this was no joke. In 1919, as Chapter 2 notes, several papers had rumoured that Woodrow Wilson was dead while his presidency was carried on behind sick-room doors. Such rumours were hardly likely in 1955 (and were of no real consequence in

1919), but Eisenhower's passive style made the visibility of the President's person essential as soon as possible after his illness. Total frankness, the policy quickly established by Hagerty, was the most effective way of maintaining public confidence. As to his character, Eisenhower was unique among modern presidents in being a national hero before he came to office. He needed neither to build up an image in the primaries and the campaign, like a Kennedy or a Carter, nor to transcend the personality of his predecessor, like Truman, Johnson and Ford, vice-presidents thrust unexpectedly forward. Eisenhower had the relatively easy task of not falling down, rather than of laboriously heaving himself up.

'Reigning' meant, again, projecting the President as a symbol. Unlike Roosevelt or Carter, Eisenhower did not consciously communicate *in* symbols. But – if only in default of other goals – his self-consciousness *as* a symbol seems greater. Even his bumbling speeches and press conferences, ostensibly occasions for verbal communication and persuasion, were effective despite, not because of, their manifest content. ('He is still the most difficult President in recent years to follow on pencil and paper', commented the veteran United Press International correspondent Merriman Smith. 'This is due to his speed of speech, plus what has been described as his "circular" sentence construction.'[28]) The symbolic president, unifier of the nation and cleanser of government, might paradoxically be closer to the people by staying at a distance. Eisenhower's distaste for the ruck of politics encouraged him to avoid 'pressing the flesh'. Too much familiarity could demystify his presidency and shatter illusions. 'The Press no longer has any respect for the privacy of the President in his fishing', ex-President Hoover complained after holidaying with Eisenhower in 1954.[29] Jim Hagerty tried to keep the wall round Eisenhower's private life as high as possible. Eisenhower himself, as Chapter 2 noted, developed the intriguing habit of referring to himself in the third person: ' "The President feels – " and "it seems to the President – " have become standard marks of his speech, supplanting the widespread and overworked "I".'[30] One might see the quirk as comparable to the royal 'We' – a sign of Eisenhower's consciousness of the dignity of office, perhaps of the office being larger than the man and with a private sphere closed to public communication. The private Eisenhower, observers have noted, was surprisingly unlike the public.[31]

The image of a 'reigning' president was further emphasised by the Eisenhower practice of delegation. Besides delegating the appointment of office-holders, he deputed to Vice-President Nixon the task of sacking Sherman Adams. At press conferences he freely admitted ignorance of internal incidents and conflicts which constitutionally were his responsibility. When journalists suggested he should have known of them and expressed surprise at his admissions, his angry reactions showed up the simplicity of his assumptions about communication processes.

All these features of his presidency reduced the importance Eisenhower attached to public communication. His administrative style devolved decision-making on to cabinet members and the White House staff. Eisenhower himself occupied an exalted position in which the functions of ruling and reigning were barely distinguishable. That position was reinforced by the limited range of his presidential goals. His previous record, moreover, provided in his public communication a potential weapon that was very much greater than he needed.

The product of these factors was an impression of effortlessness and lack of bother in Eisenhower communications. 'His remarkable rhetorical success,' comments David Barber, 'seems to have happened without either great skill or great energy on his part.' He won 'almost casually what so many other candidates and Presidents have sought so intensely through artifice: popular confidence in himself as man and President'.[32] Undoubtedly there was artifice: on a day-to-day basis it was supplied by his press secretary, James Hagerty. Hagerty enjoyed great discretion. A White House policy of 'no leaks' seems to have been unusually effective, and staff members channelled reporters' inquiries through him. He developed an extremely thorough system of briefings before the President's press conferences, to anticipate questions and rehearse the answers. His management of press relations during the President's illness – especially his heart attack in 1955 – was masterly.[33] At all times he was assiduous in using techniques of question-planting and head-line-catching to minimise the hazard of the Eisenhower presidency – the appearance of inactivity. 'Woodworking' was the name attached to his practice of worming through the administration to look for news items that could be announced from the White House. ('Boy, I sure had to dig into the woodwork for that one', he had once remarked.[34]) He also encouraged background meetings and dinners for journalists to talk off the record with senior officials, including White House staff. His own conferences with the White House press corps were held morning and afternoon – twice as often as his predecessors'.[35]

Much of this activity just replaced what F. D. Roosevelt and

Truman had tried to do themselves. Eisenhower gave no 'exclusives' and did not cultivate journalists at any level. Like most presidents, he was chronically suspicious of columnists. In the summer of 1959, at Hagerty's suggestion, he started holding White House dinners for about a dozen senior press people, but they aroused sufficient jealousies for the idea to be dropped after only four. Despite the claim that he had determined to hold press conferences weekly he actually held fewer than Roosevelt and Truman – two a month on average, compared with Roosevelt's 6.9 and Truman's 3.5.[36] For long periods he held none at all – two months each summer in the first term, plus a gap from 4 August 1955 to 8 January 1956 during his convalescence. The press conferences became more formalised too, partly because of his willingness to admit television cameras, though not for live transmission. In Cornwell's authoritative study one finds the ironic judgement that this development helped to inform the viewing public not only because of Eisenhower's answers but because 'the reporters had to provide factual background for *Eisenhower's* benefit'.[37]

Eisenhower recognised the importance of press conferences, but his attitude was dutiful and defensive. Emmet Hughes claims that his apparent approval ('I think this is a wonderful institution . . . . It does a lot of things for me personally') hid a different view: 'Eisenhower resented the institution as an intrusion, a bore, and a burden, but he could hardly have been expected to announce this to the national press.'[38] Unless his often observed tension and occasional outbursts of anger are taken as signs of defensiveness, the best illustration is his own implicit equation of survival with success. Discussing criticisms of his oral syntax, he concludes in his memoirs,

> By consistently focusing on ideas rather than on phrasing, I was able to avoid causing the nation a serious setback through anything I said in many hours, over eight years, of intensive questioning. One problem . . . is security. The more a President knows, the less likely he is to remember at any given moment what is in the public domain. It is far better to stumble or speak guardedly than to move ahead smoothly and risk imperilling the country.

Moreover, 'Admitting that one does not know all the details of everything going on in all departments of the government seemed preferable to pretending to an intimate knowledge no one man can have.'[39]

This last quotation epitomises the Eisenhower plain-man's attitude to public communication. Facts were facts and should be recognised as such. Make a speech? 'What is it that needs to be said?' he is supposed to have grumbled; 'I am not going out there to listen to my tongue clatter.'[40] The idea that it might be sensible to make a speech even if one had nothing to say – for example, in order to divert headlines from an opponent (as Johnson used to do), or because the failure to make a speech might itself be understood to mean something – was foreign to him. Indeed, the remark shows him looking at the speech for its impact on *himself* instead of on his audience. So self-centred an attitude is the polar opposite of 'news management'. Eisenhower is the supreme case of a modern president who sees good communication as keeping the channels in working order and 'letting the facts speak for themselves'. Communication as a factor in the exercise of power is of secondary importance, at most something which oils the machinery rather than fuels it or comprises an essential part. For Eisenhower's purposes, however, that was generally enough.

III NIXON'S PERSPECTIVE

Richard Nixon is the extreme contrast to Eisenhower. No modern president has attached more importance to managing his public communication. As David Barber puts it, 'Nixon lives rhetorically'. His speech-writer William Safire felt that his 'personal' (though not his greatest) failure was being 'concerned too much with how he would be perceived, occasionally creating a mask that became the man'. Where Eisenhower fretted at hearing his tongue clatter, Nixon observed, rather, 'The mark of a true politician is that he is never at a loss for words because he is always half expecting to be asked to make a speech.'[41] It is ironic that such a man struggled so long against the unsympathetic public image of 'tricky Dick', and that he carried on a running battle with newsmen and fell from power as a result of their disclosures.

(a) On the proper uses of presidential power

Richard Nixon spent eight years as Vice-President, but he became

President in 1968 with little experience of actual governing and administering, beyond his years as a congressman from 1946 to 1950 and senator from 1950 to 1952. He 'lived rhetorically' in the sense that talking and arguing were both his way of doing things and, since he was a lawyer and legislator, what he did.

How much did he think about the nature and uses of power? His two volumes of biography approach the subject obliquely. The first, *Six Crises*, was commissioned in the political wilderness in 1961. He wrote it in a hurry before campaigning for Governor of California next year.[42] The second volume, *RN: The Memoirs of Richard Nixon*, published in 1978, is a chronicle in form – 'a book of memories'.[43] Neither book dissects the notion of power. The first concentrates on people's behaviour during six major crises of Nixon's political life up to 1960, not on the detailed effects of that behaviour upon the consequences of the crises and hence on how the crises may have involved the exercise of power. The *Memoirs*, in turn, were predictably an *apologia* for Nixon's years in the White House. His attitudes to presidential power therefore have to be largely inferred from his incumbency. This, especially its dirty linen, has been so tumbled in the laundries of instant history that the barest details are needed to fill out an analysis here.

Arthur Schlesinger Jr's *Imperial Presidency* provides a familiar critique. By 'imperial' Schlesinger meant that the constitutional balance had progressively shifted between Congress and the presidency to the point where the presidency had appropriated powers 'reserved by the constitution and by long historical practice to Congress'. He was not much concerned with the political balance ('as exhibited, for example, in the increasing presidential domination of the legislative process') but more with powers in the sense of functions and responsibilities the presidency had managed to acquire.[44] Nor was this a shift that occurred only in the Nixon years. Nixon, rather, was the culmination, extending the shift into domestic affairs and threatening to produce a 'revolutionary presidency', characterised by Schlesinger as 'plebiscitary'.

In the tradition of the France of Louis Napoleon and Charles de Gaulle

the President [would be] accountable only once every four years, shielded in the years between elections from congressional and public harassment, empowered by his mandate to make war or to make peace, to spend or to impound, to give out information or to hold it back, superseding congressional legislation by executive order, all in the name of a majority whose choice must prevail till it made another choice four years later – unless it wished to embark on the drastic and improbable course of impeachment.[45]

Obviously Nixon himself did not describe his approach to the presidency as imperial, still less as plebiscitary. 'The "Imperial President"', he wrote in his memoirs, 'was a straw man created by defensive Congressmen and by disillusioned liberals who in the days of FDR and John Kennedy had idolized the ideal of a strong presidency.'[46] But the practices deserving Schlesinger's characterisation were real enough. Nixon, first, was determined not to be taken as an Eisenhower president. Although he used Eisenhower's desk and hung an Eisenhower portrait in the Cabinet Room, his claim in 1968 that 'the next President must take an activist view of his office' was more than campaign rhetoric.[47] 'Hell, if all we do is manage things 10 per cent better, we'll never be remembered for anything', he said to William Safire. 'Republicans are supposed to manage things better, after Democrats break new ground – that's the old cliché. We have bigger things to do.'[48]

Many of those bigger things were likely to be in foreign policy. Nixon was apparently fascinated with 'how things work' (despite, or perhaps because of, being extraordinarily inept with simple machinery). But he had no 'philosophical position' and was uninterested in 'issues'. His progress consisted in winning office and then in waiting for problems to present themselves (certainly an echo of Eisenhower there). He was said to have spent about forty hours working on the 1971 budget and to have been bored by it.[49] Foreign affairs were another matter. His background in the Navy, the importance of anti-communism in his early political career, and his ambassadorial trips as Vice-President, all brought him to office with foreign policy a major interest.

The war in Indochina gave this interest impetus; and the main weight of the imperial-presidency thesis is on the strong construction which Nixon, following Johnson, put upon the President's war power and role as commander-in-chief. He behaved, Schlesinger argues, as if those powers were not only inherent but exclusive.[50] The so-called 'principle of troop protection' and the precedent of the 1962 Cuban missile crisis were used to justify the invasion of Cambodia without consultation of Congress. The State Department too was downgraded by the installation of Henry Kissinger and his staff in the White House.

Other Nixon tactics aimed to thwart Congress in the domestic field. Notorious was his extension of the previously limited practice of impoundment of moneys voted by Congress. He even tried to abolish a government agency by this means – Lyndon Johnson's Office of Economic Opportunity. He extended also the limits of the pocket veto, using the Christmas break of Congress in an unprecedented way as though it were the adjournment at the end of a session, and declining to return an almost unanimously supported bill, which thereby lapsed.[51] He made frequent use, again, of the claim to 'executive privilege', to protect himself and members of the entire executive branch from testifying or providing documents to Congress. He thus cut off Congress, sometimes formally and sometimes by prevarication, from important sources of information.

Other means were less defensive. After getting nowhere with legislative proposals to reorganise the executive branch into four super-departments Nixon tried to advance the same goal by appointing four Cabinet members as Counsellors to the President with overall responsibilities for policy co-ordination in the areas that would have been established by the passage of the legislation.[52] The same period (the beginning of the second term) saw the development of a strategy in which domestic goals were to be realised by the despatch of White House loyalists into the Departments: 'The President's men – trusted lieutenants tied closely to Richard Nixon and without national reputations of their own – were to be placed in direct charge of the major program bureaucracies . . . .'[53]

That kind of administrative evangelism followed, and was possible only as the result of, a previous steady concentration of policy-making and decision-taking inside the White House after Nixon's first year. From the start foreign policy had been located there under Kissinger, but other Cabinet members besides Secretary of State Rogers became progressively downgraded. For example, Nixon's controversial and much vaunted revenue-sharing proposals in 1971 were drafted by the White House staff and the Office of Management and Budget so secretly that the four Cabinet members who would be most involved subsequently were kept completely in the dark until the day before the State of the Union message in which the proposals were announced. On a trivial level, stories abounded of Cabinet members suffering minor humiliations in their relations with the President, particularly over difficulties of access. Altogether, what started as a 'Cabinet-centred government' in domestic affairs and a 'White House-centred government' in foreign affairs became a government in which the White House sucked in more and more, with unfulfilled plans eventually to people the departments with its products.[54]

Nixon's behaviour may be seen as the symptom of a general disinclination to listen and consult – of what Nelson Polsby calls 'a systematic trampling of his political fences'. To most of the people with whom a president ordinarily does business – 'the bureaucrats, interest group leaders and journalists, Congressmen and party leaders of official Washington . . . Nixon gave intentional offence'. Instead of the 'normal political accountability involved in the day-to-day activities of governing' – building and sustaining a governing coalition – there was, towards certain groups, 'an entirely new level of coordinated hostility'.[55] This might, if one looks for rationalisations, even be an axiom of decision-making: 'I realized that although others could help direct my thinking,' Nixon reflects in *Six Crises* (discussing the 1952 election-fund story), 'the final decision in a crisis of this magnitude must not represent the lowest common denominator of a collective judgement: it must be made alone by the individual primarily involved.'[56]

Such an attitude *could* be generalised into a view that 'normal political accountability' meant bowing to illegitimate pressures. A sympathetic interpretation, however, is less appealing given that the other expression of the urge to trample was the practice of clandestine and illegal operations against groups and individuals. These are epitomised for ever in the break-in at Democratic Party headquarters in the Watergate building in the 1972 election campaign; but they preceded that by many months. As well as 'dirty tricks' there were wire-taps, as when thirteen National Security Council staff and four pressmen were tapped without warrant after leaks about the bombing of Cambodia in 1969. There was John Dean's famous 'enemies list' of 1971 ('how we can use the available federal machinery to screw our political enemies') and the plainly unconstitutional 'Huston plan', authorised by the President but almost immediately retracted, for surreptitious breaking and entering and similar activities. There were the 'plumbers', set up because Nixon did not trust the FBI to conduct an adequate investigation of the leaker of the Pentagon papers in 1971, Daniel Ellsberg.[57]

With squalid activities as well as with high-sounding but constitutionally untenable behaviour, Nixon seemed to approach, perhaps actually to espouse, a belief that the end justifies the means.

In his interpretation of the constitution, his use of agencies like the FBI and the Internal Revenue Service and his creation of new units in the White House, his rule appeared to be, 'If you can get away with it publicly, it's legal. If you can get away with the illegal privately, it's legitimate.' 'National Security' was the great legitimator. So it is for any leader who wishes to break the rules: for, without security, what use are rules anyway? And who is better placed to judge security than the leader? In one of his Watergate speeches (23 May 1973) 'Nixon invoked "national security", or a synonym, thirty-one times in defense or explanation of his questionable actions'.[58]

Presidents before Nixon had certainly stretched and snapped the Constitution – Lincoln and F. D. Roosevelt among them. But, as Schlesinger points out, there was one big difference: 'History had shown that an emergency had to be genuinely imperious and its identification widely shared if a President were to be upheld in his invocation of prerogatives.'[59] Nixon failed to carry conviction; and this, in a plebiscitary conception of the office, was a fundamental failure.

(b) On the nature of presidential power

Nixon's behaviour in office suggests that he saw the kinds of power open to him as rather restricted, in range if not in strength: a mixture of persuasion, coercion and selective use of people within his domain. Two aspects of his personality and background seem to have formed his view. One was a feeling that 'life is a battleground'; the other, his training as a lawyer.

All kinds of observers – academics, journalists, people who worked for him – attest that Nixon went through public life with an exceptionally strong sense of being surrounded by enemies, of life consisting in 'Us' against 'Them'. 'They' needed avoiding: the importance of privacy and seclusion is a frequent Nixon theme. When he became President this sense of polarity took on extra significance. As Nelson Polsby points out, 'They' dominated the Washingtonians with whom he had to deal. They seemed a self-important elite, 'out of step with the dominant mood of conservatism in the country at large'. His election thus conferred 'not only an extraordinary measure of legitimacy upon him, but also a kind of illegitimacy upon [them]'.[60]

The polarity is illustrated most typically in Nixon's attitude to crisis. Pondering ideas the night before the publisher of *Six Crises* arrived to discuss what he might write about, 'I decided that what particularly distinguished my career from that of other public figures was that I had had the good (or bad) fortune to be the central figure in several crisis situations with dimensions far beyond personal consideration.'[61] This claim will not bear the smallest scrutiny. Every public figure (many of them more so than a vice-president) is involved by definition with 'dimensions beyond personal consideration'; and Nixon's six crises, even by the standards at the time, neither threatened cataclysm nor were especially untypical. What was distinctive, it is clear, is Nixon's conception of the role of crises in politics and of when events constitute a crisis. For Nixon crises typically involved confrontation. All six in his book, except for Eisenhower's heart attack, were eyeball-to-eyeball (or TV camera) performances of *High Noon*. A crisis meant a dramatic clash between Nixon, the champion of 'Us', evoked, late on, in the image of the 'silent majority', and some champion (Hiss, Kennedy, Khruschev) of 'Them'. It was a crisis precisely because the confrontation (as in *High Noon*) could not be avoided.

Such a conception, as David Barber emphasises, is not destructive. In a natural disaster or an 'energy crisis' no one need win: resolution means minimising losses. But in a battle of champions 'We' may win. To Nixon, crises were a creative opportunity. Moreover, they were always relational; not a problem, like an energy crisis, to which power is applied, but a means *through* which power is exercised, in consequence of the champion's victory. Nixon's notion of crisis, therefore, is highly suggestive of his notion of power.

Nixon was the first lawyer since Coolidge to be president, and his notion of power was certainly what one might expect of a lawyer. He liked, first, to surround the exercise of power with formality. The confrontational approach was a part of this, with its supposition that a dispute may be so narrowed and defined that it is settled through intense, regulated contestation. Relentless consequences, in the Nixon view, then follow, with seemingly endless ripples – the 'dimensions beyond personal consideration'. There is a storybook quality of 'for want of a nail the shoe was lost' in Nixon's descriptions of the implications of failure in a crisis. The allegations about an improper election fund for his expenses as vice-presidential candidate in 1952 were 'an acute personal crisis', to be sure. But they would also affect his family and friends, Eisenhower ('and his personal future'), the Republican Party ('and the millions of its members who have put their faith in me'), and thence 'the future of my country' and – the ripple on the furthest shore – 'the cause of peace and freedom for the world'. All that, hanging on Richard Nixon's election fund. After Eisenhower's heart attack, similarly, 'Every word, every action of mine would be more important now than anything I had ever said or done before because of their effect upon the people of the United States, our allies and our potential enemies.'[62] Yet Nixon is silent about how and why the ripples flow. When the battle is won in the court-room, the cell door slams. The execution of justice is automatic. The point where power is exercised is in the formal decision not in its implementation. It is a hypodermic view of power.

The same attitude recurs in Nixon's memoirs. A good example is the televised speech on 3 November 1969, in which he coined the phrase, and invoked the support of, 'the great silent majority of Americans'. Nixon's judgement, from the perspective of 1978, is this: 'Very few speeches actually influence the course of history. The November 3 speech was one of them.'[63] Do the effects he lists truly merit that description? 50,000 telegrams and 30,000 letters, mostly of approval, arrived the following day. 77 per cent of the respondents in a telephone poll also supported him; and over the next few weeks the regular Gallup approval index rose to its highest point in his presidency so far (68 per cent). Three hundred congressmen and fifty-eight senators sponsored resolutions of support. That may not seem so historic. But to Nixon the point was that all this, the response to this speech alone, gave him the public support – the jury's verdict, the needle's jab – that justified a policy of continuing the war in South East Asia while negotiating a peace settlement in Paris. Thus 'the November 3 Speech was both a milestone and a turning point for my administration'.[64] If the speech was a success, that was all he needed. It was the crucial step in a chain reaction.

A well-defined arena for the exercise of power, then, was one aspect of formality. Agreed rules were another, dignified by rituals and style. Somewhere in the exercise of power is a judge, and if things are not done properly he may be confused. Mr Nixon, Theodore White noticed during the 1960 election debates, 'was debating with Mr Kennedy as if a board of judges were scoring points; he rebutted and refuted, as he went, the inconsistencies or errors of his opponent'. Kennedy, on the other hand, 'was addressing himself to the audience that was the nation'.[65] 'Scoring points', for Nixon, was how power is exercised; and for this there must be rules and a scorer. Perhaps some of the venom for his enemies – in the press, for instance – stemmed from a lawyer-like belief that they did not 'play fair' and stick to the rules as Nixon saw them.

Meticulous care in preparation, briefing, paperwork, was another lawyer-like characteristic. 'He is very methodical,' his senior domestic policy aide in 1969, Pat Moynihan, told a *New York Times* interviewer. 'He likes to get it on paper; he likes to get it in a big book. I think he is a lawyer. He goes off in a corner; he sits down; and reads through it all.'[66] The habit of seclusion is important again here. Nixon spent long hours agonising alone. Before the 'silent majority' speech he worked through the night. The 'silent majority' phrase went in at about 4 a.m. He slept fitfully for two hours, then worked again. 'By 8.00 a.m. the speech was finished. I called Haldeman, and when he answered, I said, "The baby's just been born"!'[67]

The last lawyer-like quality of Nixon's conception of power was his heavy emphasis on rhetoric. He preferred, first, the formality of rhetoric to the informality of personal relations. Not for him the clubbable approach of an Eisenhower or Johnson. Secondly, he was supremely someone for whom 'action is words'. 'Nixon has been a very hard worker,' David Barber comments, 'but with very few exceptions this has been hard work in preparing and delivering speeches.'[68] 'The baby's just been born!' Nixon's phrase is embarrassingly revealing. Gestation, labour, birth: through delivery, deliverance. Most of Nixon's 'crises', including Watergate, consisted in winning or losing an argument. Such is the nature of lawyers' work.

All those lawyer-like characteristics gave Nixon's attitude to power a strong emphasis on persuasion. The other factor, his view of life as a battleground, produced an inclination for command or coercion: the time comes when you simply have to confront and overcome someone. These two elements can now be explored further.

If it is right to say that Nixon saw politics as a court, then the electorate were judge and jury and 'They', the enemy, were the lawyer and his clients opposed to Richard Nixon. Nixon's main efforts at persuasion were thus directed at the general public. Power was exercised over them on the basis of their acceptance of presidential legitimacy and expertise. (Nixon had no illusions about being loved – the potential for 'referent' power. He often made wry references to his unlovable appearance.[69]) A Nixon gaffe on television about Americans being like children shows how he perceived the relationship.[70] Persuading the public was important on general grounds: through elections, it renewed the presidential mandate. Later, in particular crises like Cambodia and Watergate, it was crucial to the maintenance of credibility. In addition, persuading the public could in some circumstances persuade 'Them' (some special group, probably among Washingtonians) that what Nixon wanted was popular and should thus be done. Spiro Agnew's round of major speeches attacking the news organisations can be construed as just such an effort. He attempted to mobilise mass audiences so that news controllers would feel obliged to treat the administration more generously. The approach is summed up in this comment in Nixon's memoirs: 'Armed with my landslide mandate [in 1972] and knowing that I had only four years in which to make my mark, I planned to force Congress and the federal bureaucracy to defend their obstructionism and their irresponsible spending in the open arena of public opinion.'[71]

That kind of persuasion, however, shades off into 'persuasion' – the world of offers-you-can't-refuse and of power based on command and coercion, rooted, in Nixon's case, in hostility. To judge by his behaviour – 'the systematic trampling of political fences' – Nixon's view was that 'They' were not normally open to persuasion.[72] (One's opponent and his lawyer never are.) How, then, were they to be overcome? One method was to duck and slip past, the favourite Nixon device of avoiding confrontation. Instead of working hard to persuade a recalcitrant legislature, Nixon bypassed it with the devices discussed in the previous section.[73] Saddled with hostile news commentators, he shrugged them off and used face-to-camera addresses to the nation, leaving Agnew to 'take on' the networks. For his re-election in 1972, he bypassed the regular Republican Party channels. Faced with mass demonstrations in Washington and across the nation, he conjured the 'silent majority' to bear him witness.

A policy of avoidance involved two practices, each relying on command power. One was to bring a desired action within the scope of people in the President's domain who could legitimately be commanded. An example was the executive reorganisation designed to achieve results that congressional inaction had prevented. The other was to assert, until contradicted, the power to command people previously thought to be open only to persuasion. Here the extensions of executive privilege and the dubious uses of the FBI and Internal Revenue Service for surveillance and political pressure may be quoted.

Two variations on avoidance were sometimes possible. First, enemies may be defeated by infiltration, in the way that Nixon's 'loyalists' were intended in his second term to change the bias of the departments. (This consists really in 'avoiding' enemies by planting allies alongside them.) Secondly, the enemy may be undermined clandestinely by dirty tricks, such as helped to destroy Muskie as a contender for the Democratic nomination in 1972.

Consistent with Nixon's view of the proper uses of presidential power, his view of the nature of power can thus be roughly summed up in the maxim 'Find someone to do what you want; rationalise your action to the public.'

(c) Communication implications

Eisenhower's view of the uses and nature of power meant that he needed to bother little about public communication. Nixon's view meant the opposite. For him, public communication was a crucial instrument of power, and there was an absolute need to try and control it. Modern presidents, the *Memoirs* say,

> must try to master the art of manipulating the media not only to win in politics but in order to further the programs and causes they believe in; at the same time they must avoid at all costs the charge of trying to manipulate the media. In the modern presidency, concern for image must rank with concern for substance – there is no guarantee that good programs will automatically triumph.[74]

Similarly, a lesson that Nixon took to heart from his defeat in 1960 was that 'I paid too much attention to what I was going to say and too little to how I would look. . . . One bad camera angle on television can have far more effect on the election outcome than a major mistake in writing a speech . . . .'[75]

'Let the facts speak for themselves' would thus have been lunatic to Nixon as a policy. It must have been axiomatic to him as a lawyer that 'the facts' can be presented in differing lights. 'As I worked with Bill Safire on my speech that weekend,' a characteristic passage in the *Memoirs* recalls, 'I wondered how the headlines would read: would it be *Nixon Acts Boldly*? Or would it be *Nixon Changes Mind*?'[76]

It is no surprise that the rhetorical emphasis in Nixon's style, as David Barber says, 'can hardly be exaggerated'; nor that William Safire, looking back, felt that Nixon was 'too conscious of the need to create a myth'.[77] Yet this over-concern was a mistake that a plebiscitary president was wise to risk. For Nixon's plebiscitary style gave public communication exceptional weight as an instrument of power. His mode of legitimation was the direct appeal to the public, principally every four years but periodically in between – often at moments of crisis. In this appeal the populist resonances of the 'silent majority' are especially significant. The idea, first, stresses quantity as well as quality. The silent must number a majority: for thereby they give a democratic endorsement of the President. Their silence, secondly, gives the President authority to interpret the meaning of that endorsement how he wishes. Legitimate expertise is arrogated to himself: the expertise of specialists can be ignored as the selfish interest of minorities – particularly 'elitists'. The silence of the majority implies more generally a lack of interest in feedback. The majority are in touch with Nixon only through the ballot box, polls, and their own gut feelings. They enjoy no privileged forum like the media. At best, specific feedback is superficial, an expression of support or disapproval. At the end of his 'Checkers' speech on television in 1952 Nixon appealed directly for feedback, and the experiment worked.

Nixon's need to control his public communication was even greater because of his hatred of 'Them'. For 'They' might destroy his armament of popular support. 'They' would misinterpret, distort, deride – and impugn his motives and intentions. The paramount 'Them', moreover, was the ogre of mass media, 'a force to be feared in its own right, but even more important, a magnifying glass and public address system that gave strength and attention to all the other "thems" '.[78] The press was the enemy. It had been so, to Nixon's mind, since 1948 and the Hiss case, 'which left a residue of hatred and hostility toward me – not only among the Communists but also among substantial segments of the press and the intellectual community'.[79]

The priority given to foreign affairs, finally, made Nixon's public communication an important instrument. Stephen Hess summarises the foreign policy of the first term as 'based on the Nixon–Kissinger assumption that the most pressing world issues could be best resolved by direct negotiations among the super-powers, each represented by a strong leader. The players were limited, the means were secret.'[80] It was an ideal policy for a populist. Dramatic decisions could be conveyed portentously over the networks and foreign visits relayed at length. (One New York cable television station showed twelve hours of continuous live coverage of Nixon's China trip.) 'Action' in this diplomacy was largely verbal. His expertise and office gave the President maximum latitude to control, by secrecy and timing, the presentation of policy.

All these factors led Nixon to the most massive operation in managing presidential public communication in American history. It had many parts, soon familiar through the post-Watergate literature. Secrecy and surprise were manipulated institutionally in order to rationalise the conduct of the war in South East Asia; while for Nixon personally they were a natural technique of his lawyer's rhetorical style. He communicated direct to the public through television addresses, in preference to press conferences. This maximised his control over what the public might understand him to say, as well as enabling him to keep the explanation of complex problems on a superficial level. In the White House, according to Safire, press conferences became 'news' conferences, because Nixon 'wanted to leave the impression that the conference was the *President*'s conference to make news and not the *press*'s conference with the President'.[81] There were fewer of them anyway than under any president since before F. D. Roosevelt. No conference with the Washington press corps took place at all, for example, between 30 July and 5 November 1970 – the longest gap since Herbert Hoover's day (barring Eisenhower's illness). Even on 5 November, only a select group of ten were allowed to interview him. Added to this, his press secretary, Ron Ziegler, started in 1969 with severely reduced status compared with his counterparts under previous presidents. Even the title he kept only after a struggle.[82] With time and a mounting sea of troubles, however, Ziegler became increasingly important, and he finished as one of Nixon's closest confidants.

While the television address went to the electorate over the heads of 'Them', elaborate public relations campaigns were aimed at special publics, initially under the direction of Nixon's long-time aide, Herb Klein, and then under Jeb Magruder.

Magruder's greatly expanded operation used a computer, pro-grammed with 150,000 names, to send presidential statements to groups as differentiated as 'middle-aged black dentists'. It also was used to 'stimulate letters to the editor and to members of Congress in support of the President'. A White House aide ran a speaker's bureau. A White House aide lined up TV appearances for administration spokesmen. A White House aide wrote speeches for members of Congress.[83]

Nixon evidently referred to news operations generally as 'the PR problem' and to his advisers in that area, at least in the early years, as 'the PR group' – a name that made Safire, a member, wince. ('I could never get the President to stop using that name.'[84])

The obverse of promotional blitzes were the deliberate anti-media activities. The media must be 'effectively discredited', wrote Nixon in a private memo on 20 June 1972.[85] The context was the forthcoming re-election campaign, but the application was general. We are back again in the world of Agnew's attacks, of the harrassment of men like Daniel Schorr of CBS, of discrimination between friendly and unfriendly journalists, of action to plug leaks and of leaks to plug enemies.

Nixon set himself an heroic task of public communication and he failed with an appropriately total collapse. He paid too little attention to feedback from the public, especially by his alienation of 'Washingtonians'. He perhaps underestimated the importance of tertiary communication: for, however much he spoke to the people, hugged information to his chest and kept away from newsmen, hostile interpretations of his motives and behaviour would continue to circulate. Indeed, they might be the more hostile for being ill informed. One returns, whence one started, to the ironies of his situation. His conception of power and its uses put a premium on credibility and popular affection. Yet his awkward personality and hostility to news media made him the least likely of modern presidents to make a plebiscitary presidency work. 'The media are far more powerful than the President in creating public awareness and shaping public opinion,' he acknowledged in his memoirs, 'for the simple reason that the media always have the last word.'[86] Nixon triumphed in the 1972 election, but the fragility of his power was perfectly shown by the capacity of the Watergate break-in, an intrinsically trivial episode, to become the symbol of great awfulness and to fuel his destruction. He tried to be a plebiscitary president in a system without plebiscites. 'Washingtonians' destroyed him, but they rather than he by that time held the confidence of the people.

IV   OTHER PRESIDENTS: TRUMAN TO CARTER

To write more briefly about other presidents involves even cruder generalisation and greater risk, no doubt, of error. It is probably better, none the less, to attempt encapsulations of each than a directly comparative critique discussing all the presidents under a series of headings ('Use of TV', 'Relationship to Press Secretary' and so on). Differences between the presidents should become clear. The argument of the book involves no need to rank them. Eisenhower and Nixon have been presented as extremes but without the implication of a continuum between them on which the others could be precisely plotted. The purpose, rather, is to sum up for each what can be simply said about their use of communication as an instrument of power.

(a)   Harry Truman's perspective

Of all the presidents since 1945 Truman comes closest to Eisenhower in his lack of sensitivity to communication as an instrument of power. Indeed, the two men seem to have shared similar attitudes to the nature of power, if not to the role of presidency. But, where Eisenhower was able to achieve many of his goals without a more active communications policy, Truman, utterly lacking the status of national hero, would have benefited from seeking to manage his public communications more effectively, especially since he was not content, like Eisenhower, to stand aloof from the ruck of politics. His ineptitude was typified by his famous 'shooting from the hip' at press conferences. Put crudely, he dropped bricks – which the press then heaved at him.

Truman never wanted the presidency nor apparently expected it even when Vice-President. Certainly he did not wish to aggrandise the office. With ten years' experience in the Senate he felt that the balance of power needed tipping back from the President to Congress; and he hoped at first to develop the potential of the Cabinet.[87] Least of all did he aspire to project the President as a superman (even for ritual head-of-state purposes). 'The objective and its accomplishment is my philosophy and I am willing and want to pass the credit around', he noted in his diary in May 1948.[88]

Consistent with this was Truman's well-known view that 'a great many people, I expect a million in the country' could have done the job better than he. He saw himself, as Neustadt elegantly puts it, 'not as a man for whom the job was made, but as a man who had the job to do'. In an image not far from his own trade of haberdashery, he may be said to have taken the presidency off the peg rather than to have had it tailor-made. To quote Neustadt again, 'he saw the President as man-in-charge of government, as maker of a record for his party, and as voice for the whole body of Americans'. His business was 'to make decisions and to take initiatives; those were the duties of the boss-and-spokesman'. In sum, he had a formalistic view of the office: it had its proper place in the Constitution and should be used appropriately. The potential of the office and the personality of the incumbent were far apart. In Neustadt's judgement, 'Truman's image of the Presidency and of himself as President kept job and man distinct to a degree unknown in Roosevelt's case or Eisenhower's.' 'I've had as usual a very hectic week', he wrote to his sister Mary one day in 1948; ' . . . But there's no use crying about it. I'm here and the job has to be done.'[89]

This formalism reflected something of Truman's view of the nature of presidential power. His method of running the government, Stephen Hess considers, 'was at almost midpoint between the designed chaos of his predecessor and the structural purity of his successor'.[90] He instituted pieces of presidential advisory machinery that Eisenhower and his successors took over, such as the Joint Chiefs of Staff, the National Security Council and the Council of Economic Advisers. He emphasised staff work, routine, clear lines of responsibility, and delegation based on mutual loyalty. Like most such systems, this one was tidier in principle than in practice. It adapted partly with the passage of time and partly because of Truman's determined accessibility to people (regardless of lines of authority) and because of his feel for personalities. But the very aspiration to administrative tidiness implied a rational, mechanistic view of power not unlike Eisenhower's. As R. T. Johnson writes, in Truman's approach 'there is an emphasis on facts, staff machinery, funeling information to the top, and the President sitting like a magistrate making the final decision'.[91]

The idea of 'the facts' – an unambiguous body of knowledge

about a situation – is crucial to Truman's notion of power. For he believed, like Eisenhower, in a sort of levitational power of facts – that they would 'speak for themselves'. This simple faith acquired part of its significance from Truman's depreciation of the role of personality in politics. The separation of the office and person of the President in his mind gave him no incentive to ram home a presidential version of 'the facts'. He did not seem to realise that 'personal aggrandisement', whatever the folly of fame, might be instrumental to that 'accomplishment of objectives' which he defined as the purpose of the presidency. Beyond that, Truman's willingness to 'pass credit around' meant that he yielded opportunities to others to define 'the facts' on his behalf. This might not have mattered had he not numbered among his aides men like Harry Vaughan and Matt Connelly. These and others sullied Truman's administration through their involvement in cases of perjury, bribery and conspiracy to defraud. Truman's attachment to loyalty (Vaughan, for example, was a friend since the First World War) simply reinforced the harmful effects, for he was most reluctant to dissociate himself, unlike, say, Lyndon Johnson in similar circumstances. Loyalty, indeed, while an important unifying principle when exacted from aides, was a self-imposed limitation on presidential power when practised indiscriminately by the President himself.

The other important aspect of Truman's belief in the power of 'the facts' was the assumption of their unambiguousness. This too had roots in the detachment of the idea of power from personality. It stemmed in particular from reliance upon a system of advice and decision-making that stressed the free flow of information. The notions of 'free flow' and unambiguous meaning are related. To say that information should flow 'freely' means that it should be available to all who might find it useful: bits should not be concealed or distorted. A 'free flow' is thus by inference an increased flow – because it is fuller than when it is not free. A full flow implies in turn that information should be available uniformly. Uniform information, however, loses its value in circulation to the extent that it is not uniformly understood. The greater the emphasis put upon the importance of 'free flow', therefore, the greater is the assumption that the information will be unambiguous. (If one believed the opposite – that more information increased the potential for misunderstanding – one could not consistently prefer a free rather than a limited flow.)

Truman's system was geared to producing decisions – which he evidently much enjoyed taking. But the emphasis in the system was on the formulation of possible solutions more than on argument about what needed solving. The exercise of power thus meant persuading people of the rightness of a particular decision more than about what had to be decided. Rational men, possessed of the facts upon which a decision was taken, would surely see why the President had taken it. The facts would indeed have 'spoken for themselves'; and, that being so, it would make no difference to the outcome whether they were explained by the President or by an aide.

The pitfalls of the assumption that facts are unambiguous were glaringly illustrated in the saga of Truman's relations with MacArthur. These need no recapitulation here. But President and Commander-in-Chief in Korea left an encounter between them in Wake Island with rival views of what had been agreed about the extent of MacArthur's authority; and the subsequent confrontation and dismissal were inevitable if presidential authority was to be maintained. There are many well documented, if less dramatic, examples in the field of domestic policy that illustrate the unreliability of Truman's assumption that aides would be 'funnels' not 'filters' and that Congress would accept 'rational' legislation on the same terms as Truman construed it.[92]

In an electoral context, the same simple faith in 'the facts' is illustrated by the repeated importance Truman attached to letting people know 'where he stood'. 'It will be the greatest campaign any President ever made', he wrote to his sister in October 1948. 'Win, lose or draw, people will know where I stand and a record will be made for future action by the Democratic Party.'[93] One thing he always liked about Andrew Jackson, he remarked in his memoirs, 'was that he brought the basic issues into clear focus. People knew what he stood for and what he was against . . . .'[94]

Truman's notion of 'the facts' was plainly too simple to bear the weight necessary if the achievement of his goals was to be aided without an active communications policy. If the facts were going to 'speak for themselves', much more care was needed in managing the definition of what they were – even if the manipulative potential of presidential personality and office were not exploited on the scale of a Johnson or Nixon.

Truman certainly recognised the power of words, as any politician must. In childhood, 'I learned that a leader is a man who has the ability to get other people to do what they don't want to do, and like it', he wrote.[95] His own capacity to do that, at least through word-spinning, was slight – and he knew it. 'I may have to become an "orator"', he reflected in his diary on 1 May 1948, after an experimental off-the-cuff radio and television speech. 'I heard a definition of an orator once – "He is an honest man who can communicate his views and make others believe he is right." Wish I could do that.' He liked the plain speaking of the military man. Margaret Truman comments that his speeches shunned 'big words and flowery language because they gave the audience the impression the orator was showing off'. Moreover (and how characteristic of Truman), 'they also interfered with the communication of the facts'.[96]

Truman was happiest communicating in relatively small groups. When electioneering, for instance, he was in his element in whistle-stops. The problem with his press-conference clangers was caused largely by insensitivity to the echoes resounding to the wider public. The public were not to know, for example, that some of the more damaging phrases were put into his mouth by reporters, under the convention that their phrases became his if he expressed agreement with them. (His description of the worsening war in Korea as a 'police action' was one; his apparent readiness to use the atomic bomb there was another.) Within the confines of the conference itself, these remarks, though still disconcerting for their lack of qualification, did not carry quite the stark connotations. With his naïve view of 'the facts', Truman, as Douglass Cater puts it, 'never was able to comprehend both the culling process of the press and the printed impact of his words'.[97]

It was a reflection of Truman's discomfort in public communication, however, that his attitude even to presidential press conferences, which Roosevelt had developed as an informal institution thoroughly under his own control, was highly defensive. Far from seeing them, like Roosevelt or Kennedy, as an opportunity to explain new programmes and 'educate' the press, he approached them more like Eisenhower as 'an ordeal, or at best a contest of wits'. One result was a greater reliance than before upon the President's opening the conference with a prepared statement – over 60 per cent of the time in 1946 and 1947, and still 50 per cent in 1951–2. Much more elaborate briefing sessions were held in advance, too. The conferences were held only once a week – a practice intended to last only while the new President was finding his feet but which in fact became a habit. (Wilson, Harding, Coolidge and Hoover had all held conferences twice a week, as did F. D. Roosevelt.[98])

Defensiveness is perhaps further evidenced in Truman's less extensive informal contacts with reporters. Nor were his press secretaries, despite their inclusion in the 'loyalty' bond, incorporated into substantive decision-making like their counterparts under Roosevelt, Kennedy, Johnson and Carter. Their exclusion was yet one more illustration of the triumph of 'the facts'. If 'the facts' speak for themselves, problems of the presentation of policy need have no bearing upon the practicability of that policy and hence upon its desirability. The press secretary can just be given the facts to hand down the line.

The decline in press-conference intimacy was reinforced by two other factors. One was a change in venue in 1950 from the President's office to a much larger room seating some 230 reporters. Quite apart from the size, this bred formality because reporters had to rise and preface their question with their name and affiliation. The second factor was Truman's willingness to go on the record. Eventually his conferences were taped, with sections released for radio and transcripts of the whole made available to congressional Democratic leaders. Roosevelt, in contrast, had been very reluctant to allow direct quotation.

Truman thus moved the presidential press conference away from an intimate, private, educative meeting towards the institutionalised performances refined by his successors, especially from Kennedy onwards.[99] This was doubly paradoxical: first, in that it happened under a president who rightly felt he lacked the skills of public communication; and, secondly, because he did so very little to use the new instrument in order to influence public perception of 'the facts'.

Truman enjoyed his successes as President (however one rates them) despite, not because of, his use of public communication. Other modern presidents – Kennedy, Johnson, Ford – were undistinguished public speakers. But Kennedy made up for it with Camelot; Johnson with his formidable antennae and appreciation of news-management techniques. Eisenhower, as we have seen, could trade (had he so chosen) on his status of national hero. Nixon used television skilfully until overwhelmed by Watergate, in spite of bad personal relations with newsmen. Carter for a time used the media effectively to project his populist style. Even Ford tried (admittedly with no success whatever) to mobilise opinion behind his anti-inflation policy, by leading a 'Whip Inflation Now' campaign. Only Eisenhower, in other words, equalled Truman's lack of interest in exploiting public communication as an instrument of power. Such passivity suited Eisenhower's conception of the presidential office. It did not suit Truman's. He liked taking decisions. He wanted the presidency to get things done. Whether by lack of skill or lack of insight, he failed to use one of the tools of the job.

(b) John F. Kennedy's perspective

Kennedy's administration provides a sharp contrast to both Truman's and Eisenhower's in its attitude to public communication. The difference was less in technique, where Eisenhower's Hagerty, for example, had already set new standards as press secretary, than in a heightened awareness of the potential of public communication in the aid of an activist presidency.

Clinton Rossiter's essay *The American Presidency*, a standard text when Kennedy entered the White House, carries an epigraph from Macbeth. Kennedy's aide Theodore Sorensen tells how Kennedy suggested to Rossiter that it be changed. A more appropriate quotation, he thought (it was evidently a Kennedy favourite), would be the famous exchange in *King Henry IV, Part I*: 'I can call spirits from the vasty deep', cries Glendower. 'Why, so can I, or so can any man', Hotspur retorts. 'But will they come when you do call for them?' The story is a Kennedy equivalent of the Truman prediction about Eisenhower: 'He'll sit here and he'll say, "Do this! Do that!" *And nothing will happen.*'[100] While both presidents saw the gap between intention and results, Kennedy was far the more perceptive about what public communication could do to keep the gap small. As an orator Kennedy was poor. But as a communicator who engaged public sympathy for his aspirations he must rank, during his nearly three years in office, as the most gifted president since Franklin Roosevelt. His conception both of the scope of his office and of the nature of presidential power made him pay meticulous attention to matters of communication, not, as Arthur Schlesinger puts it, for 'hortatory and explicit public education' – for which the times were unsuited, lacking tangible crises such as Roosevelt or Truman had faced – but in subtle, oblique and largely unhistrionic ways.[101] He rarely sought to mobilise public opinion against a hostile Congress – fearing, no doubt rightly, that the tactic would be unproductive. His legislative record is weak. But in setting an agenda for domestic politics and maintaining public confidence in his conduct of foreign policy, despite the Bay of Pigs fiasco three months after taking office, his leadership of public opinion was skilful.

Kennedy was a third-generation politician; a man of action marked by his wartime experiences at sea; yet at the same time an intellectual with a capacity for self-awareness who, starting with his essay *Why England Slept* (1940), had closely studied the practice of government. Government, not politics, seems the right word to use. His congressional career and White House record show him not to have been cut out for legislative politics; and his interest in the machinery and detail of administration was negligible. (In the former he was the antithesis of his successor, Johnson; in the latter, of his immediate predecessors.) Kennedy's absorption was with executive power; more precisely, with executive leadership. He sought to govern not by command but by leading.

The balance between the man of action and the intellectual is neatly illustrated by the fact that Kennedy read Richard Neustadt's *Presidential Power* before taking office – and then, according to Sorensen, was 'slightly annoyed' by the newspaper fuss over his enjoyment of it.[102] He wanted to get on with things, to stretch the presidency and use it to activate and galvanise. Much of this process consisted in Kennedy's version of 'moral leadership'. *Why England Slept* holds the key to his attitudes. A repeated theme in the book is that 'democracies require jolts to awaken them' (the imagery of 'jolts' and 'shocks' recurs).[103] The immediate context was the problem of gaining popular approval for armament in a democracy in time to counter an external threat – at that time, Nazi Germany.[104] But the theme goes wider, and the book is permeated with a belief that democratic government is always a matter of mobilising consent.

There were twenty years between the writing of *Why England Slept* by a twenty-two-year-old and the assumption of the presidency by a mature politician. But the attitudes stayed consistent. David Barber sums them up succinctly:

To both Jack Kennedy, BA and President John F. Kennedy, the fundamental problem of governing a democracy was psychological: how to overcome the inertia inherent in man's nature. The answer was political, in the large sense of informing the nation of its true condition and arousing it from its slumbers.

Two important roles are open to the leader in this view of government. The first is to define goals for the nation. The leader sets priorities and mobilises public support; though not necessarily, it must be stressed, by exhortation and mass emotion. Secondly, and as part of this process, the leader is uniquely placed to become, not always to his advantage, a symbol. One lesson Kennedy drew from the American depression and British foreign policy in the 1930s was about the way blame became attached to the democracies' leaders.

> I believe it is one of democracy's failures that it seeks to make scapegoats of its own weaknesses. A nation takes a long time to change its mind: but, although the change may be gradual, one slight shock may make it change with lightning speed from one position to another. It then frequently forgets the reasons for its previous point of view; it cannot understand how it could have believed as it formerly did. Seeking to explain this, it places the blame on the men who were then in office.[105]

Thus Hoover was blamed for the Depression, even though to attribute to himself the causes of the slump was absurd. (Might Kennedy have seen the defeat of Carter in 1980 in these terms?) The consequences of such personalisation must be countered if the right lessons of experience are to be drawn. But the tendency to personalisation in the first place gives the leader unrivalled opportunities for symbolic leadership.

In Kennedy's view, then, the President has both the duty and the opportunity to lead the people by advocacy and example. His own leadership was epitomised in the rhetoric of the New Frontier, with its contrast to the passivity of the Eisenhower years. Neustadt picks out three essential commitments: to containing the risk of nuclear holocaust through miscalculation, to civil rights, and to management of the economy for growth in order to finance programmes such as Johnson later dubbed the 'war against poverty'. The Peace Corps is often quoted as a dramatic instance of Kennedy's gift for inspiring, as Barber puts it, the release of practical idealism. At first Congress authorised 500 volunteers: the applications poured in, and by 1964 10,000 were authorised. As to civil rights, Carl M. Brauer concludes in his study *John F. Kennedy and the Second Reconstruction* that Kennedy 'committed the moral authority of the President to racial justice in the most clear-cut terms ever . . . . Under Kennedy civil rights became a focal point of public policy and political debate.'[106]

Aside from substantive goals, Kennedy's notion of presidential leadership was reflected in his staffing arrangements. His suspicions of inertia in the State Department and his penchant for talking to relatively junior officials quickly attracted attention. 'After all,' he explained to a television interviewer (15 December 1962), 'the President can't administer a department, but at least he can be a stimulant.' Cabinet meetings he felt to be useless except as a public symbol of orderly government. He held only six in three years.[107] Relations with his staff had a 'band of brothers' image contrasting sharply with the hierarchical structure of Eisenhower and the comings and goings under Johnson. As for the Kennedy family, they were 'the greatest boon since paper' to the nation's magazines.[108]

Kennedy's conception of the presidency transparently supposed that power, which in the domestic sphere was virtually synonymous for him with leadership, was exercised through persuasion or by argument, example and the appeal to symbolism. He was of course perfectly prepared to use command, rewards and sanctions where these were available. Characteristic of his management of crises, for instance, which Stephen Hess regards as the activity (along with the public aspects of the office) that received much of the emphasis in the Kennedy White House, was the establishment of a 'personal command post'.[109] The development of his response to the Cuban missile crisis involved group discussion and advice; but, as noted in Chapter 2, observers sensed an air of detachment about the President inseparable from the fact that the ultimate decisions were solely his.

In the business of defining an agenda for the nation, however, Kennedy relied especially on affective appeal ('referent' power, in the terms of Chapter 1). Again and again he seeks ways of identifying people with his aspirations. 'The New Frontier sums up not what I intend to *offer* the American people,' he told the Democratic Nominating Convention in 1960, 'but what I intend to *ask* of them' (author's emphasis). The technique is beautifully illustrated in his attitude to the space race. The Soviet Sputnik launched in 1957, ahead of any American launch, was a 'jolt', in the terminology of *Why England Slept*. It symbolised the lagging American endeavour of the 1950s. This must change. The challenge to get the first man on the moon, therefore, should awaken in every American a sense of sharing. 'In a very real sense,' Kennedy told Congress, 'it will not be one man going to the moon . . . it will be an entire nation. For all of us must work to put him there.' In a different and ludicrous vein, which Kennedy regretted subsequently, Americans identified with him in droves by buying fallout shelters following his television address on civil defence during the Berlin crisis in 1961.[110]

Reliance on affective appeal is evident also in the administrative style referred to above. The 'band of brothers' shared an identity of interest. The Bay of Pigs invasion taught him, in Stephen Hess's words, thereafter 'to turn first to those he trusted most and, conversely, to trust little in those he knew least'. He preferred, similarly, to deal with individuals not institutions. He was far from being a 'fixer', like Lyndon Johnson. But his liking for a personal approach suggests a preference for persuading people to do things because they want to rather than in recognition of legitimacy, in response to command or in plain anticipation of reward.[111]

Kennedy's emphasis on giving people a sense of involvement made him naturally more alert to the importance of feedback than either of his immediate predecessors or than Richard Nixon. Especially after the Bay of Pigs he perceived, too, that alternative lines of advice effectively increase the President's power when a decision is needed. 'I can't afford to confine myself to one set of advisers', Schlesinger reports him as saying. 'If I did that *I* would be on *their* leading strings.'[112] The urge to avoid isolation, to remain receptive to outside information, is well shown in a remark to Sorensen: 'I sit in the White House, and what I read . . . and . . . see is the sum total of what I hear and learn. So the more people I can see, or the wider I can expose [my mind] to different ideas, the more effective [I] can be as President.'[113]

The desire for feedback was one reason why Kennedy kept in close contact with journalists. He was well aware of the press as a two-way system of communication. His unprecedented willingness to give exclusive interviews (a practice eschewed even by Franklin Roosevelt), and his readiness to drop round to journalists' houses, attend their parties and invite them to the White House, paid dividends in sympathetic coverage (and avoided rancour because he was seen over a period not to play favourites). But it also helped to provide this essential contact with the world beyond the White House.[114]

Given Kennedy's conception of the presidency and his view of the nature of presidential power, it is no surprise to find Sorensen observing that 'no problem of the Presidency concerned [Kennedy] more than that of public communication – educating, persuading and mobilizing that opinion through continued use of the political machinery, continued travelling and speaking and, above all, continued attention to the mass media'.[115] He was alert to press routines, having had a little journalistic experience after the Second World War; to the ultimately conflicting interests of press and presidency, including the ability of the press to influence the political agenda; to the hostility of many publishers compared with the sympathy of reporters; to the danger of increasing congressional hostility by too many or crude appeals to the nation as a means of pressure; and to the probability of good publicity turning sour.

Above all, since he was the first president for whom television had come of age, Kennedy was alert to the advantages of the medium in bypassing journalistic intermediaries and reaching Americans direct. More than once he described television as his 'greatest weapon', though he was careful to use it selectively. He realised, too, that the presidential press conference had developed under Eisenhower to the point where it was public theatre appropriately directed through television at a national audience; and he sought to exploit it in that way.[116] 'The reporters grew to feel that they were extras in the recurring drama', Elmer E. Cornwell Jr observes. Relatively few took notes, and only those in the first three rows tended to get called. Kennedy himself took great care over pre-conference briefings; used the opportunity normally to make quite a significant opening statement; and sometimes resorted (through press secretary Pierre Salinger) to question plants.[117] On one occasion, faced with a steel-price rise running counter to his economic policy, Kennedy used the conference to involve public opinion to get the steel leaders to back down.

Quite apart from the press conferences, such other activities as speech-writing ('a major White House activity')[118] and presidential image-building (truly awe-inspiring')[119] were developed by Kennedy on a scale which simply would not have been possible in the limited presidential machinery of so publicity-conscious a president as Franklin Roosevelt and which was not sought by Truman, Eisenhower or, later, Ford. Once introduced, many of the practices became routine.

Kennedy's approach to public communication thus seems to have been generally consistent both with his goals and with his view of how these could be achieved. The difficulty of making a judgement – as with any judgement about his presidency – is the truncated term of office. As Neustadt points out, it is like assessing

Roosevelt before January 1936, Truman before enactment of the Marshall Plan, or Eisenhower if he had not survived his heart attack.[120] Kennedy is accused of arousing expectations he did not fulfil; and, in so far as these required legislative action rather than popular will, his record of course was poor. Moreover, his public communication, as Speaker Rayburn and Vice-President Johnson both advised him, was unlikely to make much impact on an unsympathetic Congress. It was for Johnson as President, with his personal skills rooted in a congressional career – backed up, to be sure, by skilful publicity – to legislate the New Frontier. In foreign policy, on the other hand, public communication was a matter of maintaining public confidence, and Kennedy's methods worked.

(c) Lyndon Johnson's perspective

Just as Eisenhower came to the presidency with a view of power shaped by a life-time in the army, so Johnson brought the experience of thirty-two years on Capitol Hill – as staffer, congressman and Senate Majority Leader. His successes and failures as President, commentators agree, depended on how far his objectives could be achieved by the kind of power he had learnt to use in those years. His attitude to public communication was shaped by that experience too. He was acutely sensitive to public opinion – to the way it was a factor in the calculations of politicians and to the critical difference shades of timing and expression in the flow of information might make to the turn of events. To that extent he was much more like Nixon and Kennedy than Eisenhower. But, unlike Nixon and probably more than any president since Franklin Roosevelt, including Kennedy, he thirsted too for information about those he hoped to influence; although in his conduct of the Vietnam War he came to hear only what he wanted and to yield to the hazard of presidential isolation.[121]

Johnson thus worked extremely hard at public communication. The results in the domestic sphere were broadly successful in the first two years. Thereafter they became less so – partly for the very reasons that accounted for the initial success. In foreign policy, Johnson succeeded for a time in concealing information about the Vietnam War, but at the eventual cost of public confidence in his fitness to govern.

By experience and the circumstances of the time Johnson was especially suited to pursue domestic goals. Kennedy had set the goals of the New Frontier: Johnson legislated them, in the massive programme of the 'Great Society'.[122] He was a great believer in the paramountcy of presidential legislative leadership. Congress had neither the time, nor the expertise, nor the organisational structure to bring an issue into legislative focus. 'If an issue is not included in the presidential agenda,' he told his biographer Doris Kearns, 'it is almost impossible – short of crisis – to get the Congress to focus on it.'[123] By a combination of his own skills, fortunate economic conditions at home and few distractions abroad, Johnson by the end of 1965 had had remarkable legislative success. In the rest of his presidency, by contrast, he floundered in the slough of South East Asia, which sucked out his energies and hampered the implementation of the programmes he had legislated.

The failure of the war, moreover, was a particularly presidential – indeed a personal – failure, because Johnson took an even stronger view of congressional limitations in national security affairs than in domestic legislation. He held this view long before he became President himself, and it led him to pursue the war secretively, in the hope that he could avoid jeopardising the Great Society (for example by a war tax or the dissent that an open war would bring in Congress). In the event the domestic and the foreign policies were incompatible, and Johnson simply prepared the ground for the 'imperial presidency' of Richard Nixon.

Beyond these immediate goals, it seems fair to say that Johnson sought a simple social harmony. This sounds trite; but the search for consensus was supremely his method of exercising power, and it was so much an article of faith as to constitute a goal in itself. Doris Kearns sees his entire career as 'marked by a continuing effort to avoid confrontation and choice, to prevent passionate and emotional divisions over issues'.[124] He even disliked 'issues' being the basis of electoral choice: Johnson preferred to fight on 'the record'. The dislike may also help to explain his inattention to administration. For he did not run the Great Society programmes with the care he took to legislate them: it was as if the effort to get consensus upon the terms of the legislation meant that implementation ought to be automatic. Again, he took infinite pains in hiring staff; but then he took their loyalty for granted and used them.[125] The result was a larger turnover of aides than under most presidents. The Johnson White House itself was less compartmentalised in terms of responsibility and lines of authority than any since Franklin Roosevelt (or under Johnson's successors).[126]

THE PRESIDENT, POWER AND COMMUNICATION

The search for consensus holds the clue to Johnson's view of the nature of power. People do what they perceive to be in their own interests, he seems to have thought. For example, congressmen are moved by the desire for recognition and the fear of 'losing hold', so he told Kearns. The only way to make Civil Rights a reality, he explained after having to send federal troops to keep the peace during the Civil Rights march on Selma, Alabama, in 1965, was to awaken and exploit a popular sense of guilt.[127] For the President, power consisted in discerning what people wanted, considering whether it conflicted with the wishes of others, deciding how the conflict could be reconciled, avoided or removed; and then using the leverage of the office to achieve that result.

Although in foreign affairs and defence Johnson was ready enough to command, his natural style was to persuade through the creation of a sense of obligation in people. (Kennedy, we have noted, sought rather a sense of identification.) In this model of power the President is substantially a broker – not so much imposing his own wishes as mediating between the wishes of others; the stimulator of goals and the guide, not the commander. Power therefore may come very close to 'making people do what you want by adjusting your own wants to what they already intend to do'. Indeed Johnson seems to have thought on these lines in deciding not to run for a second term in 1968.[128] As Neustadt points out, he 'regained a measure of self-satisfaction only when he convinced himself that his withdrawal from the presidential race would help achieve his aims and serve the country'.[129] In other words, Johnson hoped to exercise power by an act of self-destruction.

For his legislative programme, Johnson could expect to create obligations in legislators and client groups to some extent by appealing to the legitimacy of his office. More important, however, was the appeal to expertise. He set ever-greater store by this as Vietnam became the major preoccupation, and he was un-characteristically ready himself to rely on experts inside the administration. Overwhelmingly, though, Johnson exercised power through the manipulation of rewards and sanctions, both practical and psychological. This he did in a process of bargaining, persuasion and adjustment that was at its most formidable on a person to person basis. It became known as the Treatment.

Johnson's own accounts of the Treatment are tame. 'Wild images have been concocted to describe this process of persuasion,' he wrote in his memoirs.

. . . But the real task of persuasion is far less glamorous than the imagined one. It is tough, demanding work. For despite the stereotyped Presidential image, I could not trade patronage for votes in any direct exchange. If word spread that I was trading, everyone would want to trade and all other efforts at persuasion would automatically fail. To say that is not to say that rewards (such as White House tours, invitations to social functions, birthday greetings, and Presidential photos) do not go to faithful Congressmen. But these are generally delivered by the White House staff after the fact, and on the basis of a pattern of voting, not by the President personally in exchange for a specific vote.

Nor could I rely on the 'big threat' or direct reprisal to produce compliance. It is daydreaming to assume that any experienced congressman would ignore his basic instincts or his constituents' deepest concerns in quaking fear of the White House. My best hope was to make a good, solid, convincing case for the administration's position.

The context in which such activity went on would typically be the search for a legislative majority. In the account from which this example is drawn (a 10 per cent tax surcharge in 1968) Johnson and his staff contacted interest groups and business and labour leaders outside Congress, to send a ripple into the country which would come back to individual congressmen. A press conference took the President's message to the public. Then, when the time came for a vote, Johnson started 'phoning again.

I had no set script. Sometimes I would start with: 'What's this I read about your opposing my bill?' Other times I would ask: 'What do you think of this bill?' or: 'Say, Congressman, I haven't seen you around in a while, just wondering how you've been.' But a common theme ran through these talks – friendship and respect.[130]

The pattern is familiar. What made Johnson's practice exceptional was its detailed character. There are many – sometimes hilarious – descriptions of the Treatment. Take Evans and Novak, for instance:

The Treatment could last ten minutes or four hours. It came, enveloping its target, at the LBJ Ranch swimming pool, in one of

LBJ's offices, in the Senate cloakroom, on the floor of the Senate itself – wherever Johnson might find a fellow Senator within his reach. Its tone could be supplication, accusation, cajolery, exuberance, scorn, tears, complaint, the hint of threat. It was all these together. It ran the gamut of human emotions. Its velocity was breathtaking, and it was all in one direction. Interjections from the target were rare. Johnson anticipated them before they could be spoken. He moved in close, his face a scant millimeter from his target, his eyes widening and narrowing, his eyebrows rising and falling. From his pockets poured clippings, memos, statistics. Mimicry, humour, and the genius of analogy made the Treatment an almost hypnotic experience and rendered the target stunned and helpless.[131]

Apart from sheer force of personality, the Treatment depended mainly upon Johnson's keen insight into the character of persons on the receiving end. For maximum effect this required the most detailed information about their personal and professional lives; and the stories are legion of Johnson's retentiveness of tiny facts and incidents that might sooner or later pay dividends.[132] As a method of persuading individuals or groups of three or four, it was superb. Virtually by definition, however, it was inapplicable to larger numbers, as Johnson found when his energies were transferred beyond the arena of legislative politics in which his information was based.

Johnson's communication needs should now be clearer. In legislating the Great Society, public communication played a secondary part (not counting the routine business of polishing the presidential image). It was relevant to his battles with Congress to the extent only that it might affect the bargaining process in which the President and those getting the Treatment were involved. Press relations needed managing to that end; and Johnson had years of experience with the Capitol Hill press corps to guide him.

Prosecuting the war, on the other hand, needed a different communication strategy – one of *non*-communication and a careful control of information flow to press and Congress. By July 1965 Johnson had committed 175,000 troops to Vietnam. His military advisers felt that twice the number would be needed, yet Congress and the public had considerably lower expectations than the President's own. As Neustadt says, Johnson's Pentagon advisers told him to close the gap between those expectations by calling up reserves, calling for new taxes, and inviting congressional approval of his aims. Johnson refused. He tried instead to wage the war without acknowledging its scale to Congress, or the public, or indeed his own economic advisers. LBJ chose not to risk his legislative program by a war, but chose at the same time to have a war and, thus, to be deceptive. Thereby he paved the way for an inflationary upsurge, turned colleges into pressure cookers, diverted energies, not least his own, from the administrative challenge in his Great Society, and moved decisively toward his later loss of public standing.[133]

Why did Johnson's secrecy fail? If the war goals had been achieved quickly, secrecy might have worked. But the cost of a war that dragged on and whose scale dawned gradually on the public was an unbridgeable 'credibility gap'. Once that opened, there was no way by which Johnson could inspire the public to accept the war. The mistrust infected his domestic policies too.[134]

Even had Johnson tried to mobilise public opinion behind an open war at the outset, he was not the ideal president to do so. His knowledge of foreign affairs was negligible. Foreign leaders could not be given the Treatment like domestic politicians; and North Vietnam simply refused to 'bargain' according to his model of politics.

Beyond that, Johnson's enormous skill in interpersonal relations was matched by a wooden incompetence at communication to large audiences, including through television and in press conferences. Again this was partly a problem of habit and personality. As Evans and Novak observe, 'In large groups, what was witty sounded crude, what was expansive became arrogant. It was inevitable, then, that when Johnson allowed the Treatment to dominate his "press conferences" a sour note entered his relations with the press.'[135] This happened even when Johnson was in the Senate, but when he became president the implications were worse. Apart from this, Johnson's public awkwardness could be put down to a residual fear of making himself vulnerable through grammatical slips or a lapse into crudity. Johnson's best speeches, Kearns writes, were those in which he departed from the text; and polls showed his most informal television appearances to be the most effective.[136]

Johnson's attempts to overcome these difficulties compounded them. He courted the press to an unprecedented degree in his first few months of office. But he assumed that, having received the

Treatment and other presidential favours, journalists would behave like legislators and reciprocate, echoing the Johnson line. Senate correspondents had needed Johnson more than he needed them, but the White House press corps and the columnists could range widely in their sources – and Johnson's clumsy attempts to keep his aides from the press backfired. He followed a deliberate policy of discrimination, using exclusive interviews and easy access as rewards and sanctions. His press conferences were held at unpredictable times and places, often at the weekend when the press corps had little specialist back-up. The conferences were frequently dominated by Johnson's own statements and gave inadequate opportunity for questioning. He changed his plans to snub reporters who anticipated them. He even changed appointees when their names leaked out in advance.[137]

All this gave Johnson control of a kind over his public communication; and certainly he managed it so that the Great Society was legislated and the war was prosecuted in secret. But such machinations stored up trouble in the longer run – not least, by creating the climate for Richard Nixon's misdeeds. When he needed the backing of the people, as he did in 1968, there was no basis on which he could get it. At root, Johnson's admittedly subtle manipulation of public communication proved effective only as an aid in procuring his legislative goals. Those, however, could never be more than the beginning of an effective presidential record. For the momentum to turn the congressional Acts into successful programmes, or to convince the public of the necessity of an Indo-Chinese war, Johnson's strategy was inappropriate and self-destructive.

(d) Gerald Ford's perspective

Ford's presidency is for present purposes even more difficult to assess than the foreshortened term of Kennedy. He served under two-and-a-half years, of which the first few months were overshadowed by the transition from Richard Nixon and the last year by the 1976 election. His power was further constrained by the circumstances which brought him to the White House, by congressional and public reactions against the imperial presidency, and by his lack of a popular mandate.

Although Ford might win his own mandate in 1976 (if he won the nomination first, which was not a foregone conclusion), his primary purpose was to restore public trust in the presidency and rebuild relations with Congress and other political constituencies. In an address to a joint meeting of Congress on 12 August 1974, three days after his succession, he invoked the principles of 'communication, conciliation, compromise, and cooperation'. Unlike Lyndon Johnson when he was propelled suddenly into office, however, Ford had to draw a distinction between the office and the administration. Where Johnson needed to emphasise continuity for reassurance, Ford needed to distance himself from Nixon.

As time went on, underlying continuity could be acknowledged more easily. In pursuance of the four principles, for example, Ford quickly met with members of the congressional Black Caucus, fifteen of whose sixteen members (all Democrats) had opposed his nomination to the vice-presidency; but this and similar meetings made no difference to his subsequent anti-bussing stand, which was entirely consistent with Nixon's. Continuity in foreign policy, including key advisers like Henry Kissinger, was more predictable.

The main difference from Nixon, and arguably the top priority, was that Ford's presidency should be different in style. This came naturally to him anyway. After twenty-five years in the House of Representatives, including nearly ten as Minority Leader, he instinctively did business by collective discussion, much of it in formal meetings. (By the end of his term he was said to be relying rather more on paper-work.) The style was illustrated best in his efforts to construct as broad a coalition as possible for his anti-inflation policy. In a series of 'summit' conferences he sought to involve representatives from a wide range of groups as well as Congress, backed up by a publicity campaign to 'Whip Inflation Now'.[138] The policy had little success but the style was the antithesis of Nixon's. Unlike Nixon, too, Ford kept himself accessible to departmental and agency heads; and his chief of staff did not have a near-monopoly of control over his schedule.

The need to demonstrate how different he was from Nixon must have made Ford conscious of the importance of public communication. His press secretary, indeed, was his first appointee. He chose for the job Jerald ter Horst, a journalist he had known since his earliest campaign for Congress. He gave him considerable discretion as well as 'open door' access.

But Ford's own skills as a communicator were poor. As one survey of his record put it before the 1976 election, 'He carries an unfair reputation for being a bit thick – a caricature aggravated by such

Ford habits as making a three-syllable word out of "judgement" and an obstacle out of a helicopter door.'[139] On the stump in Cincinnati he referred to Representative William Harsha as his old friend 'Jim' Harsha. In San Diego he thanked the Serendipity Singers for entertaining a crowd by praising 'those super singers, Serebinity'.[140] 'Very frankly,' admitted his close adviser, former governor William Scranton, 'he is not the best verbalizer in the world. Some people talk well. Other people do well. And some people, once in a while, can combine both. The President is not a brilliant vocalizer . . . but he thinks soundly and thoroughly and is a good decision maker.'[141] The temptation to link verbal clumsiness with physical stumbles caught by the cameras led his press secretary to complain of misrepresentation, saying Ford was 'the most athletic President within memory and the most coordinated in history'.[142] Not since Eisenhower and his 'circular sentence construction' had there been a public performer more inclined to provoke ribaldry among the press corps.

Is it unfair to take Ford's performances as symbolic of a more significant lack of sensitiveness to public communication as an instrument of power? One suspects that at heart he was in the Truman–Eisenhower tradition of 'letting the facts speak for themselves'; and his style had a certain element of 'reigning not ruling'.

Easily the strongest evidence of insensitiveness was Ford's dramatic use of presidential prerogative in declaring – indeed signing – before the television cameras a complete pardon for Richard Nixon. (Characteristically, he misread the proclamation, saying 20 July 1969 instead of 20 January 1969, as the date Nixon took office.[143]) The decision was reached without wide consultation. Shortly before he went on the air, Ford was still calling congressional leaders like House Speaker Carl Albert to break the news. Ford, obviously, saw the pardon as 'wiping the slate clean'. Inevitably it was construed otherwise, and Ford found his motives and judgement impugned. The pardon could be interpreted as reasonably to link him with Nixon as to enact a final separation. Poll figures varied, but overnight Ford's popularity plummeted. A *New York Times* poll showed 62 per cent disapproving the pardon, and Gallup found his approval rating fallen from 66 to 50 per cent during the month of the pardon. The immediate fall was probably the steepest for any one action by a president since polling began.[144] As a result both of the pardon and of not being consulted, ter Horst resigned as press secretary the same day with a backlash of public support. Ford, according to ter Horst, conceded privately that he had underestimated public feeling and had got 'egg on my face'. A different decision might have led to equally hard decisions later – if Nixon had actually come to trial, for example. But Ford certainly showed lack of feeling for the management of public communication. It is tempting to conclude that the failure was characteristic.

(e) Jimmy Carter's perspective

Jimmy Carter's communication problem was one aspect of the general problem of 'Jimmy Who?'. His national obscurity, until his candidacy, was part of the appeal of a new broom, unsullied by Vietnam, Watergate – indeed, by the cobweb corners of Washington itself. But, once in the White House, he had an unusually large task in establishing his authority both among 'Washingtonians' and the American public. For this reason the hallmark of Carter's public communication was the use of symbols. In place of a record, he had attitudes; instead of policies, he had values. Records and policies are built over years by action and argument; attitudes and values lend themselves to instant symbolic expression. Other people have foreign-aid programmes; Jimmy Carter had a mother in the Peace Corps.

Carter captured the White House in a public reaction against the 1970s. He aimed to restore dignity and integrity to the presidency. At the same time, he must have known that, in the wake of Watergate, Vietnam and Cambodia, the scope of presidential power would be curtailed. Initially, therefore, he adopted a low-key style, expressed in the first dramatic symbol of his incumbency – the hand-in-hand walk with his wife down Pennsylvania Avenue after the Inauguration Ceremony. Feet were good enough for Carter: no chauffeur-driven President he.

But the obligations of presidential leadership remained. At home Carter faced the energy crisis and rising inflation. Abroad, his initiatives over the Panama Canal, the SALT II Treaty and the Arab–Israeli conflict were overshadowed by the challenges of Iran and the Soviet invasion of Afghanistan. Ironically, the holding of American hostages in the Teheran embassy was a symbolic act not uncharacteristic of Carter's own style. (The real leverage it gave was a consequence only of the Americans' reluctance to lose lives. In a 'hot' war those lives would have disappeared in the statistics.) Carter's response to Afghanistan was quintessentially symbolic. Boycotting the Olympic Games, he opposed in an arena of ritual conflict the real war fought elsewhere.

Carter's new broom in Washington had plenty of old bristles. New faces at Cabinet level were comparatively few. The White House staff was dominated by the 'Georgia mafia', who certainly contrasted with Nixon's entourage but suffered from their own personal problems. Most importantly, Carter's 'Nothing but the Best' image took a major knock when his budget director and confidant Bert Lance was forced to resign in the face of congressional scrutiny of his financial practices.[145] The damage to Carter was increased by his premature commitment to stand by Lance. Inexperience in legislative liaison might have been expected to result in early misunderstandings with congressional leaders (House Majority Leader Tip O'Neill smarted from some unintentional slights). But the trouble proved deep-rooted, and Carter failed to secure the passage of his major legislative proposals on energy, the crisis he dubbed the moral equivalent of war.

By the 1980 election, Carter's record was widely regarded as exemplifying vacillation and ineptitude. An AP–NBC News poll in mid-September 1979 recorded the lowest approval rating – 19 per cent – for any president since such polls began in the 1930s (including the 24 per cent for Nixon just before his resignation).[146] Arguably, Carter's symbolic communication had helped bring this about. His very success in manipulating symbols at the outset accustomed people to read his actions for their symbolic content. As his troubles grew, his aides compiled lists of 'problems other presidents did not have to face'. Perhaps no one else would indeed have been more successful in the late 1970s. The early symbolic acts (walking down Pennsylvania Avenue; carrying his own hand luggage; dropping in on town meetings) had no other purpose. Other acts did have other purposes; but their consequences may have been the more serious for the President because strong symbolic meaning was none the less attached. To call a programme the 'moral equivalent of war' yet not to win the war is crass. (Presidents, after all, have exceptional power to win wars.) To launch a programme with that image was a hostage to fortune. A more precise, disastrous example is the abortive attempt to snatch the embassy hostages from Teheran. For a president trading in symbols, it was especially humiliating – again in a sphere where presidential action did not require the overcoming of checks and balances. The U2 spy-plane incident in 1960 was a similar humiliation to Eisenhower, who could not be up for re-election anyway; but did that damage his reputation as much? In a last example, the Olympic boycott was perhaps justifiable on grounds of moral purity. If it was that alone, did it not simply highlight the President's inability to exert other influence over the Russians? If it was intended to achieve more, then its failure was plain as news coverage of the games unfolded.

Carter's view of the power of his office thus seemed to involve the use of public communication first to establish the image of himself as providing a fresh start in the White House and to build up public confidence in his capacity by the expression of simple symbols. Secondly, it may be claimed that like Kennedy he sought ways to enable people to identify with his policy goals. The best illustration is not the round of town meetings and stagy sessions in citizens' porches, but the Carter phone-in on 5 March 1977. The odds against a caller's getting through were astronomical; but there was a real number that anyone could dial and that 9 million did, and a recorded message encouraging you to try again. The President was quickly on first-name terms with the forty-two callers who succeeded. He had conversations, not a question-and-answer session. This, not Franklin Roosevelt's, was the first 'fireside chat'. 'Chat' is a two-way process. Listeners could not talk back to Roosevelt. Most could not talk to Carter; but they listened in on the token few who could. As a demonstration of the desire to keep in touch with ordinary citizens, to fight the dangers of presidential isolation and keep an open mind, the phone-in was a unique and beautifully managed symbol. The same desire was evidenced much later, in the procession of more than 130 prominent Americans to Camp David in July 1979, when Carter went into retreat, took counsel and emerged days later to announce a reconstruction of his administration and a new set of priorities.[147]

These uses of public communication amount, again, to the familiar 'moral leadership'. This may have been a sensible strategy for Carter. However, leadership was not the image he conveyed, either to Congress, business and labour leaders and other groups, or to the electorate. He never succeeded in communicating the substance behind the symbols. Only, perhaps, when he achieved the reconciliation of President Sadat of Egypt and Prime Minister Begin of Israel at Camp David and emerged between them to tell the world, was substance momentarily and triumphantly achieved. Generally, however, despite a competent publicity machine, and a press secretary, Jody Powell, who was an innermost adviser, Carter by 1980 remained 'Jimmy Who?'.

V CONCLUSIONS: PRESIDENTIAL GOVERNMENT AND PARLIAMENTARY GOVERNMENT

How far, then, does a President's public communication help him exercise power?

The question has to be answered in two parts. First, is the President's communication strategy (admittedly too grand a phrase to describe, say, Truman's or Ford's) suited to what he wishes to achieve? Secondly, is it implemented successfully? Failure might be due to a strategy that either was inappropriate or was appropriate but poorly executed.[148]

In answer to these questions, the studies of individual presidents suggest no tidy generalisation. Truman had an inappropriate strategy because he did not try to exploit his communication opportunities enough. Eisenhower's strategy was consistent with his modest goals and competently carried out: the intriguing question is whether he could have put his hold on public affection to use in a more active presidency. Kennedy, the most gifted communicator of the group, adopted the right strategy for his goals and carried it out effectively on the whole. It did not help him with his legislative programme, but it is doubtful whether through public communication he could have done more. Johnson, antennae flapping, succeeded with Congress where Kennedy failed; and where Kennedy succeeded, in capturing the popular imagination, Johnson failed. His use of secrecy in pursuing the war in South East Asia was effective in the short run but ultimately self-destructive. Nixon's strategy was effective in his diplomacy but disastrous at home: if anyone were to succeed with a plebiscitary presidency, it would not be he. Ford's communication was adequate for his primary role – that of steadying public confidence in the presidency – but for little else. Carter chose a good strategy for establishing his authority; but symbols too easily ring hollow, and in pursuit of his policies on energy and inflation his communication was ineffective.

Thus summarised, the record is not dismal but hardly impressive. The successful presidents (in the context that concerns us) have been so because they have not tried to achieve much – or certainly not to use public communication intensively as an instrument. Kennedy is perhaps the exception, but the problem of the truncated term hampers assessment. Others (Johnson, Carter) have found a communication strategy that helped achieve some goals was a hindrance to others. Very few have been skilful public performers. This seems odd, given that politics is a life of words, even of theatre.

A surprising number of presidents, too, appear not to have been alert to the implications for their power of efficient lines of communication up to them. Feedback increases a president's options by heightening his awareness of the range of the possible.[149] Perhaps because of the awful consequences of error in defence or foreign policy, especially in crises, the dangers of tunnel vision or 'hearing only what you want to hear' have been emphasised in that part of the President's domain. But, as George Reedy argues at length, isolation is a hazard throughout the presidency. The lesson of Lyndon Johnson is that surrounding yourself with people (Johnson liked his information by word of mouth), TV sets, Wire Service tickers, newspapers and opinion polls does not mean you listen to what they say. Kennedy, with less fuss, heard more and probed deeper. By comparison Truman and, especially, Eisenhower paid less attention to securing a variety of information sources; and Nixon, working through a strong chief of staff and cutting himself off from Congress and interest groups, became exceptionally isolated. Attention to feedback is a revealing index of a president's sensitiveness to the relation between communication and power.

Is it to be expected that presidents are not able to use public communication more effectively to advance their objectives? The answer, foreshadowed in Chapters 1 and 2, must be Yes. To the extent that the President cannot control his public communication, he cannot predict its effect upon his power. Yet different types of power require different patterns of communication, and he needs to be able to control it. Moreover, the sources of power open to the President mainly require rather skilful – and thus controlled – communication. The Constitution gives the President the opportunity to do certain things which will be obeyed because the Constitution itself gives them legitimacy: the President does not have to convey his own legitimacy independently. These powers are the bread and butter of the presidency – the commander-in-chief powers, the veto, the power to pardon, to call extraordinary sessions of Congress and so on. Not all rest solely on legitimacy: the patronage power in the office of chief executive, for instance, involves rewards and sanctions.

It is the simple essence of the Constitution, however, that those powers available to the President through the constitutional legitimacy of his office are balanced or limited by powers given to others. His constitutional powers give him part of the means to achieve goals; rarely the whole means. To complete the achievement, the President has to root his power in some other ground than 'legitimacy derived from the Constitution'. He must win hearts, or demonstrate superior wisdom, or find a means of invoking rewards and sanctions. All these, it is here claimed, require more subtle or complex communication than is needed for the demonstration of constitutional legitimacy. The President does not have to persuade anybody before he can make his veto power effective. Persuading a Senate committee to release a bill, on the other hand, will probably be hard work.

Different types of goal, moreover, require different kinds of power. This, too, increases the President's need to be able to control his communication. It is easy to talk of goals as if they were goods in a supermarket, to be ticked off a list and bundled at the check-out counter; but Presidents do not take office in a vacuum, with a brand new programme. Goals are reactive, formulated on the job. Problems press the President: they do not wait upon his initiative. Stephen Hess has brilliantly summarised the shifting concerns of a President's four-year cycle with its pressures back and forth between foreign and domestic problems.[150] Any comparative study has to acknowledge, too, that a president is unique in his times. The developing response of the presidency since 1945 has seen, in the foreign sphere, cold and hot wars, European, Middle Eastern, Asian and Latin American crises; and, at home, changing problems of economic growth and stagnation, urban crisis, minority rights. In addition the structure of politics has changed: both close to the presidency, with the sprawling Federal bureaucracy on one hand and an increasingly splintered Congress on the other, and, further afield, with the decline of party organisation and voter allegiance. Communication patterns have changed fundamentally with the rise of television.

The 'objective opportunities' for presidents to exercise power, in other words, have naturally varied. Great presidents, it is commonly observed, are bred by great events. A president engrossed in

defence and foreign policy has the benefit of operating in a sphere
with 'command powers'. When domestic problems press, the scope
for shaping events is less – especially if they are not susceptible to
administrative or simple legislative solution.

The President's control over the formulation of his goals is thus
limited, quite apart from his difficulties in controlling the communication apt to secure them. Chapter 2 emphasised these latter
difficulties. Set beside the present considerations, one can see how
difficult it must also be for a president to judge what the most
appropriate kind of communication is – let alone carry it out
effectively. Is it the right time for an address to the nation? Or a
speech to a special interest? Or to have someone speak in his name
and keep his own prestige in reserve? More often than not,
presumably, such calculations are guesswork, if they are made at all;
yet their impact on the policy outcome may be decisive. They are
made in a context, too, where the President has competitors. These,
sometimes, may be more successful in calling spirits from the vasty
deep than he is.

This study of the President's power in terms of his public
communication can be no more than sketchy and indicative. It
stems, itself, from the author's inadequate store of primary,
secondary and tertiary communication about modern presidents.[151]
From whatever pen, it could never be more than a view of
presidential public communication derived *from* presidential
public communication and open to endless possibilities of
misinterpretation. Observers closer to the White House could
develop the same ideas with greater sophistication. Even this
tentative study, however, suggests that a proper emphasis on public
communication as a factor in presidential power inclines towards a
'weak' view of the presidency. Some presidents work very hard at
public communication. Not to do so would be unwise, even though
the results are so uncertain. The office of press secretary may be
taken to epitomise the problem. 'When he speaks to you at a
briefing,' said Carter of Jody Powell at a post-election press
conference (15 November 1976), 'then you can take it for granted
that he speaks for me when he says he does.' Such discretion –
normal in press secretaries – provides them with the scope for
mistakes. Yet 'their mistakes are the President's mistakes,' to quote
George Reedy, 'even when he is unaware of their activities.' Press
secretaries can therefore injure the President by unintentionally
misleading journalists. The exercise of power by the President

involves a ceaseless struggle to be understood – the precondition of obedience. That struggle starts right outside the Oval Office. Small wonder if he often fails.

Do chief executives in comparable political cultures do better? Can they control their public communication more effectively to achieve their ends? In the prescriptive tradition of presidential studies, this question may be asked in conclusion, in case the answer has lessons for the United States.

Parliamentary government has frequently attracted students frustrated by the delays, uncertainties and failures of executive leadership endemic in presidential–congressional relations. Only link the President to Congress, with a secure, probably partisan, majority, such as a British or Canadian prime minister or a West German chancellor normally enjoys, and the process of government would be more purposive and rational – especially in the domestic field. How much more satisfactory could be the response, say, to the energy crisis of the 1980s. Students of British government, conversely, increasingly frustrated after 1945 with the incompetence of the House of Commons to make a constructive contribution to legislation and control the bureaucracy effectively, have often looked with envious eyes on the strong committees and the staffs of Congress.

One's view depends ultimately on one's attachment to the separation of powers. Does one, in short, wish to tilt the scales of power towards the presidency? Parliamentary government certainly does not guarantee a strong executive, as the experience of France from 1945 to 1958 or contemporary Italy demonstrate – to quote two obvious European examples. A prime minister's strength rests on his majority, and in multi-party systems such as the French and Italian this may be unstable or – if coalition is impossible – nonexistent. The composition of the party system is the key to executive strength and weakness, not the constitutional rule alone that the prime minister is responsible to parliament for his continuation in office. It is true, too, as West Germans have shown since 1945 and the Scandinavians somewhat longer, that a strong committee system is perfectly consistent with a stable executive in a parliamentary system.

Constitutional tinkering that joined President and Congress in some way would thus not necessarily make the President dominant. To join the institutions could still leave the powers shared. There are, none the less, features of the 'communication context' of parliamentary government that do give prime ministers a comparative advantage over the American President.

Perhaps the most important feature is the parliamentary forum. Prime ministers do not have to build soap boxes. Whatever the contribution of a legislature to the executive branch, it is a steady object of public attention. Imagine the difficulties for a Canadian chief executive, who lacks the extra status of a head of state, if he had to govern that diverse string of provinces containing a major but geographically concentrated cultural division, without a forum in the House of Commons at Ottawa. Prime Minister Trudeau proved himself a master of parliamentary publicity in the 1970s, grafting television onto the parliamentary institution through the development of informal press conferences outside the Chamber, as well as holding conferences in the style of an American president and, eventually, seeing the cameras come onto the floor of the House itself.

At Westminster, as at Ottawa, prime ministers are sure of a forum. The careful rituals of parliamentary procedure provide them with refinements through which they can signal to news media the precise significance of what they are saying – through such choices as when and whether to intervene in a debate, or make a formal statement, or deal with some predictable matter in the regular question-time.

The British press gives far less space to Parliament than it once did. In a sense, it always has: that is, parliamentarians tend to have a 'golden age' myth about parliamentary reporting and assume, at any one time, than it used to be better formerly.[152] This assumption, however, is just a reflection of the weight they attach to parliamentary publicity. If the quantity of it is less, it remains the touchstone of public communication about the Government. Prime ministers can be confident that their own version of events, presented to Parliament, will be reported with accuracy albeit compression. Competing versions appear too – by Opposition leaders, interest groups or whoever finds access to the media; and prime ministers are at risk like presidents from tertiary communication. But the presence of the parliamentary forum is an invaluable opportunity for them. A final measure of it is the reluctance shown by the House of Commons to allow televising of its proceedings. Repeated decisions about this in the 1970s were left to a non-party vote. The reasons for exclusion therefore varied; but one was the fear of backbenchers that Government (and Opposition) leaders would tend to feature disproportionately in the edited programmes and thus enjoy a prominence which back-benchers already thought too great. Radio broadcasting, seen as less threatening, was introduced in 1976.[153]

Public communication about British government, then, remains substantially a Westminster view. A symbol of the fact is the public obscurity of the Prime Minister's press secretary. He has no need to mediate the Prime Minister's views to the public: the House of Commons is the intermediary, or else the Prime Minister may talk to journalists himself or go on radio or television. Conventionally, prime ministers from time to time meet the carefully defined group of political journalists known as the lobby correspondents (so called as a result of one of their privileges of access to Downing Street and the lobbies of Westminster). These meetings are off the record: there has never been a regular public prime-ministerial press conference. Again, the House of Commons is a more familiar and perhaps predictable forum for the Prime Minister – one in which, backed by his party supporters, he can normally expect to avoid undue embarrassment. At the same time, it is a jealous institution which dislikes being bypassed by ministers making announcements else-where which traditionally it is entitled to learn first.

The press secretary certainly briefs journalists at twice-daily meetings and round the clock in response to calls. Overwhelmingly, however, the briefings are non-attributable. This element of secretiveness is a small example of the widespread and persistent secretiveness throughout British government. Its roots are deep and gnarled. Undoubtedly one of them is the Government's collective character – a feature which is highly relevant to prime ministerial communication. Although the Prime Minister hires and fires other ministers and is often considered to be so dominant that the system might properly be described as prime-ministerial government, he governs with and through the Cabinet. They are collectively responsible to the House of Commons. When the Prime Minister resigns, all resign. If a minister cannot in conscience publicly endorse Cabinet policy, he must go.

The practice developed in the eighteenth century as a defence by ministers against the monarch, on the principle of strength through unity. ('If we do not hang together we shall all hang separately.')

Now it is justified by reference to the dynamics of maintaining party discipline, and hence the parliamentary majority, in the face of the Opposition. Clearly, secretiveness aids solidarity.

The effect of collective responsibility and its corollary secretiveness upon communication about the Government is, first, to blur it. Except in the open forum of Parliament, news stories customarily quote 'Whitehall sources', 'official circles', 'ministers', or some other periphrasis. Secondly, opinions, motives, intentions – the stuff of tertiary communication – are often attributed not to the Prime Minister or colleagues individually but to the Cabinet collectively. Problems of 'Who speaks for the President?' or 'What President?' do not arise so sharply as in the United States. In a collective executive, it is the collectively endorsed view which, generally speaking, matters. Whatever the rows in Cabinet before a decision is reached, the eventual decision is a Cabinet decision. The third point, then, is that much of the Prime Minister's communication is on behalf of the Cabinet as a whole. When he says 'the Cabinet has decided', he may be reporting a decision actually taken by himself or a committee of civil servants or a small group of ministers, and subsequently ratified by the full Cabinet. From the point of view of the governmental consequences of the decision, however, that fact is immaterial: the stamp of Cabinet approval is the key.

In reality collective responsibility is bound to be a façade. It is possible only because behind the public solidarity lie private opportunities for disclosure of the inevitable disagreements. Partly these exist in the machinery of informal party meetings at Westminster and the gossip of its bars and tea-rooms. Partly they arise from the practice of leaks. You leak; I 'give guidance'. Ministers generally wish their perspective on events to be put on record – but unattributed, so as not to jeopardise the façade of unity against the Opposition. If their opinion loses out, the need is all the greater. If it has prevailed, the record must naturally be kept straight. Just like American presidents, prime ministers fight leaks by their colleagues, fretting at the implicit challenge to their control over the definition of reality. They never succeed in blocking them – not even Harold Wilson, who made particular efforts to curb his ministers and blackball offending journalists. The fact is that leaking is built into the collective cabinet system of government. 'Leaks' are what happens when you are the *victim* of undesired publicity. 'Guidance' is what you give in order to be the *beneficiary* of desirable publicity. When Harold Wilson once complained to the

Cabinet about leaks, one minister noted in his diary that the Cabinet was 'exasperated', as '99 per cent of the so-called leaks' came from Wilson himself and a couple of close colleagues.[154]

Media coverage provides a benchmark by which governments judge their own performance: that is one reason for their preoccupation with leaks. None the less, these undercurrents of publicity do threaten a prime minister's power. Arguably, though, it is in only the broadest sense. That is to say, they jeopardise his ability to pass his legislative programme only on extremely rare occasions; and then not by defeat on the floor of the House so much as by revolt in his own party leading to withdrawal of the offending bill (as happened with Mr Wilson's industrial relations legislation in the late 1960s). Even in these cases, the wider public knowledge of dissension is only a background factor: it is among parliamentarians themselves that the revolt is stirred. The public impact lies in the effect parliamentarians believe (rightly or wrongly) that popular awareness of a split government and a weak leader may have on voting behaviour at the next election; and, secondly, in the leverage that powerful interest groups like the trade-union movement believe it gives them. The latter point is particularly important, perhaps, for its implications about industrial-relations legislation. Such legislation has been notoriously difficult to put into effect if trade unions dislike it.

In a collective system, in sum, the prime minister exercises power by managing his party majority – especially its parliamentary wing – and his cabinet. He may call in aid one to help manage the other. His public relations are a factor in both; but the institutional context, with its levers of prime-ministerial patronage, control of parliamentary business and the timing of elections, plus the existence of an 'external enemy' – the opposition – give him weapons that reduce the weight public relations need to bear.

Two final key considerations in a collective system are the path to power and the 'moral leadership' factor. In each a prime minister has advantages over the American President. With the exception of the first Labour prime minister, Ramsay MacDonald, no modern British premier has come to office without previous Cabinet experience. All have had substantial parliamentary careers. The custom of choosing a chief executive only among parliamentarians had its critics in the 1960s and 1970s, when managerial skills enjoyed a vogue. But one advantage is that an incoming prime minister already has high public 'recognition' and proven parliamentary competence. The American phenomenon of the fight for nomination, requiring in the TV age an appropriate communication strategy, followed by the learning process and adjustments of the transition to office, has nothing comparable in the Westminster system.[155]

As to 'moral leadership', a collective government and parties with a fairly strong ideological character largely remove the need and opportunity for one person to exercise this kind of political vision. Only in wartime has the British Prime Minister been a rallying point; and then the monarch has shared in the personification of patriotism. Prime ministers certainly help to define crises and set priorities, but within a programmatic framework in whose continuous reconstruction party professionals and parliamentarians expect a share. Prime ministers go on television to alert or mobilise the nation. But their power goals, commonly understood, do not include the kind of activities for which Kennedy, for example, wins approval. Even were they to do so, the responsibility would be shared.

Compared with an American president, a British prime minister need fear bureaucratic inertia or obstruction less (and need not use public communication to combat it); enjoys the opportunities of the routine parliamentary forum (though these include the opportunity to fail, if continually outfaced); enjoys no less the opportunity to seek publicity elsewhere; and communicates in the context of a collective cabinet system, buttressed by disciplined parties. Overall, it is probably fair to say that he needs to try and manage his public communication less than the President as an instrument of power, and that he can manage it more effectively.

Not all those factors apply in other parliamentary systems. Nor are some capable of introduction to the United States by Constitution-mongering, even if they were wanted. The example may serve to show in one further way, however, how dependent the President is on effective communication and how poorly placed to practise it.

Notes

NOTE TO THE INTRODUCTION

1. The encounter took place at dawn on 9 May 1970. It is described in fascinating detail in William Safire, *Before the Fall* (New York: Belmont Tower Books, 1975) ch. 2.

NOTES TO CHAPTER ONE: POWER AND COMMUNICATION

1. A convenient short bibliography on power is in Steven Lukes, *Power: A Radical View* (London: Macmillan, 1974). Dennis Wrong, *Power* (Oxford: Basil Blackwell, 1979), has a longer but unannotated bibliography. On power and communication, David C. J. Bell's *Power, Influence and Authority* (New York: Oxford University Press, 1975) is a suggestive essay.
2. Peter W. Sperlich, 'Bargaining and Overload: an Essay on *Presidential Power*', in A. Wildavsky (ed.), *The Presidency* (Boston, Mass.: Little, Brown, 1969) p. 183.
3. Benjamin C. Bradlee, *Conversations with Kennedy* (New York: Pocket Books, 1976) pp. 81–2.
4. Doris Kearns, *Lyndon Johnson and the American Dream* (New York: Signet Books, 1977) pp. 9–10.
5. See the case study in Richard E. Neustadt, *Presidential Power* (New York: John Wiley, 1980) ch. 2.
6. For a discussion, see Arthur Schlesinger Jr, *The Imperial Presidency* (New York: Popular Library, 1974) pp. 177–82.
7. Valenti ruefully accepted the ridicule but pointed out in his memoirs that the remark was generally quoted out of context. Jack Valenti, *A Very Human President* (New York: Pocket Books, 1977) p. 73.
8. Richard P. Nathan, *The Plot that Failed: Nixon and the Administrative Presidency* (New York: John Wiley, 1975).
9. Bob Woodward and Carl Bernstein, *The Final Days* (New York: Avon Books, 1977) pp. 97–8.
10. Neustadt, *Presidential Power*, p. 17.
11. *Rolling Stone*, 19 May 1977. Cf. Erwin C. Hargrove, *US News and World Report*, 2 May 1977.
12. Pierre Salinger, *With Kennedy* (New York: Avon Books 1967) p. 160; John Dean, *Blind Ambition* (New York: Pocket Books, 1977) p. 38.
13. Theodore C. Sorensen, *Watchmen in the Night* (Cambridge, Mass.: MIT Press 1975) p. 106.

14. Eric F. Goldman, *The Tragedy of Lyndon Johnson* (New York: Dell, 1974) ch. 16.
15. Jerald F. ter Horst, *Gerald Ford and the Future of the Presidency* (New York: The Third Press, 1974) Epilogue.
16. Robert F. Kennedy, *Thirteen Days* (New York: Signet Books, 1969) pp. 94–5.
17. George E. Reedy, *The Twilight of the Presidency* (New York: Mentor Books, 1971), is a particularly illuminating discussion of the isolation of the President.
18. See Neustadt, *Presidential Power*, pp. 215–16.
19. Interview with David Frost, *New York Times*, 20 May 1977.
20. Bradlee, *Conversations with Kennedy*, p. 197.
21. Sorensen, *Watchmen in the Night*, p. xv.
22. Ibid., Introduction, p. xi.
23. Quoted in David Wise, *The Politics of Lying* (New York: Vintage Books, 1973) p. 433.
24. For instance, Anthony Summers, *Conspiracy: Who Killed President Kennedy?* (London: Fontana, 1980).
25. Robert F. Kennedy, *Thirteen Days*, p. 111.
26. Quoted, Wise, *The Politics of Lying*, pp. 28–9.
27. Ibid., pp. 41–2.
28. Ibid., pp. 68ff. Wise quotes particularly from National Security Action memo of 6 Apr 1965.
29. For a useful comparative analysis see Itzhak Galnoor (ed.), *Government Secrecy in Democracies* (New York: Harper & Row, 1977).
30. Wise, *The Politics of Lying*, p. 58.
31. Ibid., p. 42.
32. Sorensen, *Watchmen in the Night*, p. 102.
33. *Newsweek*, 23 May 1977, quoting the second interview in Nixon's series with David Frost.
34. Neustadt, *Presidential Power*, esp. ch. 2.
35. Jeb Stuart Magruder, *An American Life* (New York: Pocket Books, 1975) pp. 77–8.

NOTES TO CHAPTER TWO: THE PRESIDENT AND COMMUNICATION

1. James David Barber, *Presidential Character* (Englewood Cliffs, N. J.: Prentice-Hall, 1972) p. 148; Howard H. Quint and Robert H. Ferrell, *The Talkative President* (Boston, Mass.: University of Massachusetts Press, 1964).
2. John M. Blum, *Joe Tumulty and the Wilson Era* (Boston, Mass.: Houghton Mifflin, 1951) pp. 214–15.
3. Neustadt, *Presidential Power*, ch. 2.
4. Patrick Anderson, *The President's Men* (New York: Doubleday, 1969) p. 220. Buchwald's column included the following:

> *Q.* Jim, whose idea was it for the President to go to sleep?
> *A.* It was the President's idea.
> *Q.* Did the President speak to anyone before retiring?
> *A.* He spoke to the Secretary of State.

Q. What did he say to the Secretary of State?
A. He said, 'Good night, Foster.'
Q. And what did the Secretary say to the President?
A. He said, 'Good night, Mr President.'

5. Woodward and Bernstein, *The Final Days*, p. 170.
6. Ibid., pp. 230, 357–8, 365–7, 434, 444.
7. See, for example, *Time*, 4 Oct 1976; Sander Vanocur and David Broder, *Washington Post*, 29 Sep 1976.
8. *Rolling Stone*, 19 May 1977.
9. Neustadt, *Presidential Power*, p. 76. See pp. 73ff. for an interesting discussion of such points.
10. Reedy, *The Twilight of the Presidency*, p. 102.
11. William E. Porter, *Assault on the Media* (Ann Arbor: University of Michigan Press, 1976) p. 68.
12. Reedy, *The Twilight of the Presidency*, pp. 101–2.
13. Wise, *The Politics of Lying*, p. 8. Nixon told David Frost that the war part of the film 'didn't particularly interest me', but the character sketch of Patton was fascinating. Third Frost interview, *New York Times* transcript, 20 May 1977.
14. The conference was called for 1 a.m. on 11 Apr 1951. James E. Pollard, *The President and the Press* (New York: Macmillan, 1947) p. 15.
15. Neustadt, *Presidential Power*, pp. 75, 256.
16. Marriner S. Eccles, *Beckoning Frontiers* (New York: Alfred A. Knopf, 1951) p. 336; quoted in Neustadt, *Presidential Power*, p. 33.
17. Reedy, *The Twilight of the Presidency*, p. 107.
18. Ibid., p. 38.
19. Neustadt, *Presidential Power*, p. 76.
20. Ibid., p. 16.
21. Cf. Murray Edelman, *Political Language* (New York: Academic Press, 1977) ch. 3.
22. Wise, *The Politics of Lying*, pp. 373–4.
23. *The Times*, 16 Feb 1978.
24. *Time*, 3 Apr 1978.
25. Theodore H. White, *Breach of Faith* (New York: Dell, 1975) pp. 270, 283–4, 337, 394, 442.
26. See the summary analysis in R. T. Johnson, *Managing the White House* (New York: Harper & Row, 1974) pp. 142ff.; and Irving L. Janis, *Victims of Groupthink* (Boston, Mass.: Houghton Mifflin, 1972); Robert F. Kennedy, *Thirteen Days*.
27. There is a good summary of the crisis in Louis W. Koenig. *The Chief Executive*, 3rd edn (New York: Harcourt Brace Jovanovich, 1975) pp. 369–77.
28. Thomas E. Cronin, *The State of the Presidency* (Boston, Mass.: Little, Brown, 1975) pp. 240–1.
29. Cf. Daniel J. Boorstin, *The Image: A Guide to Pseudo-events in America* (New York: Harper Colophon Books, 1964).
30. See, for example, Schlesinger, *The Imperial Presidency*, pp. 59–60, 374.
31. Kennedy Archives, memo dated 26 July 1962.
32. *Newsweek*, 9 Dec 1974, pp. 33–4; quoted in Cronin, *The State of the Presidency*, p. 241.

33. See, for instance, R. T. Johnson, *Managing the White House*, pp. 109–11.

34. For a discussion of how far the crisis had 'passed' once Kennedy made it public, see the Afterword by Richard Neustadt and Graham Allison to the Norton Books edition of *Thirteen Days* (New York, 1969).

35. Quoted in Robert S. Hirschfield (ed.), *The Power of the Presidency* (New York: Aldine, 1973) p. 150.

36. *New York Times*, 10 Aug 1974.

37. The articles are too long to quote here. They include frequent reference to such activities as 'making false or misleading public statements for the purpose of deceiving the people of the United States', planning to 'conceal the existence and scope of . . . unlawful, covert activities', etc. See the useful book by the staff of the *New York Times*, *The End of a Presidency* (New York: Bantam Books, 1974) p III.

38. 'I'll never lie to you' became the title of a book of 'Jimmy Carter in his own words' put together in the 1976 campaign by Robert W. Turner (New York: Ballantine Books).

39. Hirschfield, *The Power of the Presidency*, pp. 129, 150. The Ford press conference was on 28 Aug 1974.

40. Ibid., pp. 126–7.

41. Ibid., p. 183.

42. John E. Mueller, *War, Presidents and Public Opinion* (New York: John Wiley, 1973), is a salutary overview.

43. On Nixon's reorganisation, see Nathan, *The Plot that Failed*; the gist is summarised on pp. 7–8.

44. Stephen Hess, *Organizing the Presidency* (Washington, D.C.: The Brookings Institution, 1976) p. 25; pp. 18–25 provide a brilliant encapsulation of the presidential life-cycle.

45. 'Truman, although candid, is not discursive. Roosevelt's most valuable conferences were those in which he talked at length on one or two subjects. From these the correspondents . . . got insight into his mind and objectives which they could not have got so well in any other way' – Ernest Lindley, *Newsweek*, 28 Oct 1946; quoted in Elmer Cornwell Jr, *Presidential Leadership of Public Opinion* (Bloomington: Indiana University Press, 1965) p. 331.

46. Doris Kearns also describes gradations in presidential gifts: *Lyndon Johnson and the American Dream*, pp. 9–10.

47. Goldman, *The Tragedy of Lyndon Johnson*, p. 115.

48. *Rolling Stone*, 19 May 1977.

49. Safire, *Before the Fall*, p. 664.

50. Quoted in Koenig, *The Chief Executive*, p. 165.

51. Rowland Evans Jr and Robert D. Novak, *Nixon in the White House* (New York: Vintage Books, 1972) pp. 122–4.

52. Academic literature, including studies such as this one, also involves tertiary communication.

53. Woodward and Bernstein, *The Final Days*, p. 447.

54. Excerpted transcript in the *New York Times*, 26 May 1977. In a covering story James M. Naughton wrote, 'Refusing to use the names of the two reporters, Mr Nixon called them and their book "trash". He said he could understand and even "respect" Mr Woodward and Mr Bernstein for seeking professional advancement by "pandering" to a liberal audience, "but when it

comes to fictionalizing fact and doing it in a vicious way, that I will not forget and I consider it to be contemptible journalism."' The first of these TV interviews attracted an audience of 45 million.

55. Wise, *The Politics of Lying*, pp. 342–3.
56. *The Economist*, 16 July 1977.
57. Reedy, *The Twilight of the Presidency*, p. 109.
58. See the section on Truman in Ch. 3 below.
59. These quotations are cited in, respectively, Pollard, *The President and the Press*, p. 776; William Hillman, *Mr President* (New York: Farrar, Straus & Young, 1962) p. 219; Dwight D. Eisenhower, *Mandate for Change* (New York: Signet Books, 1965) p. 291; Wise, *The Politics of Lying*, p. 333.
60. The pattern was set, characteristically, by Franklin Roosevelt, who founded his presidential library at Hyde Park, N.Y., in 1939. A Federal law of 1955 requires libraries to be built with private funds but provides for their operation at Federal Government expense.
61. John Hersey, 'Mr President', *New Yorker*, 7 Apr–5 May 1951. Hersey repeated the formula with his book about Gerald Ford, *The President* (New York: Alfred A. Knopf, 1975).
62. Bradlee, *Conversations with Kennedy*, pp. 219–21.
63. Kennedy Archives, Presidential Office Files Box 129; note by Evelyn Lincoln.
64. *New York Times*, 14 Apr 1977. The Carter programme was shown on the NBC network on that day, having been filmed on 4 Apr.
65. Richard M. Nixon, *RN: The Memoirs of Richard Nixon* (London: Sidgwick & Jackson, 1978).
66. H. R. Haldeman, *The Ends of Power* (London: Star Books, 1978) pp. 227, 244.
67. Patrick Anderson, *The President's Men* (New York: Doubleday, 1969) pp. 226–7. Ileitis is an inflammation of the lower part of the small intestine.
68. White, *Breach of Faith*, p. 247.
69. Omar Bradley, 'Some Thoughts on the Presidency', *Reader's Digest*, Nov 1968; quoted in Hirschfield, *The Power of the Presidency*, p. 118.
70. Richard M. Nixon, *Six Crises* (London: W. H. Allen, 1962) pp. 149–50.
71. *New York Times*, 2 Feb 1977. Cf. her press secretary's 'difficult adjustment' to calling Rosalynn Carter 'Mrs Carter' – *New York Times*, date not noted (Jan 1977?). Eric Goldman noted that Mrs Johnson's press secretary, Liz Carpenter, 'who had known Lady Bird Johnson for years as "Bird", now called her Mrs Johnson with complete naturalness' – Goldman, *The Tragedy of Lyndon Johnson*, p. 430.
72. Barber, *Presidential Character*, p. 54; quoting Hugh Sidey, *A Very Personal Presidency*, (New York: Atheneum, 1968) p. 167.
73. Wise, *The Politics of Lying*, pp. 27–32.
74. William E. Porter, *Assault on the Media* (Ann Arbor: University of Michigan Press, 1976) p. 25.
75. Wise, *The Politics of Lying*, p. 480.
76. *New York Times*, 3 Mar 1977.
77. For instance, Clay and John Blair, *The Search For JFK* (New York: Berkley, 1976).
78. Sherman Adams, *Firsthand Report* (New York: Popular Library, 1962), p. 350.
79. Neustadt, *Presidential Power*, p. 128.
80. See, for example, the White House statement of 19 Oct 1973 and the

argument of Nixon's lawyers before the House Judiciary Committee, discussed in White, *Breach of Faith*, pp. 337, 367–9.

81. Quoted, Barber, *Presidential Character*, p. 250.
82. See Kearns, *Lyndon Johnson and the American Dream*, ch. 7; and Goldman, *The Tragedy of Lyndon Johnson*.
83. 'To Mr Nixon, Camp David seems to have become less a Shangri-la, more a Berchtesgaden, less a Walden, more a prison' – Simon Winchester, *Washington Post*, 26 June 1973; quoted in White, *Breach of Faith*, pp. 419–20.
84. Timothy Crouse, *The Boys on the Bus* (New York: Ballantine Books, 1974) pp. 128, 369–73.
85. Wise, *The Politics of Lying*, p. 492.
86. Anderson, *The President's Men*, p. 222.
87. Bradlee, *Conversations with Kennedy*, pp. 108–13.
88. Evans and Novak, *Nixon in the White House*, pp. 430–5.
89. *New York Times*, 8 Feb 1977; *Boston Globe*, 29 May 1977.
90. Wise, *The Politics of Lying*, p. 461.
91. Margaret Truman, *Harry S. Truman* (New York: Pocket Books, 1974) pp. 546–8.
92. There was naturally much attention to her pets, especially the hamsters. Salinger, *With Kennedy*, pp. 385–8.
93. Eisenhower, *Mandate for Change*, p. 80.
94. 'By the time Nixon left office', to quote Stephen Hess, 'the number of people employed by the White House and the Executive Office had nearly doubled from its size under Johnson, just as Johnson's staff had nearly doubled from its size at the time of FDR's death. Over the course of forty years the White House staff had grown from 37 to 600, the Executive Office staff from zero to many thousands' – Hess, *Organizing the Presidency*, p. 9.
95. Address to the Anti-Defamation League of B'nai B'rith, 20 Nov 1977.
96. *Time*, 12 May 1980.
97. W. L. Rivers, *The Opinion Makers* (Boston, Mass.: Beacon Press, 1965) pp. 145–6.
98. R. T. Johnson, *Managing the White House*, p. 56.
99. Lyndon Baines Johnson, *The Vantage Point* (New York: Popular Library, 1971) p. 159.
100. Wise, *The Politics of Lying*, p. 334.
101. Nixon, *RN: Memoirs*, p. 411. The speech was made in Des Moines, Iowa, on 13 Nov 1969.
102. Neustadt, *Presidential Power*, p. 17.
103. For an analysis of the Lance affair in the context of the 'hazards of transition', see ibid., pp. 225ff.
104. Arthur M. Schlesinger Jr, *A Thousand Days* (London: André Deutsch, 1965) p. 569.
105. Kissinger memoirs, *Time* excerpt, 8 Oct 1979.
106. Goldman, *The Tragedy of Lyndon Johnson*, p. 488; Kearns, *Lyndon Johnson and the American Dream* (e.g. pp. 43–5).
107. For the origins see Goldman, *The Tragedy of Lyndon Johnson*, p. 484.
108. Magruder, *An American Life*, p. 78.
109. Bradlee, *Conversations with Kennedy*, p. 71.
110. Wise, *The Politics of Lying*, p. 33.

111. Charles W. Dunn (ed.), *The Future of the Presidency* (Morristown, N. J.: General Learning Press, 1975) p. 292.
112. The articles of impeachment are reprinted in *New York Times, The End of a Presidency* (New York: Bantam Books, 1974) pp. 318ff.
113. Hess, *Organizing the Presidency*, p. 66; quoting Townsend Hoopes, *The Devil and John Foster Dulles* (Boston, Mass.: Little, Brown, 1973) pp. 500–1.
114. Neustadt, *Presidential Power*, pp. 220–5.
115. President Carter's press conference, 29 Apr 1980.
116. Hess, *Organizing the Presidency*, pp. 5–7.
117. Interview with Bill Moyers, Public Television network, 13 Nov 1978.
118. Quint and Ferrell, *The Talkative President*, pp. v–vi.
119. On the development of White House press relations, see Cornwell, *Presidential Leadership of Public Opinion*; and M. L. Stein, *When Presidents Meet the Press* (New York: Julian Messner, 1969).
120. Anderson, *The President's Men*, ch. 4 *passim*.
121. Martha Joynt Kumar and Michael Baruch Grossman, 'The Manager of the Message: the Press Secretary to the President of the United States', paper delivered at the 1977 Annual Meeting of the Southern Political Science Association; quoting Dom Bonafede, *National Journal*, 25 June 1977, and White House sources.
122. Stein, *When Presidents Meet the Press*, pp. 38–9, 137.
123. Goldman, *The Tragedy of Lyndon Johnson*, p. 142.
124. Communication to the author.
125. Anderson, *The President's Men*, pp. 231–2.
126. George E. Reedy, 'Speaking for the President', in R. E. Hiebert and C. E. Spitzer (eds), *The Voice of Government* (New York: John Wiley, 1968) p. 106.
127. Goldman, *The Tragedy of Lyndon Johnson*, pp. 135–9; Anderson, *The President's Men*, pp. 378–86; George E. Reedy, 'The President and the Press: Struggle for Dominance', *Annals*, vol. 427 (Philadelphia: American Academy of Political and Social Science, 1976) p. 68.
128. *Time*, 21 Aug 1978.
129. Rivers, *The Opinion Makers*, p. 156; Anderson, *The President's Men*, p. 221.
130. Charles W. Colson, *Born Again* (New York: Bantam Books, 1977) p. 38.
131. *Washington Post*, 16 July 1980. The leaked story concerned an alleged split within the administration over military aid to Morocco.
132. Sherman Adams, *Firsthand Report*, p. 82.
133. Goldman, *The Tragedy of Lyndon Johnson*, pp. 142–3.
134. *Guardian*, 10 Feb 1979.
135. Woodward and Bernstein, *The Final Days*, p. 174.
136. Magruder, *An American Life*, pp. 113–19.
137. Ibid., p. 8.
138. Bradlee, *Conversations with Kennedy*, p. 123.
139. ABC television interview with Howard K. Smith, 22 Mar 1971; repr. in Hirschfield, *The Power of the Presidency*, p. 183; Safire, *Before the Fall*, pp. 349–50.
140. Goldman, *The Tragedy of Lyndon Johnson*, p. 492.
141. Anderson, *The President's Men*, p. 231.
142. Bradlee, *Conversations with Kennedy*, p. 74.
143. Reedy, *The Twilight of the Presidency*, p. 103.

144. Murray Edelman, *The Symbolic Uses of Politics* (Urbana: University of Illinois Press, 1964) ch. 5.
145. See Lyndon Johnson, *The Vantage Point*, pp. 479–85, for the details of this somewhat backhanded compliment to Glassboro.
146. Pollard, *The Presidents and the Press*, pp. 13–15.
147. *New York Times*, 27 Feb 1977.
148. Nixon, *RN: Memoirs*, p. 411.
149. Reedy, *The Twilight of the Presidency*, p. 65.
150. Ibid., p. 158.
151. For example: 'After 750 combined hours of analysis, we have discovered major verbal and nonverbal communication differences between the candidates in the three Ford–Carter debates. The research was based upon an analysis of 7,378 specific nonverbal behaviours and 955 verbal references found in the 30,852-word transcripts', etc. – Gerald M. Goldhaver, D. Thomas Porter, Jerry K. Frye and Michael Yates, Department of Communication, State University of New York at Buffalo, reported in *Washington Post*, 14 Nov 1976.
152. It should be added that projecting the President *as* a symbol need not be done exclusively through symbolic means. Identity with common citizens can be demonstrated in the substance of the President's words and in his priorities of legislation and administration, as well as in the symbolism of an unpretentious lifestyle.
153. See, for example, the articles by Anthony Lewis, *New York Times* 22 Dec 1976; and Charles Mohr, *New York Times*, 6 Feb 1977.
154. Anderson, *The President's Men*, pp. 224–5.
155. *Time*, 19 Mar 1979.
156. Robert E. Goodin, 'Symbolic Reward: Being Bought Off Cheaply', *Political Studies*, xxv, no. 3 (Sep 1977) p. 395.
157. *The Times*, 20 June 1975.

NOTES TO CHAPTER THREE: THE PRESIDENT, POWER AND COMMUNICATION

1. A convenient source is Nelson W. Polsby, *Congress and the Presidency*, 3rd edn (Englewood Cliffs, N.J.: Prentice-Hall, 1976) p. 64.
2. Cornwell, *Presidential Leadership of Public Opinion*, pp. 5–6.
3. David L. Paletz, 'Perspectives on the Presidency', *Law and Contemporary Problems*, xxxv, no. 3 (Summer 1970) pp. 429–44.
4. Page references are to Clinton Rossiter, *The American Presidency*, revised edn (New York: Mentor Books, 1960).
5. Koenig, *The Chief Executive*, p. 325.
6. See, for examples of each, Cronin, *The State of the Presidency*; Hess, *Organizing the Presidency*; Charles M. Hardin, *Presidential Power and Accountability* (Chicago: University of Chicago Press, 1974); Reedy, *The Twilight of the Presidency*; Schlesinger, *The Imperial Presidency*; Sorensen, *Watchmen in the Night*. A useful general discussion is in John Hart, 'Presidential Power Revisited', *Political Studies*, xxv, no. 1 (1977) pp. 48–61.
7. For example, Wise, *The Politics of Lying*; Crouse, *The Boys on the Bus*; Porter, *Assault on the Media*.

8. See *Presidential Power, passim*, esp. chs. 1 and 8.
9. Reedy, *The Twilight of the Presidency*, pp. 100, 106.
10. Peter W. Sperlich, 'Bargaining and Overload: an Essay on *Presidential Power*', in Aaron Wildavsky (ed.), *The Presidency* (Boston, Mass.: Little, Brown, 1969) pp. 168–92.
11. Ibid., p. ix.
12. Emmet John Hughes, *The Living Presidency* (Baltimore: Penguin Books, 1974) p. 20.
13. Some paperback editions of Bob Woodward and Carl Bernstein's *All the President's Men* had cover pictures not of the authors but of Robert Redford and Dustin Hoffman, who played them in the film.
14. The quotations are respectively from Barber, *Presidential Character*, p. 146; Rossiter, *The American Presidency*, p. 171; Erwin Hargrove, *The Power of the Modern Presidency* (New York: Alfred A. Knopf, 1974) p. 11; Neustadt, *Presidential Power*, p. 121; Emmet J. Hughes, quoted in Hirschfield, *The Power of the Presidency*, p. 125.
15. Rossiter, *The American Presidency*, p. 162.
16. Quoted in Hirschfield, *The Power of the Presidency*, p. 123.
17. Hargrove, *The Power of the Modern Presidency*, p. 60.
18. Ibid., p. 125.
19. Wise, *The Politics of Lying*, p. 50.
20. Rossiter, *The American Presidency*, p. 159.
21. Barber, *Presidential Character*, p. 173.
22. Rossiter, *The American Presidency*, p. 162.
23. Quoted in Hughes, *The Living Presidency*, p. 125.
24. R. K. Gray, *Eighteen Acres under Glass* (New York: Doubleday, 1962) pp. 62–3.
25. Hess, *Organizing the Presidency*, pp. 69–70. Fred Greenstein and Robert Wright describe Adams as 'able to function as virtual clone'–'Reagan . . . Another Ike?', *Public Opinion*, III, no. 6 (1981) p. 53. Cf. Hardin, *Presidential Power and Accountability*, pp. 37ff., for a discussion of how far Adams had independent decision-making power.
26. Quoted without attribution, Barber, *Presidential Character*, p. 160.
27. Eisenhower, *Mandate for Change*, p. 146.
28. Quoted in Pollard, *The Presidents and the Press*, p. 79.
29. Ibid., p. 75.
30. Quoted without attribution in Barber, *Presidential Character*, p. 160.
31. See, for example, Wise, *The Politics of Lying*, p. 47; Arthur Larson, *Eisenhower: the President Nobody Knew* (New York: Charles Scribner's Sons, 1968).
32. Barber, *Presidential Character*, p. 161.
33. See, for example, Cornwell, *Presidential Leadership of Public Opinion*.
34. Anderson, *The President's Men*, p. 219.
35. Cornwell, *Presidential Leadership of Public Opinion*, pp. 185–6.
36. Ibid., p. 178; Eisenhower, *Mandate for Change*, pp. 289–90.
37. Cornwell, *Presidential Leadership of Public Opinion*, p. 183 (my emphasis).
38. Hughes, *The Living Presidency*, p. 22.
39. Eisenhower, *Mandate for Change*, p. 290.
40. Quoted without attribution in Barber, *Presidential Character*, p. 159.
41. The quotations are from ibid., p. 385; Safire, *Before the Fall*, p. 692.
42. Nixon, *RN: Memoirs*, p. 241.

43. Ibid., p. ix.
44. Schlesinger, *The Imperial Presidency*, p. 10.
45. Ibid., p. 248.
46. Nixon, *RN: Memoirs*, p. 771.
47. Ibid., p. 368; Hess, *Organizing the Presidency*, p. 76.
48. Safire, *Before the Fall*, p. 690.
49. White, *Breach of Faith*, p. 86; Barber, *Presidential Character*, p. 386; Hess, *Organizing the Presidency*, p. 131.
50. Schlesinger, *The Imperial Presidency*, pp. 186–8.
51. Ibid., pp. 237–8.
52. Hess, *Organizing the Presidency*, pp. 134–5.
53. Nathan, *The Plot that Failed*, p. 8. See Nixon, *RN: Memoirs*, pp. 761ff., for his own statement of plans at the start of the second term.
54. Hess, *Organizing the Presidency*, p. 112.
55. Polsby, *Congress and the Presidency*, pp. 51, 56.
56. Richard M. Nixon, *Six Crises* (London: W. H. Allen, 1962) p. 96.
57. Schlesinger, *The Imperial Presidency*, pp. 248ff.
58. Hardin, *Presidential Power and Accountability*, p. 24. Cf. Nixon, *RN: Memoirs*, pp. 514–15.
59. Schlesinger, *The Imperial Presidency*, p. 255.
60. Polsby, *Congress and the Presidency*, p. 51.
61. Nixon, *Six Crises*, p. xii.
62. Ibid., pp. 96, 133.
63. Nixon, *RN: Memoirs*, p. 409.
64. Ibid., p. 410.
65. Quoted in Barber, *Presidential Character*, p. 384.
66. *New York Times Magazine*, 2 Nov. 1969.
67. Nixon, *RN: Memoirs*, p. 409.
68. Barber, *Presidential Character*, p. 381.
69. For example, interview with Howard K. Smith, ABC TV, 22 Mar 1971: 'The jaw is still there. As my wife often said, there is not much I can do about my image. I was born with it' – in Hirschfield, *The Power of the Presidency*, p. 189.
70. Schlesinger, *The Imperial Presidency*, p. 224.
71. Nixon, *RN: Memoirs*, p. 762.
72. See Safire, *Before the Fall*, pt v, ch. 1, generally, and esp. p. 308.
73. 'Nixon had no more stomach for face-to-face confrontations with members of Congress than for those with anyone else' – Evans and Novak, *Nixon in the White House*, p. 107.
74. Nixon, *RN: Memoirs*, p. 354.
75. Nixon, *Six Crises*, p. 422.
76. Nixon, *RN: Memoirs*, p. 520. The context was Nixon's announcement of an important shift in economic policy on 15 Aug 1971.
77. Barber, *Presidential Character*, p. 395; Safire, *Before the Fall*, p. 691.
78. Ibid., p. 341.
79. Nixon, *Six Crises*, p. 69.
80. Hess, *Organizing the Presidency*, p. 136.
81. Safire, *Before the Fall*, p. 351.
82. Evans and Novak, *Nixon in the White House*, pp. 347–8; Safire, *Before the Fall*, p. 351.

83. Hess, *Organizing the Presidency*, p. 130.
84. White, *Breach of Faith*, p. 154; Safire, *Before the Fall*, p. 220.
85. Ibid., p. 360.
86. Nixon, *RN: Memoirs*, p. 355.
87. Neustadt, *Presidential Power*, pp. 136–7.
88. Margaret Truman, *Harry S. Truman* (New York: Pocket Books, 1975) p. 28. Clark Clifford was one of many aides who said he found Truman 'infinitely tolerant' about aides getting a better press than he did – Anderson, *The President's Men*, p. 150.
89. The quotations in this paragraph are from Neustadt, *Presidential Power*, p. 243, excepting the last, which is from Margaret Truman, *Harry S. Truman*, p. 21.
90. Hess, *Organizing the Presidency*, p. 45.
91. R. T. Johnson, *Managing the White House*, p. 53. See also Hess, *Organizing the Presidency*, pp. 44–5; Neustadt, *Presidential Power*, pp. 125ff.
92. See R. T. Johnson, *Managing the White House*, ch. 3 *passim*.
93. Margaret Truman, *Harry S. Truman*, p. 32.
94. Quoted in Polsby, *Congress and the Presidency*, p. 23.
95. Quoted in Barber, *Presidential Character*, p. 255.
96. Margaret Truman, *Harry S. Truman*, pp. 28–9. She adds, 'When it came to deciding how to phrase something, he had only two rules. No "two-dollar words" and make the statement as simple and understandable as possible.'
97. Douglass Cater, *The Fourth Branch of Government* (New York: Vintage Books, 1959) pp. 36–8.
98. Cornwell, *Presidential Leadership of Public Opinion*, pp. 162–70.
99. See ibid., ch. 7 *passim*.
100. The Kennedy story is in Theodore C. Sorensen, *Kennedy* (London: Hodder & Stoughton, 1965) p. 392. The inference that it was a favourite quotation is drawn from Arthur M. Schlesinger Jr, *A Thousand Days* (London: André Deutsch, 1965) p. 623. The Truman quotation is from Neustadt, *Presidential Power*, p. 9.
101. Schlesinger, *A Thousand Days*, p. 622. The short chapter on Kennedy's public communication, 'The Bully Pulpit', is interesting throughout, and especially for its contrast between early comments that Kennedy was not 'going to the people' enough and the opinion after his presidency that his 'educational' activities were if anything too effective in raising public expectations.
102. Sorensen, *Kennedy*, p. 389. Cf. Schlesinger, *A Thousand Days*, p. 588, which attributes the annoyance to Kennedy's belief that people might think he was *modelling* his presidency on Neustadt's ideas.
103. John F. Kennedy, *Why England Slept* (London: Sidgwick & Jackson, 1940) p. 100.
104. Twenty years later, interestingly, Kennedy contrasted the responsiveness of democracies and dictatorships to domestic problems, in an unscripted TV interview. Khruschev, he argued, must have much greater difficulty than he in such matters, since he had not the benefit of spontaneous feedback from a free press – 15 Dec 1962, quoted in Edmund S. Ions, *The Politics of John F. Kennedy* (London: Routledge & Kegan Paul, 1967) p. 161.
105. Kennedy, *Why England Slept*, p. 105.
106. Carl M. Brauer, *John F. Kennedy and the Second Reconstruction* (New York: Columbia University Press, 1977) p. 316.

107. Theodore Sorensen, *Decision-Making in the White House* (New York: Columbia University Press, 1964) p. 58.
108. Paul F. Hoye, in Providence *Evening Bulletin*, 10 Feb 1962; quoted in Cornwell, *Presidential Leadership of Public Opinion*, p. 245.
109. Hess, *Organizing the Presidency*, p. 88.
110. Sorensen, *Kennedy*, pp. 526, 613–17.
111. Hess, *Organizing the Presidency*, pp. 85, 90.
112. Schlesinger, *A Thousand Days*, p. 111.
113. Sorensen, *Kennedy*, p. 372.
114. For details, see Cornwell, *Presidential Leadership of Public Opinion*; and Rivers, *The Opinion Makers*, pp. 157ff.
115. Sorensen, *Kennedy*, p. 310.
116. Ibid., pp. 328–9.
117. Cornwell, *Presidential Leadership of Public Opinion*, pp. 192ff. According to Sorensen (*Kennedy*, p. 326), Salinger arranged plants no more than a dozen times in three years.
118. Hess, *Organizing the Presidency*, p. 89.
119. Cornwell, *Presidential Leadership of Public Opinion*, p. 221.
120. Neustadt, *Presidential Power*, p. 149.
121. See, for example, Schlesinger, *The Imperial Presidency*, pp. 178, 182–6.
122. See, for a summary, Hess, *Organizing the Presidency*, ch. 6.
123. Johnson to Doris Kearns; quoted in Kearns, *Lyndon Johnson and the American Dream*, p. 146.
124. Ibid., p. 390.
125. See, for typical examples, Rowland Evans and Robert Novak, *Lyndon Johnson: The Exercise of Power* (New York: Signet Books, 1968) p. 120.
126. See Hess, *Organizing the Presidency*.
127. Kearns, *Lyndon Johnson and the American Dream*, pp. 232, 238–41; Lyndon Johnson, *The Vantage Point*, pp. 161ff.
128. Wilson Carey McWilliams, 'Lyndon Johnson and the Politics of Mass Society', in P. D. Bathory (ed.), *Leadership in America* (London: Longman, 1978) pp. 178–9.
129. Neustadt, *Presidential Power*, p. 182.
130. Lyndon Johnson, *The Vantage Point*, pp. 457–9.
131. Evans and Novak, *Lyndon Johnson: The Exercise of Power*, pp. 115–16.
132. See Kearns, *Lyndon Johnson and the American Dream*, esp. pp. 232–48; and Goldman, *The Tragedy of Lyndon Johnson*.
133. Neustadt, *Presidential Power*, p. 186.
134. In his memoirs, Johnson concedes that he would have been wise to disclose more than he did on at least one important public occasion, his State of the Union address in Jan 1968. This came only days before the Tet offensive that proved the culmination of his troubles (Lyndon Johnson, *The Vantage Point*, p. 380).
135. Evans and Novak, *Lyndon Johnson: The Exercise of Power*, p. 117.
136. Kearns, *Lyndon Johnson and the American Dream*, pp. 389–90.
137. Ibid., pp. 258–60.
138. For details, see Koenig, *The Chief Executive*, pp. 276–7.
139. *Newsweek*, 18 Oct 1976.
140. *New York Times*, 1 Nov 1976.

141. *Newsweek*, 18 Oct 1976.
142. *Sunday Times*, 4 Jan 1976.
143. A full account is in Jerald ter Horst, *Gerald Ford and the Future of the Presidency* (New York: The Third Press, 1974) pp. 225ff.
144. Polsby, *Congress and the Presidency*, p. 63; Koenig, *The Chief Executive*, p. 93.
145. See Neustadt, *Presidential Power*, pp. 225ff.
146. *Time*, 24 Sep 1979.
147. *Newsweek*, 23 July 1979. The visitors included governors, senators, representatives, mayors and other politicians; academics; business and labour leaders; clergy, journalists and interest-group spokesmen.
148. One must bear in mind, too, a point noted by Arthur Schlesinger Jr. Of the book *Presidential Power* Kennedy once remarked, he says, that Neustadt 'makes everything a President does seem too premeditated'.
149. Irving Janis has highlighted the point in his study *Victims of Groupthink*.
150. Hess, *Organizing the Presidency*, ch. 1.
151. The author's brief exposure to primary presidential communication came, by courtesy of the White House Press Office, when he witnessed a bill-signing ceremony by President Ford in the Rose Garden shortly before the 1976 election. The main difference in this direct observation of the President from observation of his TV appearances was that Mr Ford seemed less tall in real life. This may have been because the bill concerned law and order, and many of the invited guests, crowding the President for handshakes, were very big police chiefs.
152. Colin Seymour-Ure, 'Parliament and Mass Communications in the Twentieth Century', in S. A. Walkland (ed.), *The House of Commons in the Twentieth Century* (Oxford: Clarendon Press, 1979) pp. 527–95.
153. Colin Seymour-Ure, *The Political Impact of Mass Media* (London: Constable; Beverley Hills, Calif.: Sage Publications, 1974) ch. 5.
154. Richard Crossman, *Diaries of a Cabinet Minister*, vol. 1 (London: Hamish Hamilton and Jonathan Cape, 1975) p. 580.
155. Westminster is not an altogether representative case. In Canada, for example, the federal system provides a short cut to national party leadership, with the prospect of the premiership, from provincial politics. Trudeau had not even had that experience when he was chosen Liberal leader in 1968.

Bibliography

This list includes only the main sources consulted. In addition to a number of familiar texts, it excludes a large number of biographies and newspaper and magazine articles. Editions cited are those consulted, not necessarily first editions.

Adams, Sherman, *Firsthand Report* (New York: Popular Library, 1962).

Adams, Timothy J., and Peters, Charles (eds), *Inside the System* (New York: Praeger, 1970).

Anderson, Patrick, *The President's Men* (New York: Doubleday, 1969).

Barber, James David, *The Presidential Character* (Englewood Cliffs, N. J.: Prentice-Hall, 1972).

Bell, David V. J., *Power, Influence and Authority* (New York: Oxford University Press, 1975).

Bernstein: *see* Woodward and Bernstein.

Blair, Clay, and Blair, John, *The Search for JFK* (New York: Berkley, 1976).

Blum, John M., *Joe Tumulty and the Wilson Era* (Boston, Mass.: Houghton Mifflin, 1951).

Boorstin, Daniel J., *The Image* (New York: Harper Colophon Books, 1964).

Bradlee, Benjamin C., *Conversations with Kennedy* (New York: Pocket Books, 1976).

Brauer, Carl M., *John F. Kennedy and the Second Reconstruction* (New York: Columbia University Press, 1977).

Buchanan, Bruce, *The Presidential Experience* (Englewood Cliffs, N. J.: Prentice-Hall, 1978).

Burns, J. M., *Presidential Government* (New York: Houghton Mifflin, 1966).

Cater, Douglass, *The Fourth Branch of Government* (New York: Vintage Books, 1959).

Colson, Charles W., *Born Again* (New York: Bantam Books, 1977).

Cornwell, Elmer E., Jr, *Presidential Leadership of Public Opinion* (Bloomington, Ind.: Indiana University Press, 1965).

——, *The Presidency and the Press* (Morristown, N. J.: General Learning Press, 1974).

Cronin, Thomas E., *The State of the Presidency* (Boston, Mass.: Little, Brown, 1975).

Crossman, Richard, *Diaries of a Cabinet Minister*, vol. 1 (London: Hamish Hamilton and Jonathan Cape, 1975).

Crouse, Timothy, *The Boys on the Bus* (New York: Ballantine Books, 1974).

Dean, John, *Blind Ambition* (New York: Pocket Books, 1977).

Dunn, Charles W. (ed.), *The Future of the Presidency* (Morristown, N. J.: General Learning Press, 1975).

Eccles, Marriner S., *Beckoning Frontiers* (New York: Alfred A. Knopf, 1951).

Edelman, Murray, *The Symbolic Uses of Politics* (Urbana: University of Illinois Press, 1964).

——, *Political Language* (New York: Academic Press, 1977).

Eisenhower, Dwight D., *Mandate for Change* (New York: Signet Books, 1965).

Evans, Rowland, Jr, and Novak, Robert D., *Lyndon Johnson: The Exercise of Power* (New York: Signet Books, 1968).

——, *Nixon in the White House* (New York: Vintage Books, 1972).

Fagen, Richard R., *Politics and Communication* (Boston, Mass.: Little, Brown, 1966).

Ferrell: *see* Quint and Ferrell.

Galnoor, Itzhak (ed.), *Government Secrecy in Democracies* (New York: Harper & Row, 1977).

Goldman, Eric F., *The Tragedy of Lyndon Johnson* (New York: Dell, 1974).

Goodin, Robert E., 'Symbolic Reward: Being Bought Off Cheaply', *Political Studies*, xxv, no. 3 (1977) pp. 383–96.

Gray, R. K., *Eighteen Acres under Glass* (New York: Doubleday, 1962).

Grossman, Michael B., and Kumar, Martha J., *Portraying the President: The White House and the News Media* (Baltimore, Md: Johns Hopkins University Press, 1981).

Haldeman, H. R., *The Ends of Power* (London: Star Books, 1978).

Hardin, Charles M., *Presidential Power and Accountability* (University of Chicago Press, 1974).

Hargrove, Erwin, *The Power of the Modern Presidency* (New York: Alfred A. Knopf, 1974).

Hart, John, 'Presidential Power Revisited', *Political Studies*, xxv, no. 1 (1977) pp. 48–61.

Hersey, John, *The President* (New York: Alfred A. Knopf, 1975).

Hess, Stephen, *Organizing the Presidency* (Washington, D.C.: The Brookings Institution, 1976).

Hillman, William, *Mr President* (New York: Farrar, Straus & Young, 1932).

Hilsman, Roger, *To Move a Nation* (New York: Doubleday, 1967).

Hirschfield, Robert S. (ed.), *The Power of the Presidency* (New York: Aldine, 1973).

Hoopes, Townsend, *The Devil and John Foster Dulles* (Boston, Mass.: Little, Brown, 1973).

Hughes, Emmet John, *The Living Presidency* (Baltimore, Md: Penguin Books, 1974).

Ions, Edmund S. (ed.), *The Politics of John F. Kennedy* (London: Routledge & Kegan Paul, 1967).

Janis, Irving L., *Victims of Groupthink* (Boston, Mass.: Houghton Mifflin, 1972).

Johnson, Lyndon Baines, *The Vantage Point* (New York: Popular Library, 1971).

Johnson, R. T., *Managing the White House* (New York: Harper & Row, 1974).

Kearns, Doris, *Lyndon Johnson and the American Dream* (New York: Signet Books, 1977).

Kennedy, John F., *Why England Slept* (London: Sidgwick & Jackson, 1940).

Kennedy, Robert F., *Thirteen Days* (New York: Signet Books, 1969).

Keogh, James, *President Nixon and the Press* (New York: Funk & Wagnalls, 1972).

Koenig, Louis W., *The Chief Executive*, 3rd edn (New York: Harcourt Brace Jovanovich, 1975).

Kumar: *see* Grossman and Kumar.

Larson, Arthur, *Eisenhower: The President Nobody Knew* (New York: Charles Scribner's Sons, 1968).

Lukes, Steven, *Power: A Radical View* (Oxford: Basil Blackwell, 1979).

McWilliams, Wilson Carey, 'Lyndon Johnson and the Politics of Mass Society', in P. D. Bathory (ed.), *Leadership in America* (London: Longman, 1978).

Magruder, Jeb Stuart, *An American Life* (New York: Pocket Books, 1975).

Miller, Merle, *Plain Speaking: An Oral Biography of Harry S. Truman* (New York: Berkley, 1974).

Minow, Newton N., *et al.*, *Presidential Television* (New York: Basic Books, 1973).

Mueller, John E., *War, Presidents and Public Opinion* (New York: John Wiley, 1973).

Nathan, Richard P., *The Plot that Failed: Nixon and the Administrative Presidency* (New York: John Wiley, 1975).

Neustadt, Richard E., *Presidential Power* (New York: John Wiley, 1980).

New York Times, The End of a Presidency (New York: Bantam Books, 1974).

Nixon, Richard M., *Six Crises* (London: W. H. Allen, 1962).

———, *RN: The Memoirs of Richard Nixon* (London: Sidgwick & Jackson, 1978).

Novak: *see* Evans and Novak.

Paletz, David L., 'Perspectives on the Presidency', *Law and Contemporary Problems*, XXXV, no. 3 (1970) pp. 429–44.

———, and Vinegar, Richard J., 'Presidents on Television: the Effects of Instant Analysis', *Public Opinion Quarterly*, XLI (1978) pp. 488–97.

Peters: *see* Adams and Peters

Pollard, James E., *The Presidents and the Press* (New York: Macmillan, 1947).

Polsby, Nelson W., *Congress and the Presidency*, 3rd edn (Englewood Cliffs, N. J.: Prentice-Hall, 1976).

Porter, William E., *Assault on the Media* (Ann Arbor: University of Michigan Press, 1976).

Quint, Howard H., and Ferrell, Robert H., *The Talkative President* (Boston, Mass.: University of Massachusetts Press, 1964).

Reedy, George E., 'Speaking for the President', in R. E. Hiebert and C. E. Spitzer (eds), *The Voice of Government* (New York: John Wiley, 1968).

———, *The Twilight of the President* (New York: Mentor Books, 1971).

———, 'The President and the Press: Struggle for Dominance', *Annals*, vol. 427 (Philadelphia: American Academy of Political and Social Science, 1976).

Rivers, W. L., *The Opinion Makers* (Boston, Mass.: Beacon Press, 1965).

Rossiter, Clinton, *The American Presidency*, rev. edn (New York: Mentor Books, 1960).

Safire, William, *Before the Fall* (New York: Belmont Tower Books, 1975).

Salinger, Pierre, *With Kennedy* (New York: Avon Books, 1967).

Schlesinger, Arthur, Jr, *A Thousand Days* (London: André Deutsch, 1965).

———, *The Imperial Presidency* (New York: Popular Library, 1974).

Seymour-Ure, Colin, *The Political Impact of Mass Media* (London: Constable, 1974).

———, 'Parliament and Mass Communications in the Twentieth Century', in S. A. Walkland (ed.), *The House of Commons in the Twentieth Century* (Oxford: Clarendon Press, 1979).

Sidey, Hugh, *A Very Personal Presidency* (New York: Atheneum, 1968).

Smith, Merriman, *Thank You, Mr President* (New York: Harper, 1946).

Sorensen, Theodore C., *Decision-Making in the White House* (New York: Columbia University Press, 1964).

———, *Kennedy* (London: Hodder & Stoughton, 1965).

———, *Watchmen in the Night* (Cambridge, Mass.: MIT Press, 1975).

Sperlich, Peter W., 'Bargaining and Overload: an Essay on *Presidential Power*', in A. Wildavsky, *The Presidency*.

Stein, M. L., *When Presidents Meet the Press* (New York: Julian Messner, 1969).

Strum, Philippa, *Presidential Power and American Democracy* (Pacific Palisades, Calif.: Goodyear, 1972).

Summers, Anthony, *Conspiracy: Who Killed President Kennedy?* (London: Fontana, 1980).

ter Horst, Jerald F., *Gerald Ford and the Future of the Presidency* (New York: The Third Press, 1974).

Truman, Margaret, *Harry S. Truman* (New York: Pocket Books, 1974).

Turner, Robert W., *'I'll Never Lie to You': Jimmy Carter in His Own Words* (New York: Ballantine Books, 1976).

Valenti, Jack, *A Very Human President* (New York: Pocket Books, 1977).

Vinegar: *see* Paletz and Vinegar.

White, Theodore H., *Breach of Faith* (New York: Dell Publishing Co., 1975).

Wildavsky, A. (ed.), *The Presidency* (Boston, Mass.: Little, Brown, 1969).

Wise, David, *The Politics of Lying* (New York: Vintage Books, 1973).

Woodward, Bob, and Bernstein, Carl, *The Final Days* (New York: Avon Books, 1977).

Wrong, Dennis H., *Power: Its Forms, Bases and Uses* (Oxford: Basil Blackwell, 1979).

Index

Index